5.7.80

THE FACE OF BUSINESS

The Face of Business

Business

HENRY I. MEYER

A Division of American Management Associations

Library of Congress Cataloging in Publication Data

Meyer, Henry I   1921–
   The face of business.

   Includes index.
   1. Business enterprises—United States. I. Title.
   HF5343.M49   658.4'00973   79-55064
   ISBN 0-8144-5601-4

First Printing

To Leslie

PREFACE

THIS BOOK is about business, big American business—what it is, how it is constituted, and what sort of people work in what sort of environment. The text moves from the general to the particular. The first six chapters deal with concepts true to all corporations: the management and organization of a business, its public reports, the role of money in business, the rules for paying employees, and the interesting relationship between shareholders and companies. The next four chapters look at a single typical company: at the way it is organized and at the different types of employees—line, staff, and top management. The final chapters concentrate on the individual, the businessman. We are concerned with his training, his personality, his perquisites, and his behavior up to and including sex in the office.

The goals of this book are to instruct and to entertain. Which of these is more important will have to be decided by the reader. The pragmatic person who only wants to learn will have to put up with a certain amount of digression; the one who reads for pleasure will have to tolerate facts—a book has to be about something.

A publisher's eternal question is, "Who in the world would want to read this sort of thing?" There should be several classes of people who want to read to learn, and for these people the hard facts were marshaled. Business wives can read it to find out what their husbands *do* when they go to the office. Their husbands can read to get a better perspective of their own corporation and their place in it. A businessman can learn how to take advantage of corporate peculiarities to improve his own prospects, and he can also look for his friends in these pages. Young people who are considering a business career can use the book as a guide to the business world. Investors will learn more about the product they are buying—American business.

I have few illusions, but there is one mythical character I still believe in: the intelligent person who really enjoys a good read, who appreciates careful writing and enjoys finding new ideas and following their development (though not necessarily agreeing with the author). This reader has a background enough like my own to appreciate my digressions and recognize my references, and may even be amused by the mild humor in the book. Thoughtful people *should* be interested in business in our society. It is too important to ignore.

This is a book about business as it *is*, not its history or predictions of its future. There are good books on American business history, although most seem to adopt the "noble crusade" point of view. American business must change, because its role is changing. Historically, business went about the job of exploiting the resources of the nation and dividing the spoils. It had to succeed. With the best possible protected market, an endless supply of immigrant labor, an incredibly rich store of natural resources, and cheap energy, it could hardly have failed. As we change from this world of plenty to a world where resources are getting scarce and energy expensive, and where the American market is no longer protected from foreign competition, the role of business must change. Tomorrow's corporations will be rationing organizations dispensing jobs, favors, and materiel. Social motives will at least partially replace the profit motive. As a starting point for change, thinking people should know the character and idiosyncrasies of business as it now is.

This book is not anti-business. If there are criticisms of the way things are, they are the criticisms of a friend. Business bought my home, paid for the raising and education of my children, and allowed me to retire to start a new career. It probably paid me more than I was worth. That statement is an anachronism, since gratitude by employees, even in the face of extravagant bonuses and perquisities, is almost unknown. Business has its faults, but as a way of organizing the creative impulses in a capitalist society it is so much better than any known alternative that it should be respected and preserved.

On reading the manuscript, my wife objected to its emphasis on money. The emphasis may not be esthetic, but it is honest. Money is the lifeblood of the business world. To a businessman it is many things: reward, a status symbol, the way of keeping score. Neither money nor profit is a dirty word. This striving for money is the dynamic that gives corporations their distinctive character and vitality. At the top-management level, it becomes a striving for profit, which is the final measure of corporate success. At lower levels it creates eddy patterns that may run counter to the corporate stream: patterns of self-seeking and empire building. The story must be told.

I had better clear up what may be a confusing use of first-person pronouns in this book. When expressing an opinion, the word "we" is used for the simple reason that this book is a joint effort. Although I did most of the writing, my collaborator carefully edited my work and I edited his. Apart from the fact that it is more pleasant for me to write with someone looking over my shoulder, he contributed a wealth of business experience in many fields and a sound economics training to enlarge the scope of the book and protect against error. Unfortunately my helper, who is still in the business world, preferred to remain anonymous. When it comes to telling stories or anecdotes, I use the first person singular for obvious reasons. Somewhere I say that my Dad consoled himself with bootleg whisky. If I had said "our," it would sound as if my collaborator were my brother or as if the text were written by Queen Victoria.

I have had a lot of help. The most significant is nameless: the constant association over many years with my colleagues at Pennzoil Company and its predecessor companies. The faculty at the Harvard Business School and at the Chicago Graduate School of Business were very helpful and considerate. The staff of the Louisiana State University Library was cooperative. Donald T. Mac-

Roberts was particularly helpful and encouraging. Being something of a corporate "loser," I had to write from the point of view of middle management. With his more exalted background, Don was able to help when we got to subjects involving top management.

Henry I. Meyer

FOREWORD

HENRY MEYER spent a number of years playing a key role in the success of Pennzoil Company. He has now found a second career writing books about the subjects and lessons he obviously learned well.

In this wonderfully entertaining book, Mr. Meyer says, "Business students who want to learn the operations side of American business can do worse than reading the editorial text of the (annual) reports of large corporations." There may be no better way to gain a look at how business really works than to read this excellent book. In it he gives us not just the "face" of business, but the head and heart as well. It is a wise and witty treatment of a sometimes arcane subject.

Whether you are a top executive or the rawest recruit in the ranks of business—in fact, even if you're not in the business world at all—there is ample material here to enlighten, educate, and entertain. I sincerely recommend this book as well worth the reader's time.

J. Hugh Liedtke
Chairman and Chief Executive Officer
Pennzoil Company

CONTENTS

PART ONE

Business

1

WHAT IS BUSINESS?

WHAT IS BUSINESS? The word seems to fall into the same category with love and democracy: words which are universally accepted but not well defined in any dictionary, or at least are interpreted differently by different people. Before getting on with this book, we must establish a working definition of the word as we will use it.

BUSINESS AND THE AMERICAN WAY

If vaguely defined words tend to generate adjectival forms (for example, brotherly love), "business" is no exception. There are so many variants that listing them might be an interesting word game: big, small, oil, monkey, show, funny, and so forth. As a first crack at limiting the subject matter of this text, we assume two modifiers: big and American. The first assumption gives us something important to write about, and the second restricts it to our own experience.

Big business is the soul of the American way of life. If the reader expects this book to be yet another satire on the business world, he had better smooth out these first few pages and try to get his money back. When "Engine" Charlie* said, "What's good for General Motors is good for America," he was not far wrong. When General Motors was in real trouble, we said we were in a depression or recession.

Business does have its idiosyncrasies, its charlatans and parasites. Sometimes the working of the business world is wildly funny, but on balance, its leaders are honest and responsible. The days of the nineteenth-century robber barons is pretty well over. Jay Gould, Collis P. Huntington, and Jim Fisk have gone to their dubious rewards.

The structure of national and multinational business is traditionally supported by the sanctity of contracts and by mutual trust. The in-fighting and back-stabbing dear to the heart of the business novelist occur at a lower level, a level with which this book is also concerned. If our writing at times seems carping or disrespectful, we are usually dealing with the micro rather than the macro level of the corporate world. Long association with the business environment breeds some cynicism. It also breeds respect. In spite of the doings of the consumer advocates, the environmentalists, and the politicians, it is big business that sets the tone of American society. We would not (with few reservations) have it any other way.

STEREOTYPES AND FOLKLORE

Before attempting a definition of business for our own purposes, it is reasonable to consider the usual layman's concept of what (big American) business is. This consideration is valuable for two reasons: first, common knowledge, though uninformed, is often surprisingly correct, and second, our definition must be sufficiently consistent with accepted concepts to be believable.

---

* Charles Wilson, former chairman of the board of General Motors.

What do people think about business? That they do think rather a lot about it is obvious. Governments and political parties are glibly labeled as pro- or anti-business, self-respecting newspapers have a business section (which seems to be largely concerned with real estate development), and downtown Houston has illuminated signs which track the Dow-Jones average. After giving the received concepts of outsiders a fast mull, we decided that their perceived image, or the face of business, can be examined under five categories or constraints. The organization has to be above a certain size, it must be suitably located, have an acceptable public image, involve certain types of people, and most important, it must have something to do with money. Each of these categories deserves further discussion.

Size
Size is a function of two factors: amount of money and the number of people employed. The minimum allowed of each is hard to say; it certainly changes with organization type. A small automobile maker may be much larger than a respectable carpet manufacturer. The money factor is associated with balance sheet items rather than earnings* (Chrysler, though losing money, is still big business). To an outsider, the money constraint is satisfied if the corporation spends enough money to be visible in its territory and if its checks are recognized and accepted.

To be a legitimate business in our sense, an organization must employ enough people to form a recognizable group. A two- or three-man operation, no matter how profitable, does not qualify. From the insider's point of view, this means that a valid business is stuck with a personnel department, government fair employment policies, pension plans, and other administrative baggage.

Location
It is popular belief that big business cannot exist outside of big cities. Manufacturing plants can prosper in small towns. As we

_____
* Chapter 3 gives a brief analysis of corporate "financials" and the annual report.

shall see later, these are not businesses themselves but only extensions of a proper business located in a proper city. It is almost impossible to accept the idea of big business in El Dorado, Arkansas; Waterproof, Louisiana; or Alpine, Texas. (Or in Plains, Georgia! President Carter ran an operation there, but we cannot admit him as a bona fide businessman; the image is incompatible with blue jeans. Business is not the only route to success.) The reasons are interesting.

In small towns, there just are not enough businesspeople to create the critical mass necessary for a viable operation. You cannot have a poker game without players. Business leaders *need* each other, for reasons which are both real and psychological. They must have the support of financial institutions like banks, and they require good transportation facilities and the availability of other leaders to deal with. It can be argued that with modern communications these sorts of things can be handled at a distance, but this ignores the psychological aspect of the tribal urge.

Business leaders are not an endangered species, but they are to a certain extent a persecuted one. The public may like the friendly neighborhood accountant, but it is uneasy about the people at the top. It may be envy. More likely, it is a feeling that anyone who makes that much money cannot be all good. The media do not help. We see a business leader before a congressional committee on the evening news; the guy is wearing a three-hundred-dollar suit with accessories to match, he is overweight, and he looks worried—and, by George, he should be. The congressmen are having a field day making points with their constituents by picking on a man who is playing a losing hand in a loaded game. He typically is not a good speaker (that's not his job), and his speechwriter obviously does not like him.

The only place a business leader can get proper respect is from his peers, and these are usually located in places like Chicago, New York, San Francisco, or Houston. The board rooms and the clubs of these cities are his natural habitat, and to them he goes. This herd instinct is very strong. When United Gas Corporation (a big business) was taken over by Pennzoil, corporate headquarters was moved from Shreveport, Louisiana, to Houston at great expense and for no apparent reason. The company is probably better for the move. Big business is at home only in big cities.

Image

The fact that an organization satisfies the criteria of size and location is not quite enough in the public mind to qualify it as big business; the image, the outward visible signs, must also be present.

The most obvious outward visible signs involve advertising. Advertising has two missions: to try to get consumers to buy products and to promote the image of the company in particular and of its industry in general. An increasing amount of money is being spent for the second type of advertising, known as institutional advertising. This may seem illogical, since the message is not directly aimed at increasing sales. (Sometimes the opposite! We now have electric utilities and oil companies pushing reduced consumption. The image gains are worth more than sales.) But it is not wrong-headed. Business leaders have been shot over by the government for so long that they are fighting back the only way they can. If people can be convinced that corporations are basically good (most are), then just maybe the legislators will stop looking for voter approval through harassment of business and create a more favorable environment for industry. The corollary to this media effort is that the corporation becomes increasingly accepted as a big business in its own community.

Men have fought and died following signs or symbols throughout recorded history. Some of these, like the crusader's cross, are still alive and well after a thousand years; others, like the Confederate battle flag, are retained for sentimental reasons. The business counterpart of the Union Jack is the logo: the shell of Shell, the globe of Pan Am. As a corporate signature or identifier, a logo has value, for example, to guide customers to the proper service station or as a hallmark of value on a product. It crosses language barriers. The business community seems to attach an almost mystical significance to logos. The damn things are ubiquitous: on business cards, hard hats, bumpers, tie clasps, and lapel pins.

It is questionable whether the average employee attaches any sentiment to these symbols—certainly he invents bawdy names for them whenever possible—but management people love them and are willing to spend a lot of money to change the old or to introduce new ones. The classic case is Jersey Standard, which spent more hundreds of millions of dollars than it is willing to admit to introduce the Exxon logo. Probably it was money well spent. The corporation now has a single trademark recognized in all 50 states. This opened up national television as an advertising medium, in addition to more obvious benefits. It may be that selecting or designing a logo is a pleasant change for management; it has to be an ego kick to see the piece of corporate heraldry spread all over the landscape.

While a logo provides image, it also confers prestige. A real prestige piece is a building well identified with the corporation; it is the ultimate symbol of corporate stability and big business. The Wrigley building, the Tribune Tower, the Chrysler building are old landmarks on the American scene and as significant in their way as the cathedrals of Europe. If cathedrals are statements of faith, so too are our big corporate headquarters. People do not build a home unless they plan to be around for a while.

The ultimate symbol of corporate respectability is listing in the New York Stock Exchange, often called the Big Board in statements like "We are listed on the Big Board." If a company cannot qualify to (or in rare cases does not want to) get on the New York Exchange, the next best thing is the American Exchange. Finally, for the young or hopeful, there are regional exchanges and the unlisted or over-the-counter markets, which are still better than nothing.

Not everything corporations do to enhance their image involves corporate chest pounding or trumpet blowing (not necessarily at the same time). A lot of it is simply being a good neighbor—helping local schools and scholars, supporting civic organizations, and contributing time, property, and money to make the community a better place to live. Corporations are often reluctant to advertise their generosity. This aspect of their activities should be better publicized and known, even though the shareholders may feel they could do a better job of personal philanthropy from increased dividends.

People

A common, and naive, definition of business is the people approach—business is something businessmen do. This uninformed definition is particularly prevalent among executives' wives. They see their husbands neatly dressed with dispatch case in hand board a commuter train in Connecticut or climb into their Cadillacs in River Oaks and head for downtown, there to become involved in a sort of money machine which for the wives *is* business.

This is about as valuable an exercise in backward logic as trying to prove the existence of God from the behavior of people. It does point up the fact that we are going to have to do a careful job of defining just what a businessperson is. Not everyone who wears a Brooks Brothers suit is a valid businessman. If the proper types can be identified, then we see that the people approach establishes a necessary, but not sufficient, element of definition. You cannot stage a play without actors, but you can have actors without a play to act in.

Money

Business folklore always assumes that business involves money. Money is the lifeblood and the *raison d'être* of the business community. The relationship is complicated and is the subject of whole libraries on business economics and finance. We will take a whirl at a useful description of the role of money in Chapter 4.

WORKING DEFINITIONS

Starting from the accepted folk wisdom of the last section, we can make working definitions of two key words: business and businessman. Consider the human factor first. Not everyone who works for a corporation is a businessman. There are obvious exceptions such as floor sweepers, but the taxonomy problem extends a long way up the corporate structure. It is convenient to divide all employees into two groups: managers and workers. (The term executive has been so overworked—as in "executive inns," "executive socks"—that we avoid it in this book.) Manual workers can be dismissed out of hand and we look for businessmen among the managerial group. Some identification is easy. For example, the controller can safely be counted. But how about some other highly paid people: research workers, engineers, lawyers, the eager young business school graduate who is going to spend his first few years in training jobs?

Precise classification of people is impossible. The following working rule will suffice for our purpose: *A businessman is a corporate employee who is concerned with corporate strategy and finance rather than with specific tasks.* * This is general enough to include the young business school graduate; he may be doing trivial jobs, but he is training for larger things. The research worker is generally excluded. The status of lawyers is less clear; lawyers always seem to be a problem. If a lawyer is part of the management team and is involved with policy, he is also a businessman. If his job consists in preparing briefs or trying cases, he is a hired gun—a lawyer. This separation is true of all professional types. An engineer may spend much of his career as a technician and become a businessman later when he takes his skill and experience to the management team.

Businesses include all types of workers. The businessman is of special interest because he exists only in a business environment and, as we have noted, his existence is a necessary condition for a business establishment.

With a working definition of the businessman, we can turn to a definition of business itself. In the previous section, we identified five criteria which are commonly accepted as characteristic of a business organization:

> It is involved with money.
> It is above a certain size.
> It has an appropriate corporate image.
> It is the workplace of businessmen.
> It is located in an acceptable city.

The first four can be accepted without change as part of a working definition, but the last needs some modification.

* There is another definition of businessman used, for example, in *The Wall Street Journal,* "Carter reassures businessmen...," "Businessmen talk to finance committee...." This is a subset of our definition which we shall call *business leaders.*

Big-business headquarters do not *have* to be located in certain large cities. IBM headquarters is in White Plains, and Texaco is moving to Rye, New York. These are not big cities, but they are close enough to New York City for IBM and Texaco management to have access to the money markets, to transportation, and to other business leaders. Sometimes a city becomes home territory for one particular industry, like Detroit for cars and Pittsburgh for steel. This may give the members of the group an exaggerated sense of their own importance and discourage innovation. American cars have had a look-alike identification problem.

On the basis of an insider's look at business, three more technical criteria should be added to the list. A bona fide business, in our sense, must:

- Have a management philosophy that accords with accepted business practice.
- Have an organization structure which also meets standard practice.
- Have well-defined goals and accept certain responsibilities or duties.

If the four generalities serve to identify a business organization as such, the three additional criteria describe the individual character of a given corporation. We have intentionally borrowed the convenient accounting phrase "accepted business practice" because it allows so much latitude. Within the population of business entities, there is room for great diversity of characters, even for sports. This *must* be the case, considering the myriad different missions assumed. The next chapter discusses the many different faces of individual corporations and attempts to classify them by their particular management style, organization, and goals. It is still possible to identify universal generic traits in all businesses from oil producers to sporting goods manufacturers; but as with people, it is the differences which are interesting.

2

BUSINESS MANAGEMENT AND ORGANIZATION

THE BUSINESS WORLD brings together a diversity of creatures and talents, which may range in a single company from sorting mail to solving problems in nuclear physics. These people and their capabilities are coordinated into a unified effort to achieve meaningful goals by the corporate structure (organization) and by its management (control). It is the job of the businessman to set up and maintain the organization and control system. The old word for this function is "administration," a word which is still used in academic degrees such as MBA (Master of Business Administration). The way in which a particular company handles this administration problem sets the tone of the organization—a happy ship or a lousy place to work—and determines its efficiency and whether its shares are a good or a bad speculation for investors.

We originally planned separate introductory chapters, one on business management and one on organization. It became clear that the subjects are too closely related to be treated separately. They are actually different aspects of a single business control system.

ORGANIZATION AND CONTROL

Organization is a convenient term for the structure of a business which can be shown on an organization chart. Management, as we use the term, concerns the interpersonal relations between the people who are embedded in this structure and the coordination of their efforts toward the corporate mission. Chandler defines a business enterprise as one that contains many operating units (organization) and is managed by a hierarchy of salaried executives (control).* We have no argument with his definition, but we feel that it is the style and philosophy of this control system that characterizes an individual business. You can define a person as something having a body and a soul, but this doesn't say much about his personality. In a healthy corporation, management philosophy and organization structure complement each other.

Many businesses start life without a conscious management control system. The organization is small enough and the goals (usually survival) are clear enough that it is not needed. There comes a time when such a company reaches the point where it must organize or perish. An effective system is usually built by trial and error.

Management organization is not confined to the business world. There is some sort of control system in all forms of group activity from the ant hill to Capitol Hill. Most of these are not business organizations as we have defined them, but we can abstract from these socio-, religio-, politico-, whatevero-management styles those found in business.

It is convenient to set limits on business control system philosophies. One extreme we call "Army management"; the other ex-

* Alfred D. Chandler, Jr., *The Visible Hand*, Cambridge, Mass.: Belknap, 1977.

treme we call "Baseball management." These are limits and no one business is likely to display pristine characteristics of either form. Most corporations show elements of one or the other philosophy in different parts of the organization.

THE ARMY AND THE CINCINNATI REDS

Every student of American history can see in his mind ranks of British troops, muskets and bayonets level, marching to a measured beat, advancing on the motley group of frontiersmen skulking behind trees. Every man in red knows his job. Everyone knows to put his left foot down to the beat of the drum, to raise his musket on the proper order, to ignore those falling around him and to fire only when the order is given. This is the prototype of Army management.

Under Army management, every man does his job: the innovator is likely to be shot, figuratively or actually. Promotion is largely a result of the casualty list (a highly exogenous variable), of superannuation, and of time in grade. A characteristic of Army management, the one almost immutable aspect, is an established pecking order. There are rare exceptions. An Eisenhower or a Gavin leapfrogs the grayer beards, but the exceptions are rare in a true Army organization. (Lincoln did run the part of the army under his control like a baseball team, but Army order was established below the highest ranks.) Another characteristic of Army management is reward by rank and time of service. Job security is the premium perquisite in this form of management (more about "perks" later).

The primary advantage of Army management is that it is really the only way to control large numbers of people. A horde of uncontrolled soldiers on a battlefield is easily routed. A horde of employees attacking a corporate objective without guidance and subordination is equally ineffective. The Army form of management becomes increasingly necessary with increasing organization size.

The major disadvantage of the Army system is that it stifles initiative. The excellence of any army is almost completely dependent on the *average* ability of its members (which may be high). The soldier who marches to a different drum, though he be brilliant and innovative, is doomed to failure or frustration in an Army system.

At the other end of the management spectrum, we observe what we chose to call Baseball philosophy. In this metaphor we refer to the visible baseball team and its manager, not to the front office with its legitimate business activities. We are specifically referring to the relationships between the team manager and his players.

Baseball management is essentially totalitarian. Advancement is frequently from the outside and not through the ranks. The sole criterion for advancement of the players is ability. Pay is based on performance. The competent, humdrum shortstop will eke out a humdrum existence while the superstar will spurt rapidly into the upper income group—only to wilt just as quickly when his legs or lungs weaken. Even a genuine superstar like Tom Seaver can suddenly find himself traded off to another team at the whim of his manager. This type of thing could never happen in an Army organization. (When Truman fired MacArthur, he was demonstrating again that "civilian control of the military" can be Baseball management applied to an Army organization. Truman had read about Lincoln.) Job security is not the hallmark of a baseball team.

The Baseball-style manager is much like a czar; he has no structure to hold him back. He uses people as long as they contribute and discards them when they are no longer useful. While there is little job security in an organization with Baseball management, there is a close personal relationship between the manager and the "players." It does not do, however, for a player ever to forget that this close relationship is one of convenience and that it can, and probably will, be snapped when he is no longer needed.

Baseball management philosophy is often found in organizations oriented toward sales—the early IBM comes to mind—and in advertising agencies. With brilliant, creative managers this system works beautifully. It is a riskier approach than Army management and can work poorly in the wrong situation.

If the top man is not a good judge of people or if the organization is too large, disaster looms. Even in a Baseball organization, most employees do routine jobs, and personnel problems are caused by the rapid promotion (based on merit) of a few talented people. (As we have seen, this is quite different from an Army organization, where each age phalanx marches along in step, with a few individuals forging slowly ahead toward the apex of the management pyramid.) The promotion problem can be offset by more perks or higher average remuneration at all levels. A Baseball-style organization should have a salary level higher than the industry average or it is likely to suffer serious attrition of those who are below the superstar level but who are needed to make the thing work.

This little table sums up the major characteristics of the two limiting control philosophies. Most organizations fall between these extremes.

ATTRIBUTE	BASEBALL	ARMY
Pay, perks, and promotion are based on:	ability	rank, service, and obituary column
Authority is:	direct	through channels

Army management is common in utilities and in large, sometimes decadent, organizations. It is common in trade unions, where seniority has become a fetish. If the AFL-CIO had been a business organization, George Meany would have been retired twenty years earlier and there would be a lot of younger faces in the ranks of the union hierarchy. Whether or not the members would have been better off is hard to say.

Baseball management is accepted in those cases, business and nonbusiness, where excellence is such an overriding consideration that it overwhelms the American fixation with egalitarianism.* Music is a classic example. The prodigy moves to the front rank of the violinists, regardless of age; the brilliant young conductor moves past the older, less gifted one. We accept this as quite proper. Baseball is suited to the arts.

* The French Revolution showed Baseball management gone ape. *Egalité* was one-third of the credo, but some were more equal than others! The man at the top could promote those he liked and chop off the heads of those he did not. The French peasant *sans culotte* had Baseball rammed down his throat before it was invented.

Mixed Systems

Most corporations have different management philosophies at different levels. A large business is a complex of many sub-businesses, each of which has its own, appropriate form of management and control. For example, a large multinational corporation will have its manufacturing departments, transportation department, and marketing department. It will have a research organization, a financing department, and a planning department. It will in fact have a lot of other departments, and many of them will be replicated at continental, national, and local levels—each with its own Vu-Graph projector. At these different levels and in the different departments conditions will vary, and so will the control structure. Only the Vu-Graph is certain.

Some general observations about the incidence of our two philosophies in a typical corporation are possible.

Baseball management is normally found in top management. (Remember Truman and Lincoln?) It is also found in research and in small operating groups like the Bangladesh Widget Corporation where one man is holding the whole thing together.

Most business departments gravitate toward Army control without getting all the way there. The controller's department, for example, is normally run in the same manner as an infantry division, regiment, battalion, or company, depending on its size. Only the top man of that department may be a superstar on his way to greater things. The employee relations department (surprisingly) is usually run along Army lines.

In some extremely large companies the problem of reconciling the necessity of Army style control (because of size) with the encouragement of innovation is solved by splitting management vertically. The future top executive is identified early (often by his training) and is placed in a fast management track which follows Baseball philosophy. The others, who are not expected to advance to the top rung, are placed in a slower professional track where Army philosophy prevails. Members of both groups will practice their professions side by side and will advance on the basis of merit and seniority, but at different rates. As a result, promotions may appear quixotic and unfair.

The challenge to the outsider—prospective employee or investor—is to identify the management philosophy of an organization (or department) and associate with the type he prefers. A warning is in order, though. If Baseball is the prevailing style, it is not necessarily an honest, constructive solution to the control problem: it could be the manifestation of favoritism or nepotism by top management.

THE ROLE OF THE BUSINESS MANAGER

People are more important than the control system. Good top and middle management is the one indispensable factor in a successful corporation. Given the people he has and the job to be done, the good manager can work in any system to utilize the capabilities of his people—and his own.

A business manager has three jobs: he is a *goal setter, supervisor,* and *decision maker.* At the middle-management level his goal is stark—he strives to stay afloat. Supervision is the name of his game. The problems, the questions, and the answers change hourly, but they stay at a low level. Goal setting and decision making increase in importance as one moves up the management ladder, and direct supervision becomes less important.

At the top there is extreme emphasis on goal setting and decision making. The top manager must set the corporate course. He must supervise his managers to see that the course is being followed. This differs from the direct supervision of lower levels and usually involves only the reviewing of periodic reports rather than day-to-day contact.

In addition to his concern for corporate strategy, the top manager must be concerned with a certain amount of routine necessary to keep the organization running smoothly. (Most top managers delegate this sort of thing to an administrative vice president, but they cannot ignore it completely.) This entails occasional field visits (showing the flag) in addition to conferences and report reading. Probably the most important function of the top manager is staffing his management team. Those immediately below him should be capable of excellent work without the direct supervision he has no time for.

Poor execution of any of these roles by the top manager can lead to problems. If he takes his eyes off corporate goals and fails to change course to meet changing conditions, the corporate ship may run aground. If he concentrates too much on goals and ignores routine, the organization will get sloppy and the ship will be unsafe in any sea. The top business manager steers a narrow channel. We take a closer look at his peculiar frustrations later.

Goal Setting

How does one set a proper course to realize goals? This is a difficult question. The fly-by-night trombone seller has short-term goals. He seeks to maximize immediate income to the point just before the tar and feathers and the rail arrive. The legitimate life insurance salesman realizes that he will be around for a while; he has kids to put through college and a mortgage to meet. His goals are long-term, and he is more likely to offer an equivalent *quo* for a proffered *quid*.

Colonel al-Qadaffi, the business manager of Libya (a socialist country *is* a business!), knows that his crude-oil production has peaked and that it will go down from now on. No matter how high the price of crude oil, there will be no substitute for many years, and it will be in demand. By the time substitute energy sources are developed, Libya will be almost out of oil. What target price does al-Qadaffi set for his oil under these conditions? Is fifty dollars a barrel too low?

But what about Sheik Zaki Yamani of Saudi Arabia? When Libya runs dry, Saudi Arabia will be just starting to reach its peak production. The threat of alternate energy sources such as coal-based synthetic fuels may not annoy al-Qadaffi, but it drives Yamani up the wall. A cheap, alternative energy supply would convert Saudi Arabia back to a third-class power. No wonder that Yamani seeks to maintain enough spare producing capacity to ensure an orderly market and keep the price below the critical point where the Western countries really try to develop alternative energy sources.

Goals depend on top management's perception of the future. They also depend on the resources at hand. It is one thing to take advantage of favorable circumstances. It is just as important to anticipate and prepare for trouble. Goals depend on circumstances and vary with changing conditions.

In most companies, the process of corporate planning (setting the course) to meet corporate goals starts at middle-management levels. A series of policy options, with analyses of the probable outcomes and payoffs, is prepared to meet the goals laid down by top management. As the bundle of options drifts upward in the organization, a winnowing process takes place. Frequently, the top man is presented only with one surviving plan for his stamp of approval, and no other top-level decision is required. Such single-option packages are sometimes rejected, but this is not common in well-run staff organizations where each echelon knows the likes and dislikes of the layer immediately above.

One might think that the department where the opinion-making process starts would be organized along Army lines in order to take advantage of the experience of the planners, but more often a loose Baseball-type organization is used. The process of establishing and evaluating options is frequently felt to be good training, and the departments which handle this function, even at low levels, are staffed with fast-track up-and-comers.

Supervision

It does no good to set a course unless one has some assurance that it will be followed. This is where supervision comes in. The type of supervision varies with level in the organization. Usually it is Army-oriented at the bottom and moves slowly toward Baseball at the top.

Most of what is normally regarded as supervision (bird dogging) occurs at middle-management levels where the organization is still heavily Army-oriented. At higher levels, close supervision may be deliberately avoided in order to see what the individual can do on his own. It can be costly, of course, if a rising star makes a bad mistake and wrecks a division of the company. It is less costly, however, than making the man chief executive without knowing his limitations and having him wreck the entire company. There is no need to take such gambles with men who are going to stay noncoms or middle managers all of their careers.

There are many misconceptions about supervision. A man we worked for years ago—an intelligent, gifted man—had the motto, "The good supervisor is a son of a bitch." We don't buy this approach. (Not always, anyway. See the discussion of people types in Chapter 12.) We believe there are other critical attributes of a good supervisor. It is extremely important that he understand people; that he know how they are motivated and how they respond. This does not necessarily mean that the supervisor treats every employee as that employee wants to be treated. Rather he needs to know how to get the maximum effort from each subordinate and, on the other hand, how to avoid demoralizing him unnecessarily (demoralization is sometimes necessary, and the good supervisor knows how to do that too).

A good supervisor has intelligence, dedication—and *class*.

The word "class" invokes mixed emotions. It implies prejudice, privilege, and injustice; it also implies bravery and generosity—junior officers leading their men in battle, the captain going down calmly with the sinking ship. The most successful management effort in the history of world commerce, the old India Civil Service, was based on a class system.* We still use the term; it is the highest compliment a sports announcer can pay to a courageous player. It is still the best word to describe the most important attribute of a good manager.

In the business scene, "class" refers to the relationship between the manager and the managed. The supervisor with class is genuinely interested in and likes those who work for him. He tries to help them and to further their careers rather than using them to improve his own. More important, this attitude comes from inner conviction rather than from the self-serving injunctions in management texts to "empathize" with his people. A good manager has this kind of class, a bad one does not and his people know it. Incidentally, the British in India for the most part had it. They learned the languages, respected the customs of, and liked the people they served. With America's role becoming global, may we do as well.

Back to the mechanics of supervision. The good supervisor

* Philip Woodruff, *The Men Who Ruled India*, London: Jonathan Cape, 1963.

plays two and one-half roles. He must (one) make sure that those under him are performing their tasks at least adequately. He must recognize that a firm is a bit like a hotel: people come and go, but the fabric remains, and so he must (two) recruit good people to fill the vacancies due to growth or attrition. This is one of the most important jobs a manager faces; he is normally evaluated by his superiors on his judgment of others. The ability to evaluate people is an essential ingredient for upward mobility in the business world. It is also important, for upward mobility, that the manager choose and develop his own replacement as soon as possible. The indispensable man is doomed to a lifetime of valuable, but immobile, service.

These two roles—supervising his employees and choosing new ones—take much of the manager's time, but he must play one more bit part. He must (two and one-half) spend a portion of his time with those who are departing because of a better offer, pregnancy (which may be a better offer), or just a siren's call. Such concern is a good investment. Things may not work out for the ex-employee, and he may, in due course, want his old job back. If he is a valuable man, the bet has paid off. In any event, a disgruntled ex-employee can be extremely troublesome and sometimes expensive.

The nastiest part of supervision, and that part where most supervisors fail, is in open employee evaluation. Any company of any significance has some system by which each supervisor rates his subordinates. In the more progressive companies, this procedure is institutionalized. The supervisor is expected to sit down with each subordinate and explain his rating to him. Few managers have the courage to say, like Browning's Duke of Ferrara to his last Duchess, "It is here you miss and there you exceed the mark."

As most employee evaluations serve only to determine next year's perks and the magnitude and timing of the next raise, it is probably just as well that the rating system usually breaks down. Most people take a dim view of being told they are epsilons plus,* but the proportion of employees getting top marks, the alphas, must necessarily be quite small.

* Aldous Huxley, *Brave New World.*

Decision Making

The third and last role of the business manager is decision making. He is hardly unique in this function in that everyone makes decisions once he grows old enough to think. What is surprising is the mystique which surrounds the concept in the business world. Nine out of ten prospective employees, when asked what their goals are, announce that they want to be in a position to make decisions. What the would-be decision maker means, of course, is that he wants to make *important* decisions; he wants to start at a level it takes most people years of training and experience to reach (unless they have a Fairy Godfather in the organization). In actual practice he will not even have much of a role in deciding where to have lunch at this stage of his career.

Business decisions are of two types: tactical and strategic. Tactical decisions involve day-to-day problems. Given the long-range goals, how do we get around the roadblocks that crop up daily? This is essentially a middle-management area where specialists such as engineers or accountants solve operational, sometimes exciting, problems.

At the other extreme are strategic decisions. Goal setting is clearly one of these. Others are more mundane, such as choosing an optimum debt-equity ratio or devising a policy for dealing with new government demands.

There are several important points which should be kept in mind on the subject of decision making. In a well-managed company, decisions should be made at the lowest possible levels. Authority to make relatively minor decisions should be delegated rather deeply. Another point is that above the operating level, decision making is quite unscientific and really almost metaphysical. What this sort of decision making comes down to is the balancing of a number of incommensurable factors. If we decide to take action X, it will have one effect on the profit and loss statement* (which has ramifications in the investment community), another on the competition (which may spot a vulnerability caused by the action), still another on the general public (which may or may not

* Or the income statement. More on this later.

understand the motivations and consequences, but probably will not), and finally on the employees, the shareholders, and the Feds. The manager must consider all these, and other factors, measured in different units, and strike a balance.

In the 1950s the "discounted cash flow rate of return" procedure as a decision-making tool was unleashed from the Harvard Business School and eagerly embraced by the business community. Here at last was a scientific procedure which could tell whether option A or B was more attractive in the long run! Furthermore, the procedure was so complicated that it took electronic computers to use it! Controllers, then the custodians of computers, labored mightily to implement the discounted cash flow rate of return technique on their computers and, thereby, to bring the decision-making process into the electronic age and under their control.

As it turned out, decision making did not shift to the controller's office, nor did the controller, in general, migrate to the president's chair. Decision making is still a balancing of the incommensurable—a task beyond the capability of any scrawny computer yet known to man. The men who had been making the big decisions kept on making them, using the discounted cash flow rate of return method, provided by the computers, as just another helpful tool for making difficult choices.

Goal setting, supervision, and decision making are the functions of the modern business manager. A good business organization provides a climate (usually at middle-management and certainly at the top-management level) in which the businessman can carry out these functions in an orderly way without having to spend most of his time on administrative details.

Management as a Separate Discipline

The observations of the previous sections are as applicable to the manufacture of putty knives as to the assembly of DC-10s. They were also put forth in a rather simplistic manner that suggests that management is an art (a science, perhaps?) in which one may readily be trained. This is a concept dear to the hearts of deans of business schools, to professors, and to business writers. No way! The good (real) baseball manager usually has twenty years of competitive experience behind him. The managerial talents he has are add-ons to the basic disciplines he acquired earlier. It is the same in business.

Good managers are born, not made; their class and the management skills they have acquired did not come from a textbook. Management is not like engineering, which can be learned in laboratories and classrooms. If those who are teaching management skills really understood what they are professing to teach, they would be better off abandoning teaching and taking a job in business. "Them what kin, do; them what cain't, teach." Good management is based on years of experience, sound knowledge, and an understanding of people. Officer Candidate School can put bars on a soldier's shoulders; only combat can make a good combat officer.

Management by Objectives

We had better say something about "Management by Objectives," if only because someone is going to look for it in the index. The concept is simple: if A works for B, who in turn works for C, then C sets his goals or objectives in a formal manner for B to read and understand, B then works up his objectives, compatible with those of C, and passes them on to A, and so on ad infinitum. All objectives are coordinated to a common goal. This is almost a tautology; any other way of doing business seems silly.

This simple, but sound, approach is an "in" thing and the subject of seminars and of traveling training teams. Apart from being a statement of the obvious, as taught it has its defects. The most costly is additional paperwork. The recommended implementation procedure involves long, formalized, objective statements, to be prepared at each level. The bureaucratic mind usually substitutes special forms for common sense. Another defect is the "domino effect": a high-level change in goals triggers a flurry of changes all the way down the corporate structure. The most basic flaw, however, is that the goals of top management are not, and never will be, completely compatible with those of middle management. Top management wants to increase earnings and net worth; middle management wants to survive and build empires.

ORGANIZATION CLASSIFICATION

Although business organizations have a lot of elements in common, they are far from being alike. A quick check of the members of the *Fortune* 500, for example, shows wide variety. These differences can be categorized, or classified, in terms of *structure, character,* and *mission.*

Structure

The structure of business organizations may be centralized or decentralized, or it may fall somewhere in between. Indeed, some organizations oscillate, going from one to the other. There are perils at either extreme, and it is reaction to these dangers that causes companies to fluctuate.

An organization which is highly centralized, in which most goal setting and important decision making is done at headquarters, can lose touch with the market. Unrealistic goals can be set and improper decisions made. A classic example of this danger is given by Tolstoy in his description of the battle of Borodino in *War and Peace.* According to Tolstoy, Napoleon was completely out of touch with the actual situation and it would have been physically impossible to carry out his order of battle. Napoleon lucked out. He commanded a superb army where the noncoms and the field officers knew what had to be done, rose to the occasion, and routed the Russians. The situation would have been a disaster for the French had it not been for the high quality and morale of the troops. It is equally true in the business world that high-quality staff and line people can overcome bad top-level decisions, but this is a dangerous way to run a business.

Decentralized organizations can also have problems. The more widely goal setting and decision making are disseminated, the less coherence there is in the corporation. Conflicting goals may be set in different units. Resources may not be optimally employed. Optimization for each local unit may lead to something quite different from the optimum for the whole. (A division of a large electronics corporation once procured its computers from an outside, competing manufacturer!) With substantial decentralization, there is a real possibility that a local manager will violate company policy in such a manner as to reflect adversely on the entire organization—unauthorized bribes to politicians come to mind. It is no wonder that some organizations move back and forth between the extremes, seeking some satisfactory middle ground.

Character

Organizations may also be classified as to their character: large or small or in between, single-product, multi-product, true conglomerate, domestic or international, vertically integrated or not, and so on. From an investor's point of view, there is safety in diversity but probably less action.

Unlike questions concerning control, those concerning character can be researched from outside the company. Moody's *Industrials,* company annual reports, and 10-K reports to the Securities and Exchange Commission, which we consider in the next chapter, are excellent sources of information.

Mission

The final organization classification we take up is mission: just what has the organization been set up to do? The answer to this question tells a lot about the kind of resources it will need and how it should be organized.

An example of mission type is resource development: oil and gas, coal, uranium, land, copper, and so on. Another is farming. (There are large corporate farms, although, for tax reasons, cooperatives are quite common.) Manufacturing is the most familiar business mission, although the meaning of the term is not exactly unambiguous. The *Fortune* 500, for example, include some firms which might more properly be described as resource development. Other missions include services: sports, recreation, building maintenance, health care, and all the many things people do for each other. There is a wide variety of financial missions such as insurance, commercial banking, and stock brokerage.

All organizations, business and nonbusiness, have missions. Some are obvious, like that of the American Cancer Society. The missions of government units are less evident and may even compete with each other. The departments of Labor and Commerce appear to have different, even antithetical, missions.

Any organization can be classified under these three headings: type of control, character, mission. To cite a familiar (to me) example: Pennzoil is a centralized, medium-size, predominantly domestic, resource-development-oriented company. If one is interested in a corporation, either as an investment or as an employer, it is a good idea to classify it along these lines. The degree of centralization is not always apparent to the outsider and may be one of the things a job applicant should look into during a visit.

TOP MANAGEMENT STYLE

The style of top management is usually a function of historical accident and the organization's character and mission. Style can vary widely among apparently similar companies in the same industry. Texaco, for example, has a reputation in the oil industry for being cheap and chintzy.* Gulf has a reputation for being more generous, easier to do business with, and, recently, of engaging in illegal and unethical contributions. Exxon resembles Gulf except that it has tried to avoid undercover payoffs. (It got caught in one in Italy which was the result of excessive decentralization.)

In-Group Management

Management is sometimes by an in-group. An example is where the in-group owns the majority of stock—or at least a controlling interest, which is frequently far less than 50 percent. Cases are rare among the larger companies today. Perhaps the best mod-

---

* Anthony Sampson, *The Seven Sisters*, New York: Viking, 1975, p. 197.

ern example is J. Paul Getty's control over Getty and its associated companies. Thomas Watson "ran" the early IBM just as John D. Rockefeller ran the old Standard Oil Trust. In-group management today rarely survives more than one management generation.

One type of in-group management occurs when an entrepreneur creates a new organization which he then controls. Texas Eastern Transmission Company was created by the late R. H. Hargrove. He saw an attractive business opportunity, pulled together the resources and people needed, and created a major business organization, which he ran until his untimely death.

Pennzoil illustrates another method of achieving in-group control. Two independent oil operators, Hugh and Bill Leidtke, used extensive financial leverage—and not a little *chutzpah*—to gain control of a stodgy company, Pennzoil, with assets far greater than their own. Having consolidated their control of Pennzoil, they then acquired another stodgy company, United Gas, many times the size of Pennzoil. In this case the in-group did not physically create a new company; it used financial leverage to gain control of existing firms, which it then reshaped to its liking.

Professional Management

In contrast to management by an in-group, there is professional management. This form of management is the norm today for corporations of any real size.

In most corporations the ownership of its shares is so widespread that no one individual or in-group has control through share ownership. Certain politicians are fond of citing the stake of some financial institutions such as the Chase Manhattan Bank in companies such as General Motors and Exxon as evidence of "Rockefeller control." This "control" is illusory. Much of such stock is held on deposit for others who decide for themselves how to vote on issues. Insofar as the bank retains voting rights on such stock, it usually votes as the company management suggests.

Most shareholders, in fact, normally vote as management suggests (see Chapter 6). These include financial intermediaries as well as little old ladies in sneakers. It is not uncommon for 95 to 99 percent of the owners to vote in favor of management proposals. Only on rare occasions do the shareholders rise up in anger. Generally professional management is self-perpetuating.

Much has been written about the separation of ownership and control in the business world. Learned economists have lamented the antisocial aspects of this separation. Without weighing the pros and cons of the situation, it is clear that it is this separation which has led to the development of professional managers.

In the modern large corporation, trained but inexperienced professionals—engineers, accountants, geologists, business school graduates—enter at the bottom of the pyramid. As they drift upward at differing rates, some increasingly shed their original profession and take on functions of a more managerial hue. What emerges at the top is the professional manager. Each employee is judged along the way by those above him on the ladder and is moved up—or out—on the basis of his contribution, the organization's needs, the assessment of his potential, and a little bit of luck. On balance the system works fairly well; if the best man does not get to the top, a good one usually does. The alternative approach, the selection of a son-in-law by the leader of an in-group, leaves at least as much to be desired. The shareholder who votes in favor of the management's recommendations is not normally voting against his own interest.*

The style of top management is important to the potential investor and particularly to a prospective employee. It may not be easy to determine from the outside, but it is worth investigating.

SUMMARY

How are we getting on toward our goal of exposing the business world, of revealing the face of business? We have answered a few questions but not many.

* A preview of Chapter 6 is essential here to avoid confusion. Shareholders do not normally vote directly for officers, such as the president, or for the chairman of the board. They vote for the members of the board of directors, who, in turn, elect the officers. But it is the officers who suggest to the shareholders whom they should select as directors. Since the shareholders usually follow these suggestions, the officers, in effect, elect themselves.

The place of a businessman in a corporation is now fairly well defined. He is a member of middle management (but not *all* middle management qualifies, since some managers are technicians); he may move up through the ranks of professional management, even up to the top. The duties of a manager are explained, but not the inducements which persuade him to take up this unnatural job or even the types of functions that he manages. The businessman is still a shadowy figure. We need to consider his training, motivation, behavior, and superstitions.

The definition of corporate organization is in an even more unfinished condition. Organizations are now classified in a general way by character and mission. A close look at the organization structure—the organization chart—will come later. The whole subject of reading the lines of, and between the lines of, published corporate reports in order to make this classification is still to come.

This is an unusual chapter, almost a sport, in a book on business, in that money is hardly mentioned. Money is the very essence of business, not just as static figures on financial reports but as a moving, almost living, force. We have a lot of spadework to do on money.

The shareholders have been introduced, but as usual, they have been shortchanged. The relationship between the shareholders (both as owners and as investors) and the company needs to be clarified.

3

CORPORATE REPORT CARDS

LARGE COMPANIES present periodic printed reports to the public, to the government, and to their shareholders. We call these "corporate report cards" because they are to companies what the more familiar kind of report cards are to students. In a real sense, companies are graded by the readers: by present and potential shareholders and by the financial community. An "A" awarded by investors is a stock price rise, an "F" is a decline. Marks by the financial community are corporate bond ratings: A, AAA, Aaa, Baa, and so forth. These ratings may be even more important to the company than its stock price, because they directly affect its cost of borrowing money. The first red alert of New York City's problems came when its bond rating slipped.

Bond rating (made by Moody's and Standard and Poor companies) is too technical a subject for this book. There are good references, and there are smart analysts who understand them. Most people are more interested in whether they should buy or sell a certain company's common stock or even if they should go to work for the organization. They should be able to understand corporate report cards well enough to help resolve these questions. It is to such "outsiders" that the following material is addressed. Any analyst, or anyone who has passed Accounting 201, may move on to the next chapter.

The three most available and most helpful corporate report cards are: the annual reports (with the interim shorter quarterly reports); government reports such as the 10-K; and reports made by outside commercial sources who provide ready-made report cards complete with grades. A lot of this material is readily available at large public libraries, at stockbrokers' offices, from the government, and from the companies themselves (write the Corporate Secretary). It is still amazing how many people come for a job interview who have not even read the annual report!

The Annual Report

The most widely recognized, and respected, corporate report card is the annual report to shareholders. The report of a *Fortune* 500 company is about as thick, slick, and informative as a copy of *Newsweek*, if somewhat more limited in scope. The purpose of the annual report is to tell the reader—usually the shareholder—what the company did last year and what it plans to do in the future. More exactly, it tells what management wants the reader to think about the company's past performance and future objectives. Fortunately, poetic and editorial license are severely constrained by financial and accounting reality. A single report may tell up to three different stories, which correspond to the three reporting media used: editorial text, financial reports, and the notes. The wise reader reads all three.

Editorial Text

This is often the biggest section of the report. The first section may be color pictures of top management or board members (reproving the axiom that people over forty should think twice before having their pictures taken). This is traditionally followed by a "Letter to Shareholders"—a short financial and operating summary signed by the president and the chairman of the board.

The remainder of the editorial text varies greatly from company to company, depending on corporate mission and type, problems and opportunities, editorial policy, and whether or not the company is competing for a prize for its annual report. One company may have sections on financial highlights, operating highlights, and a review of the past year; another (particularly a conglomerate) may have separate sections for each area of the business. There may be a section of colored pictures showing company people at work, including a representative sprinkling of minority workers, female workers, and pretty girls in hard hats. Everybody seems to be having a great time. Somewhere there will be a listing of executive changes in the year.

The textual part of all annual reports has the same goal: to present an interesting, fair, and factual picture of the state of the company, and to do it in as favorable a light as possible.

It is easy to dismiss the editorial text as a slick sales pitch by management, but this is not fair. If management communicates effectively with its owners and workers in the annual report, it is doing them a favor. Good communication is so important in business that any indication of an ability in this area is a plus. On the other hand—to resurrect our nautical analogy—if the report is poorly written, it brings into question the day-to-day communication between the captain and the crew, between the helmsman and the navigator. The text of most annual reports is well written. Business students who want to learn the operations side of American business can do worse than reading the editorial text of the reports of large corporations.

The Financial Reports

The most structured part of an annual report is the financial reports section. The "financials" include three pertinent reports: an income statement (often known as the P & L—profit and loss—statement), a balance sheet, and a sources and uses of funds (or cash flow) report. These are the statements, modified, as we shall see, by the notes, that earn a company the equivalent of the "A" or "F" on Junior's report card. Financials are also distributed by listed companies in their quarterly reports and by outside commercial sources. Those in the annual report are official—they carry the auditor's stamp of approval.

The only way to present an introduction to the interpretation of the financial reports is to work our way through an example (not a typical example, because there is no such thing—the reporting format varies from company to company and from industry to industry—but there is still enough conformity that the line-by-line analysis of one report will carry over to the interpretation of others). This is going to be a bit tedious. Having already suggested that the sophisticated reader leave us, we now invite those sybarites who are reading this book for pleasure alone to move on.

As our example we chose the annual report of Gulf Oil Company. This may seem a bit unfair; Gulf has had enough trouble without inflicting its financials to an amateur vivisection. Gulf is now doing fine (we give them an "A"); they put out a clean report; and we feel comfortable discussing the financials of an oil industry company. 2098968

The first financial statement in the annual report is often the balance sheet, which is a snapshot of the assets and liabilities of a company at time of record. (The income statement shows *changes*, and the sources and uses statement shows money movement.) Although there is no standard format for all companies, the balance sheet will always have two columns of figures, which add to the same total: the *assets* of the corporation, shown in the left (or top) column, and the *liabilities*, shown in the right (or bottom) column. That these two columns add to the same total is the beauty of double-entry bookkeeping. For every asset(s) entry there are equal total liability entries. Consider the simplest case, a company which has just been formed but hasn't done anything yet. The only asset is the cash put up by the shareholders; the only liability is the same amount of money labeled as shareholder's equity—what they have coming to them if nothing is done. The balance sheet of even a large and complicated company is nothing more than an extension of this simple beginning.

Gulf's balance sheet for 1976, titled Consolidated Statement of

Financial Position, is reproduced as Figure 1. Some general observations are useful before getting down to details. It has a top-bottom format—assets in the top listing, liabilities below. Both lists add up to the same total, $13,449,000,000 (that's right, thirteen and a half *billion* dollars). It is hard to grasp such huge numbers. In order to reduce the number of zeros on the report, each printed "dollar" represents one million dollars. To cope with these figures, it may be easier for the reader to think of them as representing chips in the business game: one million dollars equals one white chip. Another interesting general point is that, as we shall see, the numbers lose precision or meaning as one moves down the tables. The bottom figures in each list are little more than educated guesses.

Now to the nitty-gritty. Let's start at the top. The first asset line, *cash and marketable securities,* is known precisely, of course. But is it? What is the "Note 4" attached to this simple entry? There is more to cash and marketable securities than meets the eye, and one should detour to Note 4 to see what problems are involved. Since we are now dealing only with the printed financials as such, we defer discussion of notes. Whenever there is a note to a line entry, explanations are in order.

The next asset is *receivables (less allowance of $48 and $45 million).* This represents monies that are due to Gulf immediately or at least within a year. The allowances of $48 and $45 million (white chips?) represent money that is probably uncollectable. It is also a guess (and a lot of money). There is another nasty note reference (Note 5) which will give details and probably explain the mysterious "and" in the allowances.

Inventories comes next. There is room for creative accounting here. Inventories open up a whole world of complications which Note 7 is going to resolve only partially. To most of us, "inventories" seems a simple concept: count the number of cans on the shelves. Financial accounting deals with inventory *value,* not numbers, and this raises problems. Typically, the different units in stock have been bought at different times at different prices. How to assign a reasonable value to inventory items in this mixed bag? The "conservative" accounting approach is to carry inventory value on

Figure 1. Gulf Oil Company, statement of financial position.

	Millions of Dollars December 31	
	1976	*1975*
ASSETS		
Current assets		
Cash marketable securities (Note 4)	**$ 1,989**	$ 1,837
Receivables (less allowance of $48 and $45 million) (Note 5)	**2,907**	2,356
Inventories (Note 7)	**1,242**	1,143
Prepaid expenses and other current assets (Note 17)	**41**	137
Total current assets	**6,179**	5,473
Properties (less accumulated depreciation of $5,843 and $5,650 million) (Note 9)	**6,632**	6,236
Investments in affiliated and associated companies (Note 13)	**308**	280
Long-term receivables and other investments (less allowance of $60 and $58 million) (Note 6)	**288**	405
Deferred charges	**42**	31
TOTAL ASSETS	**$13,449**	$12,425
LIABILITIES		
Current liabilities		
Accounts payable	**$ 2,317**	$ 1,757
Notes payable and current long-term debt (Note 11)	**139**	217
Consumer sales and excise taxes payable	**151**	158
Accrued United States and foreign income taxes	**565**	618
Accrued rents and royalties	**145**	99
Liability to nuclear partnership (Note 10)	**30**	138
Other current liabilities (Note 15)	**844**	751
Total current liabilities	**4,191**	3,738
Long-term debt (Note 11)	**1,168**	1,294
Deferred production payment proceeds (Note 12)	**123**	57
Deferred income taxes (Note 14)	**483**	369
Other long-term liabilities	**145**	156
Minority interests (Note 20)	**397**	353
TOTAL LIABILITIES	**6,507**	5,967
SHAREHOLDERS' EQUITY		
Capital stock—authorized 300,000,000 shares, without par value; issued 211,910,826 shares stated at	**883**	883
Paid-in capital	**698**	698
Retained earnings	**5,800**	5,320
	7,381	6,901
Less 17,046,686 and 17,200,641 shares in treasury, at cost (Note 22)	**439**	443
TOTAL SHAREHOLDERS' EQUITY	**6,942**	6,458
TOTAL LIABILITIES AND SHAREHOLDERS' EQUITY	**$13,449**	$12,425

The notes on pages 28 to 43 are an integral part of the financial statements.

the balance sheet at cost or replacement value, whichever is the least. This normal approach can dramatically overstate or understate the real value of inventory when prices are changing rapidly. Accountants have developed better methods. Note 7 is going to have a lot of explaining to do.

Resuming the stroll down asset lane, we pass over the small item *prepaid expenses and other current assets* and move to the last items: *properties, investments, long-term receivables,* and *deferred charges.** For a change, these appear to be well-defined items representing known amounts of money laid out or forgone. Wrong! All these items are subjective and have notes to explain them. The biggest entry, properties, includes all sorts of things acquired in a variety of ways over the life of the company. Some may have been acquired through stock trades which involved income tax factors independent of underlying worth. Both the stated and the actual value of properties change from year to year. As equipment or buildings wear out, their stated value is decreased ("depreciated" or "depleted") using some accounting formula. Other properties such as land or a subsidiary company may greatly increase in real value.

The rules of thumb used by the accounting community bear little relation to actual value change. When the real value of facilities or investments deviates too drastically from the accountants' stated value, special one-time corrections may be made on the balance sheet to reconcile these differences. Such a jump can be a surprise, pleasant or unpleasant, to the investor. Adjustments are becoming increasingly common and represent the triumph of market reality over accounting convention.

The sum of these increasingly flaky (as we move down the list) asset values is the stated *total assets.* This number is of prime importance because it will indirectly determine the shareholders share of the pie after liabilities are taken care of.

Liability items are easier to understand than assets, since they are mostly a listing of monies owed by the company. The increasing

---

* These entries are called "other assets," while the previous items were "current assets." There isn't much difference.

uncertainty rule still holds: the further down the list, the less reliable the numbers and the more footnotes are called for.* The biggest items on Gulf's sheet are *accounts payable* (a solid figure unless the creditors have other ideas) and *long-term debt*. Long-term debt may be complicated where there are many debt issues outstanding, which is often the case with public utilities. If there are convertible issues (debt to common stock) in the package, this introduces further uncertainty. Bankruptcy creates the ultimate chaos—fodder for lawyers to feed on.

The last section of the balance sheet, *shareholders' equity*, is of vital interest to the investor. It does not stand alone without the other two sections, since the total equity is equal to total assets minus total liabilities. There are usually several line items in this section, but the titles are meaningless to an outsider. To list the amount paid for originally issued shares, as on the primordial balance sheet, is about as sensible as retaining the price originally paid to the Indians for Manhattan Island on New York's books. Only the total has meaning. It is the *book value* of the company; divided by the number of outstanding shares it is the book value per share.

Market share prices diverge markedly from book value for a number of reasons. We have pointed out that the listed assets and liabilities which ultimately determine the shareholders' equity are subject to uncertainties and interpretation. Since the equity account is the difference between two large numbers, the uncertainties are magnified (more on this in the next chapter, "Money Flow"). More important from the investor's point of view, the balance sheet looks backward on past performance while share price is based on cumulative investor expectations and hopes. Judged solely by book value, street car company stocks looked great in the thirties, but they were lousy investments. Conversely, many electronics stocks in the fifties and sixties had market values many times their book values and some of them (not the ones I bought) were greatly underpriced. The most valuable asset of some high-technology companies is the brains of their scientists. How do accountants put

* This is true on Gulf's report but not inevitable. Some companies follow a reverse order of reliability in their listing. See, for example, *Annual Report*, Western Union Corporation, 1977.

a value on that? What is the value of the Coca-Cola trademark? The balance sheet by itself is not enough to award corporate grades. We also need the income statement.

The income statement (or profit and loss statement) shows how things have changed since the last annual (or quarterly) report. There is a direct connection between the income statement and the balance sheet. If assets have grown more than, or shrunk less than, liabilities, the company has made a profit in the reporting interim—or conversely. Profits which are not paid out as dividends are added to retained earnings and the balance sheet stays balanced.

Figure 2 is Gulf's income statement—again under a bastard name—taken from the same annual report as the balance sheet on Figure 1. Income sheets are easier for the non-accountant to read than are balance sheets. The item names are more familiar: revenues, deductions (or costs and expenses), income before tax—these sound familiar. Every family on a budget makes a monthly income statement. In this case, profit at the end of the month is money in the bank. The annual income tax return (Form 1040) is really an income statement. Most of us are concerned with balance sheets only at times of crisis—death, divorce, bankruptcy, or when running for public office.

Taking a closer look at Figure 2, we see that Gulf had *revenues* of 18,403 white chips (over 18 billion dollars) and that two of the detail items are flagged with note references. The deduction entries seem straightforward enough, despite three note references. Don't be fooled! Costs are sensitive to accounting practice. The value (cost) of goods from inventory and the methods of computing depreciation and depletion vary from company to company and from year to year. The oil industry has special problems, particularly with inventory costing.

Oil companies have to carry large inventory stocks of crude oil in storage tanks and floating in huge tankers. To a refinery manager, one barrel of crude looks pretty much like another.* He has

---

* This is not completely true. Crudes do vary in quality, but the supply for a given refinery tends to be consistent.

Figure 2. Gulf Oil Company, consolidated statement of income and retained earnings.

	Millions of Dollars Year Ended December 31	
	1976	1975
REVENUES		
Sales and other operating revenues (Note 3)	$18,117	$15,838
Interest income	189	183
Equity in earnings (losses) (Note 13)	40	(23)
Other revenues	57	44*
	18,403	16,042
DEDUCTIONS		
Purchased crude oil and products	10,019	7,306
Operating expenses	1,400	1,251
Selling, general and administrative expenses	1,299	1,216*
Taxes other than income taxes (Note 14)	2,097	2,214
Depreciation, depletion, amortization and retirements (Note 9)	631	628
Exploration and dry hole expenses (Note 8)	364	317
Federal Energy Administration entitlements	214	224
Interest on long-term financing	109	114
Income applicable to minority interests	62	60
	16,195	13,330
INCOME BEFORE TAXES ON INCOME	2,208	2,712
TAXES ON INCOME (Note 14)		
United States	226	120
Foreign	1,166	1,892
	1,392	2,012
NET INCOME	816	700
RETAINED EARNINGS AT BEGINNING OF YEAR	5,320	4,951
CASH DIVIDENDS	(336)	(331)
RETAINED EARNINGS AT END OF YEAR	$ 5,800	$ 5,320
PER-SHARE DATA		
Net Income	$ 4.19	$ 3.60
Cash dividends	$ 1.73	$ 1.70

* 1975 reclassified to conform to presentation adopted in 1976.
The notes on pages 28 to 43 are an integral part of the financial statements.

no idea what a particular barrel cost, nor does he care; for him crude oil is fungible (replaceable). The investor is critically concerned, since cost of goods directly affects earnings. It is the accountant who must resolve the problem.

There are two general approaches: FIFO and LIFO. FIFO stands for *first in first out*; that is, a barrel of oil taken from inventory is assigned the value of the oldest oil (first in) in storage. In an inflationary situation, or in one loused up by the OPEC countries, this is lower than replacement cost. This increases current profits but will reduce future profits when only high-cost oil is left. LIFO—*last in first out*—prices inventory at the most recent cost (last in). This usually increases production cost and reduces profit.

The careful investor should refer to the inventory item (and its note) on the balance sheet—in our case, Note 7—to see what system, or mixture of systems, the company is using. This is true for any type of company; the oil companies just provide the most dramatic example at present.

In the long run it makes no difference whether a firm uses LIFO or FIFO or something in between. These different approaches really only adjust the *timing* of reporting earnings, not the cumulative total. Companies may or may not prefer to report income today rather than tomorrow. The good investor is interested in their preference. A company may not change inventory systems annually to control the earnings picture; it is stuck with what it has until it gets SEC permission to change. This is what "hurt" the oil companies when the OPEC price increase hit them. Insofar as they were stuck with FIFO accounting, they could not show the new increased cost of their supply. Hence the "obscene" profits, which had to be paid for later.

To move on to happier things, consider *net income.* This is what is left after deductions and taxes—the score, the "bottom line" of modern businessese, used in statements like "Six big ones up front is the bottom line" (translation: you get six thousand after expenses). Since net income is the difference between revenues and expenses, it includes all the uncertainties of the preceding figures. It is never completely accurate in any case, because the income tax figure is only an approximation and will not be settled for years.

With all its faults, net income is still the most important single entry in the financials. It can be compared with last year's figure to see if income is going up or down. It can be compared with dividends to see how well they are "covered." It can be divided by the number of outstanding shares to give earnings per share. The stock price can be divided by earnings per share to get a price–earnings ratio—the most abused statistic of all. Naive investors think there is a "proper" price–earnings ratio for a given stock. If it is 10, say, and earnings per share go up one dollar, then the stock price will go up ten dollars. Not true. The price–earnings ratio is only a ratio; it can change. An important performance check is to see if the rate of income increase is as great as the rate of revenue increase. If it isn't, corporate efficiency is declining.

The third major financial statement is the sources and uses of funds statement, or, as Gulf chooses to call it on Figure 3, consolidated statement of changes in financial position. There is some redundancy between this statement and the two reports we have already considered, but it does give additional information, particularly to trained analysts. It shows, for example, whether growth is being financed from healthy earnings increase or from increased, burdensome borrowing. For the average investor, the outsider, this statement has less interest than the other two.

These are the big three, the most important financial statements. They will be found in one form or another in all annual reports. Other supporting statements and long-term summaries may be included, often in the editorial text or in the notes. The members of the big three do not stand alone; they support and depend on each other. From two consecutive balance sheets and the sources and uses of funds statement, the income statement for the interim period can be constructed. The converse is not true: the balance sheet cannot be constructed from the other two reports, because the original starting point cannot be recovered. Those readers who remember their freshman calculus will recognize a logical parallel between it and accounting: the relation between differentiation and integration. As an indicator of change, the income statement is a differential; as a historical summary, the balance sheet is an (indefinite) integral. You can operate on totals to get changes but not on changes to get totals.

Figure 3. Gulf Oil Company, consolidated statement of changes in financial position.

	Millions of Dollars Year Ended December 31	
	1976	1975
FUNDS PROVIDED BY:		
Net income	**$ 816**	$ 700
Income charges (credits) not affecting funds:		
Depreciation, depletion, amortization and retirements	**631**	628
Income applicable to minority interests	**62**	60
Undistributed (earnings) losses of affiliates and associates	**(32)**	49
Deferred income taxes	**114**	109
Other	**(29)**	(7)
Funds from operations	**1,562**	1,539
Proceeds from sales of properties	**342**	226
Reduction of investments and long-term receivables	**138**	38
New financing including production payment proceeds	**156**	156
	2,198	1,959
FUNDS USED FOR:		
Properties and business investments	**1,378**	1,229
Reduction of long-term debt and production payments	**211**	225
Dividends	**336**	331
Nuclear partnership reclassification (Note 10)	**—**	138
Other—net	**20**	11
	1,945	1,934
INCREASE IN WORKING CAPITAL	**253**	25
LESS INCREASE (DECREASE) IN NONCASH CAPITAL (Note 2)	**101**	(46)
INCREASE IN CASH AND MARKETABLE SECURITIES	**$ 152**	$ 71
CASH AND MARKETABLE SECURITIES AT END OF YEAR (Note 4)	**$1,989**	$1,837

The notes on pages 28 to 43 are an integral part of the financial statements.

Before leaving the financial reports we had better exorcise one devil. Corporations *do* keep two sets of books: one for the shareholders and one for the tax collector. There is nothing sinister about this. The Internal Revenue Service insists on its own set of accounting conventions, which depart markedly from what are considered good accounting principles. This is often due to congressional tinkering with tax law for sociological rather than fiscal purposes. The accountant's first duty is to prepare meaningful reports for the shareholders. He then has to prepare different statements for the government. He publishes a public statement (schedule M–1) to reconcile the two. To do anything else would be irresponsible.

The Notes

There is a footnote (in fine print) at the bottom of all the Gulf Oil Company financial reports reproduced here: "The notes on pages 28 to 43 are an integral part of the financial statements." Sixteen pages of notes for three pages of financials! They must have something to say.

In reading the editorial text, it is a good idea to adopt a cynical attitude to counter the enthusiasm of management. It is safe to be neutral when reading the financial reports—accountants are not spellbinders. When reading the notes, be brave, keep your spirits up; this is tiger country. Whistle if it helps. The notes are the Jeremiah of the annual report bible; every possible catastrophe is documented, all corporate debt issues are laid out like dirty linen. I remember groping my way to the liquor cabinet after reading the notes in the report of one of my favorite companies. A rough computation showed that if we (I was a small shareholder) lost all our pending court decisions and had to make all threatened refunds and pay off all debts, we would have to liquidate the company and still owe enough to build a couple of Panama Canals.

Things are not as bad as they seem. We won't lose *all* the suits, we won't have to make *all* the refunds, debt retirement is planned and provided for. It is prudence ("Don't say we didn't warn you") and not the desire to scare the bejabbers out of the shareholders that causes companies to present this catalog of disaster. Besides, the auditors demand it. A look at the debt structure of some companies (not all) makes the reader wonder about business's pious denunciation of government irresponsibility. It may make him feel better about the hire-purchase Oldsmobile station wagon parked in his own driveway.

One page of the 15-page Gulf annual report notes, which includes Note 7, is reproduced as Figure 4. The notes should be read with, as footnotes to, the financial reports. To base a decision on the bare numbers of the financials is like buying a car after kicking only one of the tires. The notes to the financial statements frequently tell more about what is happening than do the reports themselves. It is a good idea to compare this year's notes with those in earlier reports. This makes it possible, for example, to track trends in inventory management, such as a switch from LIFO to FIFO accounting to spread inventory profits into future years.

It is hard work, it may be painful work, but read the notes.

The auditors' report is not really a note just to the financial statements but to the whole annual report. Under the rules of the Securities and Exchange Commission (SEC) all publicly held companies must have their books audited by an outside accounting firm. The accounting firm then puts its reputation on the line in a statement that it has examined the company's books and records and that in its opinion, the various statements fairly reflect the condition of the company. The accounting firm cannot afford to give such a clean bill of health lightly. If some corporate shenanigans have been overlooked, the auditors are subject to a lawsuit by shareholders and investors who have been misled.* Auditors are not infallible; they have made monumental blunders and have even been known to withdraw an opinion retroactively.†

Management wants a clean bill of health from the auditors and is usually willing to make reasonable compromises to get it. If agreement can't be reached, due to differences of opinion or to an honest lack of data in a complicated case, the auditor issues a *qualified* opinion, in which he states where there may be uncertainties or ambiguities. The financial community usually takes a dim view of qualified opinions, but not always if the reasons are clear. Signal Company stock, for example, has not suffered from a qualified opinion in its 1977 report.

---

* For a recent example, see "On the Rocks," *The Wall Street Journal*, August 29, 1978.
† Ibid.

We will return to the auditing function later when we take a closer look at the role of shareholders. Properly, the auditor is the shareholder's creature, not management's.

Figure 4. Gulf Oil Company, Notes 4 through 7 to the 1976 annual report.

NOTE 4—CASH AND MARKETABLE SECURITIES

	Millions of Dollars December 31	
	1976	1975
Cash	$ 54	$ 83
Time deposits and certificates of deposit	1,028	910
Marketable securities	907	844
	$1,989	$1,837
United States	$ 821	$ 819
Canada	461	232
Other Foreign	707	786
	$1,989	$1,837

Marketable securities are stated at cost which approximates market.

NOTE 5—RECEIVABLES

	1976	1975
Customers	$2,145	$1,673
Affiliated and associated companies	344	359
Other receivables	466	369
	2,955	2,401
Less: Allowance for doubtful accounts	48	45
	$2,907	$2,356
United States	$ 789	$ 683
Canada	457	422
Other Foreign	1,661	1,251
	$2,907	$2,356

In 1976 and 1975, provisions of $15 and $17 million, respectively, were credited to the allowance for doubtful accounts. Other charges and credits, principally write-offs and recoveries, were $15 and $3 million, respectively, in 1976 and $16 and $2 million, respectively, in 1975.

Figure 4. *continued.*

NOTE 6—LONG-TERM RECEIVABLES AND OTHER INVESTMENTS

	Millions of Dollars December 31	
	1976	*1975*
Long-term receivables	**$277**	$407
Other investments (at cost)	**71**	56
	348	463
Less: Allowance for doubtful accounts	**60**	58
	$288	$405
United States	**$ 33**	$ 53
Canada	**36**	36
Europe	**113**	146
Asia	**48**	77
Latin America	**30**	68
Middle East	**28**	25
	$288	$405

In 1976 and 1975, provisions of $4 and $47 million, respectively, were credited to the allowance for doubtful accounts. Other charges, principally write-offs, were $2 million in 1976 and $4 million in 1975.

NOTE 7—INVENTORIES

LIFO		
Petroleum		
United States	**$ 264**	$ 268
Europe	**141**	188
Other Foreign	**85**	25
Chemicals		
United States	**67**	40
Europe	**30**	13
Other Foreign	**5**	5
Merchandise	**12**	15
	604	554
FIFO (Canada)		
Petroleum	**324**	255
Chemicals	**12**	15
Merchandise	**18**	22
	354	292
Average Cost		
Petroleum	**19**	23
Chemicals	**2**	2
Minerals	**4**	2
Merchandise	**12**	12
Commodities	**20**	1
Materials and supplies	**227**	257
	284	297
	$1,242	$1,143

Figure 4. continued.

| | Millions of Dollars December 31 | |
	1976	1975
Total		
United States	$ 486	$ 451
Canada	384	319
Europe	197	222
Other Foreign	175	151
	$1,242	$1,143

	Millions of Barrels	
Petroleum Inventories		
United States	90	90
Canada	34	30
Europe	39	44
Other Foreign	9	6
	172	170

Decreases in certain LIFO pools increased earnings by $14 and $5 million, after considering taxes, in 1976 and 1975, respectively. LIFO inventories were $1.14 and $.87 billion less than current cost, including recognition of announced price increases of foreign crude, at December 31, 1976 and 1975, respectively.

Materials and supplies, and certain taxes on products carried in inventory are not included in the computation of cost of sales. The inventory amounts included in purchase costs, used in the computation of cost of sales, were $1.01, $.87 and $.86 billion at December 31, 1976, 1975 and 1974, respectively.

GOVERNMENT REPORTS

Companies are required to make an increasing number of increasingly detailed reports to the government. Most of these are available to the public. The most useful are those demanded by the SEC, and of these the best is the 10–K report, which every publicly held company must submit annually. The 10–K report includes all the financials and notes in the annual report plus a great deal of additional, more detailed information. The amount of information required increases every year. (At the current rate of growth these reports will soon grow to the size of the Manhattan Yellow Pages and will be useless because of a surfeit of data.) 10–Ks are available from the SEC. They are also available from the Corporate Secretaries of the submitting companies. One of the main duties of the Secretary is to see that government reports are filed on time and that they are available to others.

In earlier days the 10–K did not provide much more information than did the annual report. Recently, the SEC has demanded information which used to be considered proprietory. For example, oil companies must now report their oil and gas reserves in the United States and abroad. In the past such data were highly confidential—secret. Companies which are low on reserves can be expected to be aggressive bidders for new supplies; if competitors know this, they will respond appropriately. The new 10–K contains lots of useful information free of the editorializing of the annual report.

Another SEC report is the 8–K. Leave this one to the specialists. It is issued in cases of unusual and nonrecurring events such as major new financing in the offing, or after a company has signed a consent decree agreeing not to do what it was not doing already. The *existence* of a recent 8–K report may be of interest to the investor.

When a new stock or bond issue is planned, the SEC really gets nosy. A prospectus is called for to be distributed to all existing shareholders, to creditors, and to anyone else who is interested. This is the place for a financial analyst or corporate voyeur to pick up all sorts of information and corporate tidbits. History, plans, and prospects of the company are documented. A prospectus is also likely to give the age of each member of top management, his or her salary, bonuses, stock options, and expected retirement income. As the chairman of the board of one of our largest companies said in perusing his latest prospectus, "We sure do live in a goldfish bowl."

The sort of gossipy data provided in the prospectus may be useful to the investor. He may prefer to invest in companies with a younger (presumably aggressive) or with an older (presumably prudent) management. For the ambitious businessman in a middle-management position, age information can be crucial. If the people in top management are not much older than he is, he has problems, whatever his qualifications. Not only are the possibilities of moving up limited, but his own job may be threatened! Management is going to look for bright younger men to put on a "fast track" to the top. The older middle manager's job may be one of the way stations on that track, and he may be shunted to one side to make room. The young man in a company in which middle and top management are all older than he is may be on to a good thing.

COMMERCIAL REPORT CARDS

There are many commercial organizations which give corporate evaluations for the investor. Any issue of *The Wall Street Journal* or *Barron's* carries advertisements for such "investors' services." They range in price from moderate to extortionate and in approach from sound analysis to the metaphysical. Large brokerage houses provide free updated analysis sheets on selected companies for their customers. They may also print a modestly priced investment newsletter. The most respected sources of commercial information are publications by Moody's and Standard & Poor's.

You can't afford to buy Moody's volumes, but you may read the *Industrials, Utilities, Transportation,* or *Over the Counter Stocks* in the public library. These volumes provide all the basic financial and historical information on listed companies that most investigators will need. It is important to know which volume to use; Consolidated Edison, for example, is classified as a utility, not as an industrial. Use the proper volume.

One minor warning. The *Industrials* manual contains two sections. The first consists of data which have been verified by the company; the second section is data prepared independently by Moody's. Company-verified data should be more reliable—or some independent accounting company is in deep trouble.

Standard & Poor's is an alternative source of data. The format is much like Moody's except that industrials and utilities are mixed up together. S&P also provides information on the performance of industrial averages for the sophisticated investor. Perhaps the most useful and familiar S&P publication is the monthly stock guide. This booklet gives highly condensed data on companies listed on the major exchanges and for some over-the-counter issues. It even prints some ranking or grades. The *Guide* is a good starting place for an investment study. Copies are usually available free from your friendly neighborhood broker's office. They are passed out as promotion material.

A relatively new service is the access to both current and historical corporate and market data through computer data banks. The subscriber has a terminal through which he can call for, and get printed, all sorts of financial and stock information on most companies. Since charges are largely based on usage time, this need not involve an extravagant investment.

We referred earlier to bond rating by Standard & Poor's and by Moody's. Making such ratings is a special art which involves evaluating not only the performance and prospects of a company (or a city) but also its financial *structure*. Leave the rating to the experts, but check the rating of a company.

4

MONEY FLOW

WE HAVE STATED earlier that business, to be a business, has to have something special to do with money. This separates business from other large organizations such as military and civil service. The relationship between business and money is complicated. The classical role of business is to "make" money, but equally important from the businessman's point of view are the distribution of money and the rules, explicit and implicit, under which this is done. The object of this and the next chapter is to clarify these roles and duties, which are often not clearly understood even by middle management and which are often perverse in that they force companies to spend a lot of money for unprofitable reasons.

MAKING MONEY

How does business, or any organization for that matter, make money? From an accountant's point of view this is measured by a positive number on the bottom line of the income statement. The last chapter pointed out some of the problems of a strict accounting approach—the importance of cash flow and balance sheet items, for example—but in any event corporate financial reports do not give much guidance for future action. They are about as useful as yesterday's scorecard is to a baseball manager. Stripped of accounting language, there are only three logically possible ways of making money: to manufacture it, to take it from someone else, or to take it (that is, value) from the earth.

The first approach should not concern us, since the printing of money is the prerogative of government in most nations.* Bankers may object to this statement, since they really do create money when they lend deposits which depositors consider theirs. But these are deep waters, too deep for this book. There is reasonable doubt that *governments* can actually create money; what they really turn out are convenient IOUs (like cigar store coupons), which must eventually be cashed in for something tangible. A banana republic (or the United States) can grind out bills until it is green in the face without changing national wealth. These are problems for economists and not for the businessman who is trying to keep the corporate ship afloat. He must get his money either from someone else or from Nature.

Money from Nature

Ultimately it is energy from the sun, converted by that greatest processing plant—the earth—that provides us with all the goodies and the essentials of life. It is ironic that only primitive societies worship the sun: it would seem more appropriate for modern man to adopt this persuasion now that the sun's importance is better known. The conversion may come; we may see solar energy plants double as shrines. At least the resident priest could claim that he had a direct line to the Almighty.

Until we start getting a significant part of our material needs directly from solar energy converters (unlikely for many years), we must take them second-hand from the earth. This harvesting is of two types: by extraction (mining) and by renewal (farming).

Food and timber products can be turned fairly directly into

* In early days, some banks in the United States did print or mint their own money. This is still done in some countries.

money. The goal of agribusiness is to acquire sufficiently large tracts of land to take advantage of economies of scale, to use business management, organization, and resources to produce food efficiently and ultimately to make a profit. There are problems, current and threatening. Who owns the land? In a capitalistic society the answer seems obvious: the man who owns the deed. This may not always be true, as many deedholders in nearby Mexico painfully discovered recently.

The United States government is the largest domestic landholder. It owns about half the land west of Texas in the "lower 48" and over 95 percent of Alaska* and is constantly seeking to take land from the private sector. A recent threat has been a stirring of the aborigines; the Indians and the Esquimo have been making claims on private as well as public land with increasing success.

Unless the legislative and legal rules change drastically, the agri-businessman is still (with few exceptions) in a sound position to try and make money from farming. Given the vagaries of weather, the uncertainties of commodity prices, and vacillating government policies, he may have a hard time turning a profit, but in an abstract sense he is making money: he is turning the fruits of the earth into engraved pieces of paper.

The extractive industries, principally mining and oil and gas production, are more complicated than agribusiness, although they are also concerned with making money from Nature. The question of ownership is more complex. Problems involving mineral rights, leasing, and government participation keep armies of lawyers gainfully employed. Much more than agribusiness, the mining and oil companies are multinational, which leaves them open to harassment from foreign governments as well as their own. The complicated relations between foreign governments and the multinational oil companies have invoked several highly controversial books on the subject† as well as volumes of testimony before the Senate Foreign Relations Committee.

---

* National Atlas of the United States, Department of the Interior, 1970.

† For example, *The Seven Sisters*, Anthony Sampson, New York: Viking, 1975.

The government is at least as much to blame as the oil companies for the current disputes. It has at times turned its back on the international dealings of the big oil companies, which went about doing their own thing in their own businesslike way—honorably according to their own rules. On occasion the government has even encouraged the oil companies' activities as a matter of national policy; examples are the American presence in Iraq and the "Red Line Agreement." It hardly seems fair for the Senator Churches of this world to step in at this late date and blame the companies for carrying on in the way that the Achesons of an earlier date endorsed.

Let us bring this discussion to order and return to the subject of making money from extraction. The conversion of minerals into money is not as direct as the conversion of food, since demand for minerals is not as constant as human hunger. Only in this century has the need for energy, at least in Western nations, been as pressing as the need for food. The recent realization of this value change and the acceptance of the obvious fact that fossil fuels as an energy source have finite reserves* have encouraged hysteria in government and stubborn disbelief in the ordinary gasoline and natural-gas user—hardly a good climate in which to develop a rational policy. The businessman in the oil and gas business is caught in the middle; he is kicked around as a political football by politicians ("Break up the Yankees") and distrusted as a grasping pig by his customers. The only constant in the situation is that the oil companies are performing two critical services: providing energy (for a strong America?) and converting natural resources into money. The big oil companies will be with us for a long time to come, but they will operate under more difficulties than they deserve.

That the mining industries usually operate in a more friendly government climate than the oil industry is not logical. There *are* well-defined alternate energy sources such as nuclear energy, but

* Denis L. Meadows et al., *The Limits to Growth,* New York: Signet, 1972—a report on studies made by the Club of Rome. This provocative work has been criticized by economists for not making enough provision for cost/availability effects or for substitution. It has also been criticized by mathematicians for the form of the functions used, which predispose solutions to go to zero or infinity.

there is no way to replace the Mesabi range! Some metal uses are critical; others are not. When I was a child, my mother told me that we were running out of tin, which in my mind signaled the end of the toothpaste tube. Since then I have used aluminum tubes and plastic tubes (not too satisfactory) and still brush my teeth.

This introduces the subject of *substitution;* aluminum can be substituted for tin, and plastic for aluminum, in many uses. The mining businessman does not have a completely captive market. This means that in order to turn natural resources into money at an optimal rate, he may have to use persuasion to sell his product. It is a fatal mistake for a mining business to trust in the permanence of traditional markets. The copper industry, for example, has allowed serious substitution inroads to be made by aluminum and plastics without effective counterattack.

Metals are turned into money through the working of an open market; the commodity exchange, supply, demand, and Adam Smith* are in the saddle. If there is too much supply, price goes down, production goes down, and the price stabilizes. The problem of management is *whose* production goes down—preferably yours, not mine. There is a strong incentive to form producing cartels to keep production from all mines at a level which will ensure a good price. This is illegal in the United States for domestic producers but less distasteful in other countries.† The Arab oil embargo is only a taste of things to come, and we may be just as helpless to meet new supply threats.

Money from the earth—this seems like the most straightforward road to riches both for the corporations involved‡ and for the

* Adam Smith, *An Inquiry into the Nature and Causes of the Wealth of Nations,* first published in 1776.

† See, for example, an article entitled "Panel Finds Cartel Had a Direct Impact on Uranium Purchases" in *The Wall Street Journal,* August 15, 1977.

‡ Some corporations are more equal than others! The metal content of ores and the ease of mining varies from mine to mine. If you have a property better than the average, you will get rich. This is Ricardian rent. The farmer who owns the bottom land nets more than the hillside farmer. If he rents the land, however, he breaks even and the landowner gets rich. In mineral exploration you can still find rents; it is harder in farming.

producing nations. The Arab nations are a good case in point, and Colombia prospers as the price of coffee rises. Abundant natural resources are not always the road to national wealth. In the preceding discussion we pointed out some obstacles peculiar to extractive industries, but more general obstacles may be more decisive. The political persuasion or the social ideology of a country may be such that it is impossible for *any* business to compete in other than its own protected market. This is discussed in the next chapter.

Money from Others

If a corporation is not in business to take money from Nature, the only place to get it, since it cannot print it, is from someone else, someone who has it. How does a company go about getting its customers to hand over their hard-earned scratch? There seem to be only three ways to do this. In descending order of respectability they are (1) to satisfy a genuine need, (2) to satisfy a contrived need, or (3) to use blackmail or coercion.

Before discussing these three marketing approaches, let us consider just what the corporation is peddling. It isn't selling natural resources—we took care of that in the last section. The only things left to sell are protection against risk (insurance companies), the use of money (banks), and human effort, either mental or physical—the turning of raw materials into an automobile, the writing of a legal brief. The manufacturing company or the service company is on shakier ground than a natural-resource company (in the absence of a substitution threat) in that its success is dependent on customer preference. Also, human effort is highly substitutable. Detroit recently found out (after battling Volkswagen for years) that salable automobiles could also be made in Japan.

Genuine Needs

Fortunately for the stability of our society, the largest portion of dollar value sales does satisfy real needs. For example, a construction company buys fabricated steel shapes to build a building. The deciding elements in such sales are cost, quality, and service.

and the associated advertising must stress these points. The reduction of cost and the enhancement of quality and service are socially useful business goals.

Unfortunately, need-filling manufacturers are the most vulnerable to foreign competition. This is because a large part of their costs is determined by our social climate and by government actions (considered in some detail in the next chapter). The seller is not selling charm: the buyer of a 14-inch-wide flange section doesn't care if it is painted blue or not, he buys it from the cheapest reliable source, foreign or domestic. Steel and shoe fabricators then troop to Washington to try and change the ground rules of international competition by asking for subsidies or quotas. Unless there is evidence of "dumping" by foreigners on the domestic market, responsible government will resist such requests, because trade restrictions are usually counterproductive in that they impose an extra burden on consumers.

Advertising real needs is a good thing. Not only does it inform the public of the virtues of a product, but it can alert it to the benefits of improved production methods or even to new needs. Examples are the use of the "float" process to make cheaper plate glass and the introduction of personal electronic calculators. More important, broad advertising of needed products ensures that they will be produced in a competitive environment.

Spurious Needs
In the creation of spurious or contrived needs, American business (or politics) has its finest, or at least most creative, hour. The method is through advertising, in this case a polite term for brainwashing. If the campaign is really successful, a spurious need can be raised almost to the status of a real need. Nobody really *needs* Coca-Cola, but it is hard to imagine the American scene without it.*

---

* In many medium-size cities, the richest man in town is the Coca-Cola distributor, even though he probably has the easiest job! With national advertising and a prepared product, his job amounts to running a delivery service.

Advertising is such a strange business—it is a business, selling service—that it is hard to write about. Most of us are on the receiving rather than the throwing end. It is like trying to describe baseball pitching from the point of view of the batter. Advertising is an obvious component of the fact of business, and we cannot ignore it. Three different types of reading give insight: textbooks on advertising, nonfiction or essays on its role by informed people, and finally fiction, a lot of which has been inspired.*

It is convenient to divide product advertising into two types: hard and soft. Hard advertising is aimed at real needs, and soft advertising is aimed at the emotions of the buyer. A good way to demonstrate the difference is to compare the ads in the *Oil and Gas Journal* with those in *The New Yorker*. Being essentially honest, hard advertising is not very interesting.

Let us consider soft advertising from the seller's point of view. There seem to be three possible goals: to create the impression of real differences in similar products, to sell things the buyer doesn't really need (and which may even be harmful to him), and finally to *oversell* real needs.

An example of advertising aimed at the first goal is gasoline marketing. As any refining engineer knows, there isn't much difference between the quality of gasoline sold under different brand names (although service can and does vary). The object of this kind of advertising is to create a difference in the mind of the buyer.

Identification of the second kind of soft advertising, selling unneeded goods, can be safely left to the reader. It is tempting to dismiss this type of thing with a *caveat emptor* shrug, but it can do real damage—the promotion of junk food, for example.

The third goal, overselling, is a threat even to sophisticated buyers, to business organizations themselves. Selling a third car to a man who does not really need the two he has makes a fool of the buyer. Overselling in the name of technology is much more com-

* Three titles of general interest are: John Kenneth Galbraith, *The Affluent Society*, Boston: Houghton Mifflin, 1969; Marshall McLuhan and Quentin Fiore, *The Medium Is the Message*, New York: Random House, 1967; Frederic Wakeman, *The Hucksters*, New York: Rinehart, 1946.

mon and more expensive. The engineer-salesman for a technical hardware manufacturer is in a strong position when he takes on a businessman who long ago forgot how to solve a quadratic equation. By playing on the customer's fear ("Don't let the competition get ahead") and on his vanity ("You are a modern, progressive company"), he can move a lot of expensive hardware.

Computer manufacturers have been most successful using these approaches. Every respectable business today needs computers, good computers, staffed by competent people; it does not need an extra order of magnitude of computing power maintained by a bloated staff, but this is the way things are moving. Unfortunately, the engineer-salesman has as his allies the very people who should protect management—the resident technicians. These people want to build their empires, and their influence and increasing hardware are the most direct route to their goals.[*]

How does the advertising business persuade people? What tools does it use? The following comments are made by us only as the victims of advertising and are not definitive. Students of the field can check their references and see if we are reacting properly.

Two approaches seem to be used in soft advertising to get us to buy things: *identification* and *conceit*. (Advertisers must have contempt for their marks, the same sort go-go dancers have for theirs.) The first approach, for example, encourages a television viewer to identify with a group of handsome young people who are obviously having more fun than he (the viewer) will ever have and who (incidentally) drink Pepsi-Cola. The false inverse logic is obvious. Less obvious is third-party identification. Just because Farrah Fawcett-Majors happens to be a reasonably attractive woman, the brainwashed viewer buys a certain brand of shaving cream. Certainly he doesn't identify with Miss Majors; maybe he thinks (hopes?) that she identifies with him. It is all very mysterious.

The conceit or vanity approach is straightforward. Prestige is for sale—the big car, the swimming pool, the "world's most expensive perfume." Whether or not this is a fair trade can be answered

[*] Henry I. Meyer, *Corporate Financial Planning Models*, New York: Wiley, 1977.

only by the buyer. Some prestige items such as antique furniture and oriental rugs are good investments, but their promotion is small-time stuff compared to the moving of manufactured, self-destructing products.

Before leaving this discussion of advertising, two comments may be interesting: on the businessman's attitude toward advertising and on the medium of television. It has been our observation that many businessmen in other fields do not really like advertising people very much and look on them as an overpaid but necessary evil. Sales managers try to take subjectivity out of the issue by using rate-of-return analyses of advertising programs. If a targeted return or an expected market share is not generated, they will move on to another program or to another agency.

Years ago it was possible to take burned-out light bulbs to the light company and exchange them for new ones (of a sufficiently high wattage). This type of promotion seems to be over, which is a shame. As television programming approaches the state of commercials interspersed with trash, the advertisers really should give the sets away. It is a pity that we pay for a factor which is undermining society. When children spend more time in front of the tube than with their families, when the fantasy world of TV seems more real to them than reality, and when children are not learning to read, we are in trouble. That business contributes to this social decline through advertising dollars is unfortunate, but there doesn't seem to be any alternative if the product being sold (or oversold) does not fill a genuine need.

Blackmail or Coercion

Blackmail is a hard word. For our purposes it can be defined by the statement: "You take my services and pay me well for them or else. . . ." This sort of thing is usually practiced at a lower level by labor unions (or else we strike!), by lawyers (or else you go to jail!) and by doctors (or else you hurt bad!). Some whole businesses are in a parasitic or coercive relation to other businesses, and such companies do very well indeed.

By far the most effective method of getting money from others without persuasion is to let Uncle Sam do the arm twisting—that is, to put tax dollars into business. The spending of public money by business has a long and often unsavory past. It is an emotional and important subject and deserves more space than we can allot to it. Libraries can be, and have been, written on the subject, but for some reason it is not a popular topic in business literature. Businessmen prefer to think of themselves as operating in a free-enterprise rather than socialistic system. You don't find many courses in business school curricula such as "How to Get and Spend Public Money" or, more important, "The Morality of Spending Tax Dollars."

Wars used to provide the classic opportunity to have the government move taxpayers' dollars into business, but the transfer of funds goes on all the time and today is increasing at an alarming rate, both nationally and internationally. Spending for our own national defense is pretty straightforward, but how about building F-15 fighters for other countries, to be paid for by our own tax dollars loaned to the buyers? There is massive government spending for highways, rivers, and docks. Some of this is "pork barrel" money, but a lot of it is useful.

A recent trend is massive government spending for social reasons—urban renewal, training, make-work projects. While its official position is to view this with alarm, business is the channel by which much of these monies is spent. At least these dollars stay at home. American business also spends a lot of IMF and World Bank money in foreign countries—money which comes in large part from American taxpayers. The rationale for these investments is to improve the economies of Third World countries, a goal which is as often missed as met. Is it good stewardship to spend our tax dollars in foreign countries to manufacture goods that will eventually compete on our own domestic market? Is it good business?

An example of accepted coercion is the work of outside auditing companies. Publicly listed corporations *have* to employ outside auditors and even go through the charade of having them selected by the stockholders (see Chapter 6). Reputable corporations do not really need outside auditors; they have quite enough incentive to keep their books in order without coercion. In fact, they maintain an *inside* auditing department, which could easily pick up any additional work done by the outsiders at a fraction of the cost. The obvious rebuttal to this argument is that someone has to monitor business practice. It seems a shame that business has to pay for its own policing—it's one more cost of doing business.

Other parasitic companies grow fat at the corporate trough. Actuarial firms monitor the fiscal soundness of pension plans—by fiat. Outside consultants are required to certify the hydrocarbon reserves claimed by oil and gas companies. Different types of industry have different cowbirds in the corporate nest. These are the dues that honest companies must pay to establish credibility—a penalty businessmen pay for the shenanigans of their contemporaries and of their predecessors.

Most of these outside services are the result of government decree. In fact, each piece of restrictive legislation seems to generate a new breed. The latest example is the Washington-based consultants whose business is to prepare environmental impact statements that will stand a chance of being accepted.

Outside companies often do useful work, but the fact of their peculiar relationship tends to make them expensive and self-serving. Actuaries are a good case in point. From a mathematician's point of view, the work done by actuaries is rather trivial. The statistics haven't changed much since the principles were laid down by Fisher.* The profession keeps its membership down to a profitable level by licensing, that is, by giving examinations which tend to limit the numbers in the field. Their statistics may not be too advanced, but their private notation is obscure. Since the outside actuary has no direct stake in the client company, his projection parameters—inflation rate, interest rates, and so forth—tend to be conservative for reasons of self-protection. This conservatism can raise the funding requirements and cost the client company millions of dollars over and above the retainer fees. Most big companies do their own statistical analyses to protect themselves against, or at least to put themselves in a position to argue against, the outsider's figures.

* Sir Ronald A. Fisher, "Theory of Statistical Estimation," Proceedings of the Cambridge Philosophical Society, Vol. 22, Cambridge, 1925.

Kirchoff's Law for Business

Kirchoff's law properly belong to physics or to electrical engineering. It states that at any node in an electrical circuit, the algebraic sum of current flow in and out of the network node must be zero. There are many similar conservation of energy or matter formulas in physics and applied mathematics. The equivalent business statement of Kirchoff's law is: "There is no free lunch."

We try to keep cute little diagrams out of this book, but Figure 5 seems necessary to clarify the discussion. The arrows in the figure obviously represent money flows in a business. *Materials* is the money spent for the stuff of manufacture—sheet steel, paint, and so forth; its flow rate depends on the manufacturing rate. *Fixed costs* go on independently of operations and include items such as rent and interest. *Other taxes* (not income tax) covers a multitude of statutory costs; property tax is the outstanding example. *Government reporting* is becoming an increasingly important cost of doing business. The meaning of the other arrows is obvious.

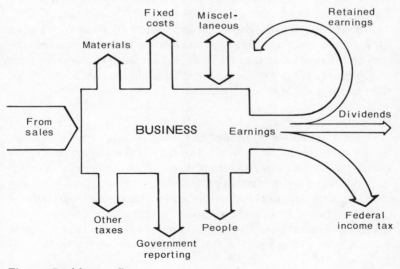

Figure 5. Money flow.

Following Kirchoff's law, money in and money out must balance. Although Figure 5 is not drawn to any scale (ratios are different for different types of business), some features of the diagram are obvious. The most disturbing, from management's point of view, is that the earnings flow is small compared with other cash flows. This is a fact of life. In these two oil company examples, the data are from 1978,* with the figures in millions of dollars:

	EXPENSES	GROSS REVENUES	INCOME
Pennzoil	1,425	1,553	128
Exxon	62,123	64,886	2,763

Similar entries can be taken from other companies' annual reports. In most cases, income is only a small fraction of sales dollars. As an income-making machine, business is pretty sorry; dividend yields are usually less than that on government bonds. Big business is a bonanza to almost everyone except to its shareholders. Management would like to do better for its owners, but it operates in a very tough environment.

Before considering these problems, let us say a rare good word for federal income tax. In one sense, income tax is the *least* obnoxious cost of doing business. Government demands its pound of flesh only out of profits (taxable income). No profit, no tax. This is more than can be said of other demands.

Instability

The classic case of an unstable solution to an applied-mathematics problem is one in which the answer is equal to the difference between two large numbers. Kirchoff's law suggests that this is always the case in computing business income. There are large cash inflows from sales on the one hand and large cash outflows for materials, labor, fixed costs, and taxes on the other; income is the difference or residual of these large cash streams. The business term for this is *operating leverage*, but more basically it is a built-in in-

* Source: Moody's *Industrials*, 1979.

herent instability. Small percentage variations in any of the major cash-flow streams have large impact on the earnings. If several factors are subject to fickle change, prediction of income is almost impossible.

This built-in instability of the earnings of large corporations is probably the reason for the psychotic behavior of the stock market. Its uncertain behavior is a reflection of the instability of business itself. There are many theories of stock price prediction: intrinsic value, stream of earnings or dividends, and so forth. There are also derived parameters which are supposed to define the state of a corporation: assets to earnings, current ratios, and others. It may be that these attempts to quantify corporations and stock market evaluation are really attempts to define reliable indices which can be used to camouflage the real prediction problem—the basic instability of business earnings.

Lack of Control

The image of fearless business leaders running their own shows for their own ends and in their own ways just will not wash. The options available to management are constrained and are getting more limited all the time. Management is constrained by government actions, by the marketplace, occasionally by its own shareholders, and severely by its own history: the skeletons in the corporate closet. An analysis of the cash-flow streams in Figure 5 shows that many of them are influenced by exogenous or historical factors.

If a corporation is historically committed to a certain type of operation, it is twice constrained by market factors: the acceptance of its products in a changing world and the cost of materials to build them. A corporation has to pay interest on historical borrowings by previous management, which is a fixed cost of doing business.* Changes in tax rates and in the cost of government reporting

---

* Total corporate debt runs about four times the national debt, and has been at that level for several years. (Source: *Survey of Current Business,* U.S. Department of Commerce, reported annually in the August issue.) Interest on this debt is eventually passed on to consumers in increased prices.

are out of corporate control. Small percentage changes in either of these cash streams will have a magnified effect on earnings.

In many companies the largest expense is payroll. Even here, management options are limited. Outside factors, rather than *quid pro quo*, have a decisive influence on wage rates. This is discussed in the next chapter. For the present it is enough to say that management has much less say than it would like in deciding how much to pay people, at least if it is to get the people it wants.

BUSINESS MONEY GOALS

It is usually assumed that the goal of top business management is to maximize profits and earnings. This is only partly true. Business leaders do want earnings to improve from year to year, but they want an orderly progression; sudden increases are almost as much deplored as sudden drops. There are good reasons for this attitude. There are also exceptions to it.

Earnings jumps are unsettling to investors, who are apt to take their profits and sell their shares. This may actually send the price down—another example of irrational market behavior. The shareholder knows, as does management, that big earnings are a hard act to follow. If the business is one of our key industries such as automobiles, steel, or oil, an earnings jump brings demagogues out of the woodwork crying "obscene profits" and demanding excess profit taxes. Large profits also bring out the barely dormant greed of labor unions. Unorganized employees are not above the share-the-wealth movement. They may be as interested in perks as pay, but they want "theirs." Orderly progression is a better operating climate. Management doesn't like surprises.

There are exceptions to this rule when new companies or new products are involved. A new company doesn't have a track record, and so the investment community and labor are inclined to be tolerant. Sometimes a corporation comes out with a new product or a new idea that captures the imagination of the investing public. Earnings jumps are not only tolerated but expected, and the listed stock price takes off like a rocket and usually follows a similar trajectory. Where there is money to be made, there is money to be lost.

Controlling the Earnings Pattern

The preceding discussions of instability and lack of control imply that there isn't a whole lot that management can do to level the earnings pattern. Although options are limited, the situation is not helpless. For one thing, the operating leverage that makes earnings sensitive to outside influences makes them sensitive to internal actions. Control responses by management can be considered under two headings: technical and actual.

Technical control involves creative accounting and tax policy. It is possible, within legal limits, to shift earnings from one year to the next, for example, to change depreciation calculations (for tax purposes) and to change the method of inventory evaluation (LIFO to FIFO). It is also possible to write off some balance sheet items of dubious quality. These activities are not illegal or even examples of sharp practice. It probably serves both the general public and the IRS (which has to give its approval in any case) to have companies present an orderly earnings pattern.

Actual control involves actions, sometimes painful actions. A usual outward visible sign is a switch from first-class to tourist travel for executives (which also cuts the number of trips). Sometimes surgery is appropriate: the elimination of redundant people or fat-cat departments or even the closing of unprofitable plants. Such actions are concerned with *reducing* expense to increase income; it is more difficult to move the other way. Middle management can go back to first-class travel, but no management in its right mind is going to knowingly hire useless people or create unproductive departments. It takes a lot longer to open plants than to close them. In a sense, management has more options to raise short-term earnings than to lower them.

In addition to the actual and technical steps taken by management to smooth the earnings time series, there seems to be a natural law that helps it out. Certain types of industry have traditional ratios of income to revenue. Insurance companies have higher ratios than manufacturing companies, who do better than oil, who in turn do better than steel companies. Why this is so we do not know—it may be a case of realities meeting expectations—but there do seem to be profit ratios where certain types of companies feel comfortable. When the OPEC nations quadrupled the going price of oil, the major companies were caught with their pants down and their profits up,* and the sound of the demagogue was heard in the land. Here was a sector of industry whose profit ratios had to improve! The product it had developed and planned to sell at one price was suddenly selling for much more. Improve they did, but the new level did not last. It took about two years for the oil industry to get back to its old familiar level. There is no attempt at explanation here; the subject will be well covered in congressional hearings.

Taking a Bath

Sometimes management does not try to soften the blow of an earnings decline. It knows its stock is going down, and it responds with a corporate "What the hell, we may as well be hung for a sheep as a lamb." Thus it writes off all the dubious capital items in sight and lets the earnings collapse. The technical term for this is to "take a bath."

After the dust settles and the stock price stabilizes, shares in a company which has just indulged in a corporate ablution may be an excellent investment, particularly if the company has combined its plunge with constructive actual control measures. The corporation should emerge leaner and tougher and look forward to better things.

Dropping the Pilot

There is a recent trend to income anomalies which are the result of change in top management. This is due to what may be called the "screw the new chairman" syndrome. The mechanism is simple. The outgoing chairman makes his last year in office look good; he recognizes all possible income and defers expenses. This allows him to leave to the accompaniment of cheering by his associates and an increase in the value of his stock options (Chapter 13). The new chairman takes over a grim situation, but one in which there is lots of room for improvement, and he can later repeat the ritual for his successor.

---

* Much of this was inventory profit, which is hard to explain and even harder to control.

5

PAYING
THE TROOPS

NOBODY IN A business organization is paid what he is worth. This statement is a reasonable starting point for a discussion of the whys of the internal distribution of money in a business organization—the calculation of the payroll.

Under our present system of fixed rates, no employee could possibly be paid what he is worth. Since performance varies, a completely rational payment would vary from week to week. How about vacations? How about overtime pay, where workers are paid a premium for working when they are probably not at their best? What is the hourly *value* of a clerical worker or of a laborer? Even economists, who have answers (not necessarily the right ones) for almost everything, can't assign reasonable values to workers' time.* Salesmen working on commission may come closer to a true *quid*

* The assignment of a "just price" or "just wage" is an old concern. Thomas Aquinas considered it at length in his *Summa Theologica*. The notion can be traced back to Aristotle. This problem is not popular with economists today.

pro quo, but as long as they continue to turn in expense accounts and work on a fixed, negotiated commission rate, they are paid only approximately fairly.

If it is difficult to set an intrinsic value to the output of routine workers, it is completely impossible to determine the worth of management people and businessmen. The higher in the organization, the more tenuous the relationship becomes. There has to be some sort of relation between salary indeterminacy and the frequency and importance of the decision making involved. The consequences of even a single high-level decision can make or cost a company millions of dollars. The manager who makes bad decisions is overpaid; on the other hand, one good decision may be worth more than any salary.

The decision-making process itself may be painful, or it may be instinctive. A lot of feasibility studies and other formal decision aids are window dressing, made to support a predetermined position. It is not only statesmanlike decisions made in the boardroom that are risky; a company is also exposed every day to dangers at a low level of decision making. A friend of mine once turned off the wrong gas valve and shut down a cement kiln full of slurry. Good sense must be worth something.

Since management is obviously not free to set arbitrary wages, and since there are no rational rules to set pay levels, there must be some irrational rules. We will try to identify and analyze these rules, both for the general reader and for the young person who is planning to enter the business world. He wants to get his, and we want him to get it. To take advantage of the system, he should know the ground rules of the payment game and not make the vulgar error of assuming that remuneration has much to do with worth.

The operating payment rules have to answer a lot of sticky questions. Why does a doctor in the United States get five times as much as a doctor in England? Why is a factory worker cheaper to hire in Mexico than in Canada? Why is the president of General Motors paid much more than the president of the nation?

Four, not necessarily independent, factors seem to be involved in wage setting: social and political environment, coercion, consensus, and ability. These factors are effective in different degree for the different classes of employees: workers (grunts), professionals and middle management, and top management.

Money is not the only reward for service, but it is the most common and the most visible. A discussion of nonmonetary compensation, which is particularly important at high salary levels, is left to a later chapter, where it is discussed under "perquisites" or "perks." Some of the limitations of money as the only reward for service are considered in this chapter.

Minimum Wages

Social and political effects on wages are most important at the lower end of the pay scale. The most visible sign of government control is the minimum wage—a legislated floor which is periodically raised by rich congressmen as a political gesture.

As far as big business is concerned, the effect of raising the minimum wage is felt later in that big labor uses it as a justification to increase union scales. Usually the only corporate workers who actually get the legal minimum are summer employees who are taken on in an eleemosynary gesture or as a favor to executives to keep their children safely stashed away for the summer. Large corporations have good reasons to pay their regular employees more than the minimum the law requires, and enough to exceed what may be called a *social* minimum wage.

To a large extent, the cherished public image of a corporation is a reflection of the morale of its employees. Today's management wants its domestic* workers, at any rate, to be contented and proud of the company; more than that, it wants them to be responsible, contributing members of society. It certainly doesn't want (relative) paupers on its payroll. This implies a socially acceptable minimum wage considerably higher than the legal limit.† Business

---

* Multinational corporations, in some cases, still operate what amount to "sweat shops" in foreign countries.

† The idea of a social minumum even extends to the armed services—quite a change from the old days when only "first three graders" were expected to be in a position to get married. If this concept extends to the Russians, war may be impossible: both sides could afford the guns and missiles but not the men.

would be willing to pay dearly to meet this social level even without the pressures of labor unions.

Although it is still an important factor in wage determination, the original premises on which a social minimum was based may already be obsolete. In its pure, outdated form the social minimum applied only to male heads of families. The concept seems to have grown out of an aspect of the American Dream and out of commendable compassion. "Anyone who works for the good old Widget Company *should* be able to have a decent home, support a wife, educate his children, and join the Elk's Club." As a residual of this attitude, big companies generally pay common (male) laborers more than trained (female) secretaries. This social model is no longer valid. The concept of predominantly male-supported households is passé. Particularly at lower income levels, both man and wife work. Labor unions and the federal government are increasingly taking over the role of exercising social conscience.

The Puerto Rican Problem

Mexico and the Caribbean nations have not developed as rapidly as the North American nations. The American or Canadian worker has a much higher skill level, better education, and, most important, a larger stock of capital goods supporting his effort. If the Mexican government were to set a minimum wage (in pesos) equivalent to that in Canada or the United States, the Mexican worker would be priced out of the market or there would be wild inflation in Mexico. This is what has happened in Puerto Rico. By a political quirk, United States minimum wages also apply to this Caribbean island. This makes the native labor uncompetititve. Unemployment in Puerto Rico has risen to 40 percent, and more than half the population receives welfare support. An unrealistic minimum wage cannot be preserved without problems.

POLITICAL CONSTRAINTS

Political factors influence both the scale of pay and the composition of the labor force. The ultimate possible domestic threat from a business point of view is the nationalization of an industry or a service. Wages could then be set by law rather than by other considerations. Nationalization is now relatively rare* in the United States, but if industries become too inefficient or the service professions too greedy, it can happen here. Socialized medicine, of course, explains the large pay differential between English and American doctors. Even without socialistic wage setting, the government controls business salary levels in the United States to a remarkable degree.

The federal government (even excluding the armed services) is the largest single employer in the United States. It competes with business for competent employees. Until recently, business felt that it had to pay somewhat *more* than civil service for comparable jobs to get the people it wanted and compensate for the liberal fringe benefits associated with government service. The generosity of the public sector in spending other people's money is now such that business can only hope to come close enough to the civil service pay scale to attract those who prefer private employment.† Fortunately for business (though not for the efficiency of public service), public policy, for ideological reasons, favors minority hiring, and this eases the competition for good people at least at lower levels. This brings up the sticky question of "fair" employment.

The civil rights movement has been successful in one respect: it has largely eliminated prejudice against the hiring of women and minorities. For the most part, business is quite willing to hire on a color- and sex-blind ability basis. This is not enough for government. The aim of its affirmative action program is to achieve the same employment cross section in corporations as the composition of the local population. If hiring is done on ability, a similar distribution is logical only if the ability spectrum of all ethnic groups is similar. This is simply not true. To try to satisfy stated goals business does two things: it competes for, and pays a premium for, truly competent minority people, and it shades job requirements for the hiring of others. Together these hiring practices tend to increase

---

* TVA, the postal service, and some railroad operations are now nationalized.

† For a definitive study of salary comparison, see the lead article in *Scientific American*, November 1977.

the average salary and lower the average effectiveness of the work force—a social cost of doing business.

COERCION

Very few workers, union or not, have a really comfortable feeling of job security. Most know that, for the kind of money they are making, their jobs could be quickly and competently filled by others. Individually the worker has little clout. His recourse is to organize, either into a union or into some sort of professional protective society. A group does have the power to coerce management into ensuring job security and paying higher salaries. There is a trend toward what is sometimes called tenured employment, and this in turn tends to divide our society into "ins" and "outs." Ins, such as civil service workers and the employees of big business, have tenure; people who work for themselves, such as artists, or who work for a small business, do not.

Although only about 25 percent of the labor force is unionized, it is the union settlements that determine the going rates and fringe benefits for all workers in the business community. Union workers do have a legitimate beef; it is their strikes that help nonunion people. The relationship between a corporation and the union(s) representing its people is complex. In some cases it is symbiotic and beneficial to both parties; often it is a necessary evil that management has to live with. The most obvious weapon of a union is the strike. Properly timed* it is a potent weapon—fixed costs continue while income ceases. Any merits of the case are submerged by this threat or blackmail. Union leaders have a value philosophy which is at odds with management or even with good sense: that people doing the *same* job are entitled to increasing wages (after inflation) as time passes. Management's position, consistent with the work ethic, is that earnings increases should depend on promotion,

---

* There are some cases where management welcomes a strike! For example, a mine with excess stocks can live off inventory while its labor costs are down. Automated operations such as oil refineries can continue production for a long time using supervisors.

which should be based on merit and involve increased responsibility or output.

Another form of coercion comes from professional groups, which are in the enviable position of setting at least a minimum going rate for their services. A college hiring a medical professor has to pay him more than an entering history professor; a corporation has to pay an entering lawyer more than a physicist. The usual explanation for this sort of injustice, based on alternative opportunity, only begs the question. Why are lawyers (or actuaries or doctors or CPAs) paid more than mathematicians?

The answer seems to be that it is the result of long-term blackmail exercised against society, reinforced whenever possible by favorable laws. That this differential is not inherent is demonstrated by the fact that the favored professions vary from country to country. Doctors in Russia, for example, are not considered special. In Sweden, engineering is the prestige profession.

Business has fought a running battle for years to keep wages tenable against social and political pressure and against labor unions. In most cases it has been able to cope, as long as labor and government operate independently. When they combine against business, industries and the country are in trouble.

LABOR–GOVERNMENT COLLUSION

Management must operate under the constraints of Kirchoff's law, discussed in the last chapter. If labor is in a position to demand and get higher and higher wages for the same amount of work, the only effective long-term response is improved productivity—more bang for a unit of work. Increasing productivity requires capital investment. The greatest current danger to American business is not socialism but the emergence of a situation where labor is in a political position to force its demands while at the same time government policy discourages investment. An obvious case in point is postwar England, but it doesn't seem fair to kick the British lion one more time. There may be a more pertinent example.

Australia is a rich country, potentially as rich on a per capita basis as any in the world, and yet Australia is in trouble.* Australia does not have the capital to develop its resources or to modernize its plants. Government policies, both of the left and the right, have discouraged foreign investment. Labor unions operate in a favorable climate and have been able to increase the standard of living of their own members without an offsetting productivity increase. American contractors found, for example, that Australian pipeline welders were more expensive and less reliable than their Stateside counterparts. Despite surface indications of prosperity—due in part to the spending of savings and capital—long-term prospects are bleak.

Australian industry cannot generally compete on the world market to sell manufactured goods. Unemployment is high and will probably get higher. Inflation was over 12 percent in 1977. All this implies that Australia is becoming a member of the Third World, in the sense that it will have to live by the export of raw materials and import its manufactured goods.

For a capitalistic country to be healthy, business must have a fair chance. Government should not discourage investment and should provide a climate in which labor and management can fight it out on something like equal terms.

TITLE AND RANK

The preceding discussion is of only limited interest to a college graduate entering business; he isn't about to go to work for minimum wages. How are salaries set for business school graduates and for the professions—for businessmen? The answer is: ostensibly by job title and actually by rank. Our eager graduate wants the best of both.

Titles

Job titles serve two purposes: they identify the pecking order and chain of command within the organization, and they serve to

* A readable reference is the article "Crisis Down Under" by Jacques Decorny in the *Manchester Guardian Weekly*, July 3, 1977.

establish social position outside the company. "What does your husband do for a living?" A title like chief engineer or data processing manager is satisfactory for the first purpose, as we will see; it is not always acceptable for the second.

The status associated with different titles varies historically and geographically. Old, honorable handles such as plant manager, chief draftsman, civil engineer, and sergeant (a legal title) have lost some of their original meaning and prestige. A few titles such as tool pusher (drilling supervisor) are picturesque and industry-oriented. Some old titles—editor, manager (of a baseball team), professor, and coach—have retained their old value, but even they are threatened by the new status symbol: vice president. Until recently this American title was not understood abroad. A smart executive transferred to a Commonwealth country would get it changed to director to get the proper respect.

An inevitable question during a job interview is, "What will my title be?" If the interviewer wants to hire the man, he had better make it good! Overly modified titles are bad; they imply a low spot in the order. (My first civilian job was junior assistant engineer. I doubt if anyone would accept this today.) Generic titles are often avoided (unless they carry their own prestige, like "attorney"). A mathematician is hired as a research assistant and a statistician maybe as an analyst. Some honorable terms like clerk are not well received. The result of all this psychological and semantic in-fighting is that people are given the most impressive possible titles that will not make a shambles of the organization chart or make the other employees angry.

Since the eventual conferral of the title of vice president can make or break a career (or an ego), we have to say something more about it.

The Vice-President Thing

A required question for the job interviewer to ask is, "What is your ultimate goal?" Very often the answer, accompanied by a diffident grin and a shuffling of the feet is, "Someday I want to be a vice president." *Not* to set up an efficient accounting system, *not* to design successful products, *not* to make important decisions, but to *be* a vice president. This is success! The three-car garage, the country club membership, the proud wife! The title has become the end-all and be-all of American business.

Used properly, the term vice president refers only to a stand-in for the president, someone who substitutes for him and shares his burdens. There is a real need for such people, particularly in the multinational companies, where the president can't be everywhere and usually stays home to mind the shop. With so many vice presidents around, it is obvious that most of them are not stand-in presidents. In order to identify the *real* vice presidents, business has invented special titles: executive vice president (second in command), group vice president, and senior vice president. Lesser orders may conveniently be classified as hyphenated vice presidents: vice president—research, vice president—accounting, vice president—systems, and so forth. Only the modifiers are meaningful; the vice president part is honorary, like "Sir" or "von."

It is not a bad thing for management to be able to hand out these corporate knighthoods.* It doesn't cost anything (a research director should make as much money as a vice president—research), and it gives the corporation a hold over middle management. A man who is any kind of vice president is not as likely to quit; his wife probably wouldn't let him. The title can also be used as bait to help entice people from other companies. The thing can be overdone. Check the list of vice presidents in the annual report for meaningless titles such as vice president—special projects; if a corporation is sloppy in making up its honors list, it may be sloppy in other things.

Rank

With the often capricious assignment of titles to middle management people, it is becoming difficult to use titles as a basis for setting salaries. Some independent sort of ranking must be estab-

---

* Banks seem to have been the first to discover this. For them it has the added attraction that people applying for a car loan prefer to deal with a real vice president. Almost anyone who doesn't actually deliver mail is apt to be a vice president.

lished. The baseball–army analogy is again illuminating. On a baseball team, players are paid according to their contribution to winning, and their titles are descriptive. A shortstop is a shortstop and not vice president—left side of infield. Army pay, on the other hand, is based on rank. A captain is paid as a captain; he may be a public relations officer or a company commander. (There are some exceptions. A captain-doctor makes a lot more than the infantry captain he patches up. This is due to the technological blackmail referred to earlier.)

Modern business practice is to pay by rank. Widely diverse titles are grouped under numbered or lettered ranks and pay brackets allowed for each. This ranking is often semiconfidential in that a manager knows the ranking of his subordinates but not his own. He could get a phantom promotion to a higher-sounding title but still have the same rank. The smart employee or job applicant should know this and find out what his fancy title *really* means in the ranking structure. Like most corporate secrets the code is not hard to break. On the other hand, there may be a few employees who really like their job and who would rather not know how they are officially rated.

CONSENSUS

Rank and coercion determine the salary of most employees, but there is one group which is above these laws: top management. In early days the general store owner paid off his employees at the end of the week and then checked the till to see how much was left for himself. Top management is often assumed to be in a similar position. A picture comes to mind of the chairman of the board, the president, and the executive, group, and senior vice presidents sitting around a conference table to divide the spoils. First, set the pay of the chairman of the board—set it high because all others will be relative—and then work down. It isn't quite that simple. Board approval of salaries has to be obtained, usually from an executive compensation committee composed of outside directors. Stockholders have a prior claim to profits, which they will have a hard time exercising. Within these restrictions, top management does set its own remuneration. It does this by consensus of its own people.

How is the range set? Profits play a minor role: it looks bad to take raises when the corporation has a poor year. The shareholders may have to do without dividends, the president will lose his bonus, but he rarely takes a statutory pay cut. The real criteria for top management compensation are *size* and *industry type*. The chairman of a medium-size oil company will probably have his salary set somewhat lower than that of the chairman of Exxon, which is bigger and higher than that of the chairman of smaller oil companies. Different industries have different traditional levels. The automobile industry has a high level. General Motors is the largest automobile company, and its president makes a lot more than the president of the United States.

The salaries top management pays to itself—over a million a year in some cases—are ridiculous; they are also bad business. Management knows quite well that a lot of these bloated amounts will be turned over to the government in income taxes, it also knows of better methods of remunerating itself, but still tradition and appearances must be kept up. The redeeming point is that *it doesn't really matter!* The number of people with their hands in the till— the "in" group—is so small in most corporations that the impact of their salaries on earnings per share is minimal. In those rare cases where shareholders do make themselves heard they usually have much more legitimate beefs to raise than high executive salaries. These may even serve as a convenient red herring to allow the venting of righteous shareholder wrath while really important management problems are ignored.

ABILITY

Yes, Virginia, ability does play a role in setting salaries. Promotions are based on many things: ability, luck, age, and simply being in the right place at the right time. If this sounds like sour grapes, it isn't. The reason that time and chance play such a large part in promotions is the overall competence of American businessmen with respect to job requirements. When a position becomes open or a man threatens to quit, there are usually several candidates who are capable of taking over. There is an embarrassment of riches. The choice is apt to be capricious or convenient. There *are* irreplaceable men in middle management in a corporation, but there are usually only a few.*

Examples of critical employees are lawyers with good connection in high places, sales executives with loyal clients, and gifted technical or creative people (Steinmetz is supposed to have been given a blank check each year by General Electric). Unusual people are often considered a nuisance by the personnel manager (himself highly replaceable), who prefers employees to fit neatly into ranks with fixed salary brackets. A common concession to the unusual man is to allow a special upper limit to pay brackets to reward ability. Unfortunately this latitude is too often used to reward good old Joe. Top management should intervene to reward and retain unusual people at all levels of the organization.

This argument seems to violate the Peter Principle (people rise to a level of incompetence).† Except for specialized work such as research or finance, we think it does. In the usual business environment most people who are competent in one job will be competent in another; those who are incompetent will be incompetent in any job. Brilliance is rarer than competence; in many business situations it is as much an embarrassment as an asset. Businessmen are comfortable with conformity.

MONEY AS COMPENSATION

Salary money is not the only compensation of the businessman but the most usual and the most obvious. There are two reserva-

---

* This is not a new phenomenon. Consider Samuel Johnson's letter to Mrs. Thrale, who was concerned about taking over her husband's business. "Do not be frighted. Trade could not be managed by those who manage it if it had much difficulty." (Robert W. Chapman, *Letters of Samuel Johnson*, #647, London: Oxford, 1952.)

† Laurence J. Peter and Raymond Hull, *The Peter Principle*, New York: Morrow, 1969.

tions which limit the effectiveness of salary as the only compensation for businessmen. First, there is a strong egalitarian tendency to narrow the pay differential, particularly with respect to the take-home pay for a wide spectrum of employees ranging from skilled craft people through middle management. Second, salary money is "new" money, which has a nasty way of disappearing as fast as it comes in.

The Equal-Pay Tendency

There is an old business tradition that middle management and professional employees make more than craft-type employees. (There are exceptions based on scarcity and risk. A deep-sea diver, for example, makes more—and deserves more—than most executives.) As social pressure and union coercion raise the pay of craft workers, the *minimum* rate to middle management then will also rise. At the same time, top management is forced to set a *maximum* rate for these same people in order to keep the corporation solvent. The whole pay range for middle management and professional people is narrowing. Median salaries do increase with rank, but the spread in each level tends to overlap those of adjacent levels. Another equalizing factor is the forced deduction for taxes, social security, and company benefits such as insurance and retirement. Disposable income varies less than apparent income.

This equalization process has gone much further than most people realize. In a small technical department such as management science, for example, the whole spread of salaries may range from $20,000 for the newest employee with a doctor's degree to $35,000 for the department head. These levels will rise with inflation. Due to graduated taxation and deductions, the real difference will decrease.

The increasing number of working wives does not, of course, increase equalization, but it does further upset the old concept of the rich boss and the struggling employee. A $40,000 manager with two children in decent schools and a wife at home has much less discretionary income than his clerk who is childless and whose wife has a cushy civil service job. Incentive is increasingly becoming a function of titles and perquisites rather than just salary.

Old Money and New Money

Old money is good money. It consists of stocks, bonds, and property *on which taxes have been paid* and which turn out regular supplemental income or capital gains. New money—paycheck money—is ephemeral and gives its possessor only the privilege of turning right around and spending most of it. All employees are faced with a personal Kirchoff's law—money coming in and money going out—and most of them arrange things so that inflow and out-flow are pretty well balanced. They don't *have* to arrange things this way, but most do.

Years ago I had a friend who, whenever he got a raise (our raises were pretty small in those days), would immediately buy something on time such that the payments would equal the raise. I asked him why he did such a dumb thing. According to him this was the only way he could get something tangible for his money; if he kept it for spending, he felt, it would evaporate.

Although they may not admit it, most middle-income people have the same philosophy. As they go up the income ladder, they acquire things and ensure that expenditures rise to meet income. The automobile provides a good all-American example. When a businessman reaches a certain level, he buys an expensive car. The fact that blindfolded he wouldn't know whether he was riding a Ford LTD or a Continental is immaterial; it is time to move up.* Why does he do it? There is no peer pressure demanding it. Maybe the man is a snob. I don't think so; snobbery is rare in American business. I think it is personal satisfaction ("I've reached the point where I *should* be driving a Cadillac")—a self-awarded prize to recognize achievement.

The prizes that the middle-income businessman usually rewards himself with—cars, boats, swimming pools, country club memberships—have one thing in common: their worth is transient. There is one notable exception to this rule; we get to that later. To make matters worse, most of these things are bought on time; as sal-

---

* This is not meant to imply that a Continental is not a better car than a Ford. I am sure it is, but our hero is not going to keep his expensive car long enough to find out.

ary goes up, debt goes up with it. Why this seemingly irrational behavior? The man should know better; he should be turning new money into old to provide for his children's education and his own retirement and to build up an estate. There must be nights when he lies awake listening to the depreciation of the furniture, the wall-to-wall carpeting, and the color television.

The income tax laws encourage a personal debt position, but there may be two other reasons for his behavior. The first is that like other people, he likes to spend money. The second is more subtle. As a large part of American business is engaged in producing ephemeral or at least self-destructing goods, the health of the business community, and of the country itself, depends on an army of willing spenders. As a member of the club, businessmen feel that they must play the game. Whether this is conscious or unconscious is immaterial—buying is the thing to do, and it is almost subversive not to.

The preceding paragraph paints a bleak picture of economic disaster in the midst of affluence. That this does not usually happen* is due to two facts. One is that corporations are increasingly assuming the big financial burdens for their employees: hospitalization, retirement, insurance, and even savings through stock and bond purchase plans. The other redeeming fact is that the young businessman is almost forced to make *one* good investment in his career: his house. Real estate appreciation is such that most businessmen get, over their career, what amounts to free housing. It is a paradox of our society that a poor black working man pays more over his working career to live in his shotgun house than does the executive to live comfortably in River Oaks.

Perhaps our free-spending businessman isn't dumb after all. The good old corporation (and the government) will take care of his old age while the (finally paid-for) house will provide a place to live and even leave a modest estate. Estate building as a separate goal seems to be a low-priority item. The concept of laissez-faire ex-

---

* An exception is when an executive loses his job. He is then forced to look at his balance sheet and may find himself to be technically insolvent.

tends to the second generation! To provide a comfortable, even lavish, home for his children and to educate them (usually at state schools) is enough parental responsibility. In most cases the cycle works, although there are clouds on the horizon, such as the energy crisis. The children grow up and make more money than the old man and adopt his spending habits.

New money keeps turning over; business prospers. We are a consuming nation, and it is increasingly difficult to differentiate the life-styles of steel workers, plumbers, airline pilots, and department heads.

So What?

That salary differences are not as marked or as meaningful as they once were does not change the traditional attitude of the businessman. He still wants to make more money than the next guy. One way to get on what is called a fast track is to be a nice person and to be in an area where performance is hard for an outsider to measure (law, for instance). Since this approach depends on a fortunate, or lucky, early career selection, it is usually not available to the entering business school graduate or to the old employee who is not getting along as fast as he (or his wife) wants. These people should try to get into a situation where things are favorable. The principles outlined in this chapter are a useful guide to making a constructive move. A good job should satisfy the following criteria:

· It should carry a sufficiently prestigious title.
· It should be in a corporate area which does not operate under close cost constraints; that is, it should be in an area where salary raises are not closely budgeted.
· It should be in an internal organization that is large enough to provide room for promotion. The manager of a small specialized department often has no place to go.
· It should be one where promotion does not depend too heavily on ability or experience, because this can make for slow movement and odious comparisons.
· It should be involved with money, either capital expenditure

or financing. Salaries always appear smaller when compared with such large transactions.

• It should involve contact with higher management—top management preferred. This is called *exposure* in business school jargon.

The list is probably not exhaustive, but it will do. Any position which satisfies all these criteria is one hell of a job—a road to the green pastures of vice-presidential country. A possible stumbling block is the last listed condition. The value of exposure is stressed in business schools, and the smart young applicant always raises the issue in job interviews. "Who will I work for? Who will I deal with?" The problem is that exposure is a two-edged sword. To complement the optimistic assumption that management will be "totally impressed" with the bright young person is the slim possibility that they won't like the pushy rascal.

Most of the listed operative criteria involve finding the right department or the right area in the corporation. The resolution of this problem, that of finding an appropriate corporate home, will have to be deferred until Part Two of this book, which deals with the organization and structure of a typical corporation. We can't do much to resolve the exposure dilemma, since reading a book is a poor way to change personality. Part Three, which takes a look at people in business, does at least suggest acceptable behavior patterns and may help the reader avoid obvious mistakes.

6

MANAGEMENT AND THE SHAREHOLDERS

MARK TWAIN had a very American interest in money and investment; it seemed to rank a strong third after piloting steamboats and writing. On a nostalgic trip down the Mississippi after the Civil War* he reported as much as anything on the economic growth of the region. Of a Natchez cotton mill that was then working 5,000 bales of cotton annually, he says, "Capital $105,000, all subscribed in the town. Two years later the same shareholders increased their capital to $225,000 . . . stock held at $5,000 per share, but none in the market."

Here is the classic definition of the word "shareholder." Someone had a good idea—build a cotton mill—but didn't have enough

* Mark Twain, *Life on the Mississippi;* see the chapter "Manufacturers and Miscreants."

money himself, so he rounded up help from friends and neighbors ("went public," we now say), who put up funds and went shares in the venture. These people must have taken a close interest in the project, because $5,000 was a small fortune in those days and there were only 45 shareholders. You can be sure that they visited the plant, were known to the workers, and participated in making major decisions. This is a far cry from the usual relationship between today's modern company and the shareholders who are its legal owners.

As a modern shareholder you get a certificate, a stock certificate, to prove your claim. If it is for 100 shares of GTE, for example, you are the legal owner of something less than a millionth of the company. You can even estimate what your piece of the action is worth in "bricks and mortar." Divide the reported "book" value by the number of outstanding shares and multiply by 100.* Don't try to collect, don't expect anyone in your company to call you by your first name unless you introduce yourself first, and don't expect to influence any company decisions. If you want to turn your share into money, you will have to sell it to someone else. You can do this—sell directly to an individual—but most people prefer to sell through a third party: a stockbroker who charges a commission for his service. A stockbroker is like any broker in things or in people: he brings buyer and seller together—"makes a market" for corporate shares.

All this seems so different from the direct participation of the shareholders described by Mark Twain (who we hope all became rich men) that there doesn't seem to be much point in owning corporate stocks. Obviously, the money paid to someone else for his shares doesn't help the parent company at all. The dividends you receive as a shareholder usually provide a lower return than do good safe bonds or even bank deposits. Why do people buy stocks, and why do companies worry about the trading price of their shares, which may have been changing hands for 50 years?

---

* We confine this discussion to "common stocks," which are the simplest and usual form of share ownership. There are other kinds: preferred, classed, and non-voting, for example, which are discussed in proper books on securities.

The logical reason to buy stocks is to make money. Adam Smith* claims that 90 percent of investors don't really care whether they make money or not, and he gives alternative reasons. We won't bore the prior reader of his fun book or spoil the plot for new readers: we stick to logical behavior. One reason to buy stock is to buy enough to gain some control of a certain company. With one forty-fifth of all the shares (like Mark Twain's shareholders) you could probably get a seat on the board and actually have some say in running the company. The more usual reason to buy stock is the hope that later it will be possible to sell it to someone else at a higher price—that the stock will "go up." This is sometimes called the "some other sucker" school of investing. Another reason to invest in the market, for a rich person at any rate, is because it is *there*, it is one of the few places where he can invest large amounts of money safely and efficiently and keep them available (liquid).

THE MARKETS

The stock markets—the New York Stock Exchange (the Big Board), the American Stock Exchange (the Curb), and the regional exchanges—provide working examples of the free marketplace. Stocks sell only at prices that buyers are willing to pay and are sold at prices that the sellers are willing to receive. Since the number of shares offered is not exactly the same as the number wanted, the exchange provides a floating inventory of shares (like a storage tank on a water main) to take up the slack.† The free market mechanism provides the only valid rule that controls stock prices: the price of a stock goes up when more people want to buy it than sell; the price of a stock goes down when more people want to sell than buy. There is no other rule of stock price movement, but this does not prevent investors from trying to "beat" the market—to anticipate movement before others do.

There are two types of market movement: general movement of the market as a whole, up or down (usually measured by the

* *The Money Game*, New York: Random House, 1967.
† Nonexistent shares can be sold, known as short selling. There are other marketing curiosities which are not our concern.

changing Dow-Jones average), and the price movement of individual stocks compared to the general trend. If a large investor has a diversified collection of stocks (portfolio), he makes money when the market rises and loses when it falls. Most funds, which do the selection for you, operate on this basis. Financial writers are often criticized for explaining general market movement *after* it happens. This is unfair; sports writers can only explain why the Red Sox beat the Yankees after the game is over.

It is more fun to try to pick individual winners. There are many schemes for doing this, ranging in method from the highly mathematical to the bizarre: from multiple correlation to the study of sunspots and hemlines. Most writers on the subject eventually recommend the "intrinsic value" theory, which is a fancy way of saying that you should buy stock in a good, well-managed company with a promising future and sock it away. Your chances of immediate profit are slim, as this depends on your doing a better job of analyzing the company *before* other buyers do. Buy and hold shares in a good company—this gets us back to Mark Twain's example and to the continuing relationship between the company and its shareholders.

Adam Smith suggests that books on investing are dangerous reading because the authors insist on giving "systems" for beating the market. Here is our contribution. It concerns predicting major changes in the general market behavior. When the market has had a sustained rise (a bull market), there comes a time when most popular writers on financial matters get carried away. They "see no reason" for the trend to change and predict the Dow-Jones to hit 2,000 "sometime next year." Sell. This is the time to get out. Conversely, when the market is in a long slide (a bear market), the same writers eventually abandon all hope and suggest that the D-J is headed for 400—half or double seem to be the critical predictions. Buy. The Bulls are about to take charge. We don't know why this system works. Perhaps the writers get bored saying the same thing day after day, like the Houston TV weatherman who said, "The weather tonight will be warm and humid; tomorrow will be partly cloudy and hot with a chance of afternoon thunderstorms. *This prediction is good for the next four months.*"

DIVIDENDS

Price rise is not the only way to make money from stock ownership. Most companies pay their shareholders regular dividends. The dividend yield on common stocks is usually less than that on good bonds, *but* stock dividends are not fixed. The stock that paid 4 percent at the time of purchase may increase its dividends to the point where it yields 8 percent or even 12 percent on the original investment. (On the other hand, the dividends may vanish.)

The payment of dividends to common-stock holders is slightly illogical; it may not even be good business. Some companies don't pay any. For years Superior Oil paid none and IBM paid only token amounts. Mark Twain's shareholders probably didn't get regular dividends; they more likely had a jolly little "melon-cutting" ceremony from time to time and passed out profits.

The shareholder, presumably, bought shares in the Widget Company because he liked the way its management uses its resources. What more can he ask than that the company *keep* the profits and reinvest them in the same good way? (Incidentally, this avoids double taxation on corporate profits and on dividends.) Companies pay dividends because the stockholders *expect* them— they wouldn't buy the stock otherwise—and to keep the price up. Unsophisticated investors would rather have regular dividend income than sell a few shares that had increased in value (due to reinvestment), even though the latter type of return is taxed at lower capital-gains rates.

There is a respected stock pricing theory that maintains that a share price should be equal to the present value of all anticipated future dividends. This is wrong, not only because of the preceding argument, but because the computed value is very sensitive to the chosen discount rate—a rate almost impossible to choose in an inflationary economy.

THE PROXY CARD

Once a year every shareholder gets a chance to express his opinion of the company. He gets a proxy card with little printed boxes on it for him to vote "yes" or "no" in answer to certain questions. The hitch is that there aren't many questions (usually just two), and they don't seem very important: voting for or against a presented slate of board members and accepting or rejecting outside auditors. The card is accompanied by a brochure which gives management's positions on some administrative questions, but the shareholder is not usually asked to vote on these things. As far as operating problems are concerned, they may as well not exist.

The new shareholder may feel a bit conned: he is asked to vote for a bunch of important-sounding people he will never know and for a multinamed accounting firm he has never heard of. He also notes that if he returns the card unmarked, management assumes that he voted as management recommends. (We haven't yet got to the Book of the Month Club system where not returning the card is taken as a "yes" vote.) Actually, these two questions are critical. In a simpler time, such as in Mark Twain's day, they would be all that was needed to give the shareholders control of the company. That this is far from true today is due to shareholder indifference, fractionation of ownership, and the rise of a professional management class.

Auditors

Why do the shareholders vote for the outside auditors anyway? The answer is that the auditors outrank management! The only people who *can* select the auditors are the owners—the shareholders. Actually, they don't select the actual auditors but only an accounting firm (accountants supply auditors) which provides the service. These people work for the shareholders and not for management.

Auditors are supposed to keep an eye on management and to warn the owners if there is any funny business rather than good business going on. This is what is *supposed* to happen; what really happens is quite different. Traveling auditors, often young men in a learning and job-seeking mode, move into the company headquarters and check to see if the company accountants can add and if the accounting system is proper—if it was last year, chances are it still is. If the company is highly mechanized, the auditors are almost helpless to make even this check. Their work is eventually presented in a series of reports, which are concerned mainly with trivial inaccuracies and loose control. The whole effort is legitimized by the auditor's report in the annual report. This is short (two paragraphs is about par), impressive—complete with the accounting firm's name and address in fancy type—and contains the statement "in conformity with generally accepted accounting principles."

This statement is the best cop-out since Pontius Pilate called for a washbowl; it is supposed to absolve the accounting firm of further responsibility. What in the hell are accepted accounting principles? What the shareholder wants to know is: is the company healthy, is management doing its job, is the dividend policy sound, will there *be* another annual report? Companies do go broke. The Pennsylvania Railroad bravely paid dividends until the last, Westec stock prices went down to zero (yes, zero). Companies fail for different reasons, but you may be reasonably sure that their last annual report contained the magic words "in accordance with generally accepted accounting practices." (Recently, a group of shareholders have sued an accounting company for not warning them of the company's imminent demise. They may have a good case, but there isn't much "come" betting.)

Actually, the shareholders don't select the auditors—management does! Whichever accounting company appears on the proxy card is going to get the job, except in those very rare cases where the shareholders organize and reject the whole package. It doesn't make much difference anyway; if you don't like Arthur Andersen, you will get Peat Marwick Mitchell, which amounts to the same act with different players. Accounting companies are prosperous, and their partners are rich as a result of their business commissions. As long as management in effect chooses the accounting firm, the partners are going to be more interested in their relations with company management than with the poor shareholders.

To be fair, it wouldn't be easy for the auditors to contact the thousands of stockholders, who range from sophisticated fund managers to little old ladies who don't know a balance sheet from a telephone bill. What the shareholders obviously need is an organization to represent them, a small group that has time to study the company and which can deal with the accounting firm. Theoretically, and legally, the shareholders *have* such a group: the board of directors whom they elect and who are supposed to protect their interests.

The Board of Directors

Let us look at an idealized diagram of the upper echelons of control in a publicly owned company (Figure 6). The shareholders are in the driver's seat. Using their proxy votes, they select the board of directors, who select the officers, who run the company. The shareholders also select auditors to keep an eye on the whole business. If there are few enough shareholders, as in the Mark Twain case, they can all be directors themselves and appoint the officers. The titles of corporate officers have a comforting old-fashioned sound: president, treasurer, secretary, controller—more like the officers of a local garden club than of a big corporation. These titles are usually lost on the annual report in a sea of vice presidents. The diagram represents the way things should be, not the way they are.

Professional managers run American business; they aren't about to relinquish their control to a mob of uninformed shareholders (which may be a good thing). In fact, management's relation-

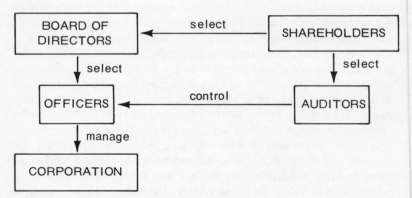

Figure 6. Corporate control.

ship with its owners is a lot like that of a political incumbent to his constituents: keep them happy, keep them docile, tell them what they want to hear, and make formal reports only when necessary. The average shareholder does not object to a passive role. He wants his dividends, he wants the stock to go up, and he can always sell if he doesn't like the way things are going.

It is obvious that control of the board is equivalent to control of the company. (As we have seen, auditing interference has been defused.) Management took this over long ago by the simple method of selecting the board members itself, subject to almost automatic shareholder approval. The method is beautiful in its simplicity; it is also legal. The officers (management) present a slate of board members to the shareholders, who then have the opportunity to vote "for" or "against" management's choice on the proxy card. Any opposition is normally so fractionated that it is completely ineffective. The elected board members then elect the new officers—an election without surprises. This sequence is so generally accepted that the highest rank in a company is not that of president but chairman of the board. The chairman, of course, is not necessarily an officer of the company.

Board members are an interesting bunch. Some may be termed "working" members—those who are already part of management and possibly officers of the company. Other members are "outside" or "guest" members. They may be chosen for business reasons, such as a representative of a bank that has a big stake in the company, or for cosmetic reasons. It is ego-building for the working directors, and image-building for the company, to have celebrities such as retired generals and politicians (who may be useful) on the board. A token black or a female is a good thing. (If Barbara Jordan ever gets tired of teaching, she can have a new career as a professional board member.) English and Canadian companies usually include a titled board member.

Being an outside board member is a good deal; the pay is handsome for the time involved, and there is VIP treatment, including transportation on company planes. The annual board meeting is apt to be as much a first-class vacation as a working meeting. If this sounds more like membership in an exclusive club than fair representation of Joe Shareholder, that is the way things are.

Such complete, incestuous control by professional managers might seem to encourage, or at least provide the setting for, management irregularities or outright fraud. Apart from little things, like moving sons-in-law into soft jobs or providing free transportation, American business usually keeps its house in order. This seems to be due to three constraints: the inherent decency and honesty of most managers, a lingering, almost pathological, respect for the faceless shareholders, and fear of the federal government.

American (Western) business methods may not export satisfactorily to emerging and Third World countries just because these countries do not have our tradition of fair play and Judeo-Christian morality to police themselves. To the outsider, American business is so obviously organized by and for management that not to take advantage of this must seem silly. In spite of its built-in leverage, management does worry about the shareholders—the great unknown. Management wants them to vote "right": 51 percent is not enough, and companies spend a lot of money getting out the vote. It is a proud moment at the annual shareholders' meeting when the presiding officer announces that the vote is over 90 percent in favor of management.

Business knows it has one implacable policeman: the federal government in all its hydra-headed manifestations—the SEC, the IRS, OSHA, FERC, and on and on. These government departments have all the natural charm of the tax collector—they assume the worst and mobilize at any sign of trouble. It is dangerous to get out of line.

THE ANNUAL MEETING

Once a year management puts on a show for the shareholders: the annual shareholders' meeting, which is a sort of State of the Union presentation. Every shareholder is dutifully informed of the meeting and is invited to attend. Any investor who made a point of going to these things would be a traveling man. A quick desk check shows that I would go to Houston and Dallas in Texas; to Washington, D.C.; to Stamford, Connecticut; to Toronto and Montreal in Canada; and to Beverly Hills, California. Obviously, most shareholders don't go. The company, which would rather have favorably signed proxy cards than warm bodies, expects a poor turnout and reserves one meeting room at a local hotel to accommodate its thousands of shareholders.

Who does go to the annual shareholders' meeting? Who doesn't? Big investors and fund managers *don't* go—they don't have to in order to find out how things are going. The typical small investor doesn't go. He bought his stock on a tip in the hopes that it will go up, and may not even know what the company does for a living. Company people go because the meeting is usually held in the headquarters city and the employees are given time off to attend, much as time is given for an assembly or pep rally at school. The directors attend. Local shareholders and friends of management go; for some of them it is a social occasion. I remember the nice little old ladies who used to regularly attend the United Gas meeting in Shreveport to hear what dear Mr. McGowen was going to say this year. They *should* have been a sympathetic audience, for he had built their fortunes along with the company.

The only way to describe the action at an annual shareholders' meeting is to describe a typical meeting. Details vary from company to company, but the following scenario will serve.

A Typical Meeting

The crowd gathers at the Hyatt Hotel and is cordially checked in at a desk by badge-wearing people especially detailed from the public relations department. Many of the company employees feel a bit diffident, as this is their first contact with Big Business. The officers and directors sit on a row of chairs on the stage, facing the audience, and try to look friendly.

After the usual shuffling and whispering, "Who's he?(she?)," the meeting is brought to order. The presiding officer, usually the chairman of the board, announces that some 80 percent of the shares are represented at the meeting (mostly by proxy) and that it (the meeting) is duly convened. Like the opening lineups for a World Series game, the members of the board are introduced; each stands and grins. Two strange people are also introduced as auditors from the accounting company; they will be available to answer shareholder questions later in the meeting.

The only real business of the meeting is then announced: to elect a board of directors and to approve the accounting firm. The slate of directors which was on the proxy cards is then declared nominated, and other nominations are solicited from the floor. There are none. A preprogrammed company man then moves that nominations be closed. The second, and last, item of business is announced: to select or reject the proposed public accounting company to provide outside auditors. The vote on these two questions then follows. As the high point of the meeting, this is an anticlimax. Anyone who has not previously voted by proxy may now fill out a ballot (very few do). With all the business of the meeting tidied up, and while the ballots are being tabulated by the judges (not much of a job since it has already been mostly done), we come to the high spots of the meeting: the president's report and the chairman's remarks.

If this is a large company, television crews swing into action. If the audience is lucky, the president is a good speaker. He points with pride to last year's accomplishments (or rationalizes last year's failures), he views with alarm the government's increasing interference, and he gives a hopeful projection for next year. The chairman's remarks which follow are less a State of the Union address. His emphasis is on certain critical problems and hopes.

After the speeches there is a special treat for the congregation: a movie of "The Company at Work." Such industrial films are usually excellent, interesting, well produced, and narrated by an actor with an Eastern accent (which can be disconcerting if the company happens to be a Southwestern oil company). There is a trifle too much emphasis on the work force, featuring nice-looking girls in hard hats. In fact, this may be the ideological intersection of the capitalist and communist ideology—the noble worker.

After the entertainment comes the question period. Someone wants to know why the officers are paid so much, someone else wants to know why the company has such a large fleet of planes, another wants to know when the dividends are going to be raised. These are expected questions with prepared answers: salaries are reviewed by the compensation committee and are in line with the industry norms; each company plane is carefully cost-justified; we preserve a consistent, prudent dividend policy and are just as anxious as you are to raise dividends (laughter). Then someone gets up and asks why the company got shut out of the Powder River Basin play. What is this guy, a troublemaker? Management has been agonizing over this one for months. "Thank you, sir, that is a very good question. I suggest you talk to our vice president of exploration after the meeting."

The secretary—Who's he? (she?)—submits the judges' reports to the presiding officer, who then reports that the proposed slate of directors has been approved by a majority of more than 90 percent. The accounting firm has done almost as well. The people on the stage try to look both gratified and humble at the same time. The meeting is adjourned.

It is easy to criticize the annual shareholder meeting with its proxy-card voting as a farce—a benign farce—but it is hard to suggest an alternative. As long as companies are actually run by professional management (with the shareholders' acquiescence) but want to keep alive the myth that they are controlled by the shareholders as they were in Mark Twain's day, something has to be done to preserve a decent appearance. The annual meeting is usually a pleasant affair, even though the voting is not exciting. It provides a useful format for the president and the chairman to present their views and the prospects of the company to the shareholders and to the media. Often good news such as a raise in dividends or a successful acquisition is saved to be announced at the annual meeting. Most important, as long as this sequence is maintained, the shareholders *do* have the mechanism to throw out an incompetent management. It is rarely done—it takes a lot of work and organization—but it can and does happen (remember Gulf). For most companies the threat is more useful than its realization.

MANAGEMENT AND SHARE PRICE

There are some listed companies that haven't sold a share of stock in this century. Shares which they originally sold for $5 a share are now changing hands at more than $100. These companies are in the position of an artist who sees pictures he painted and sold years ago at $50 each now being auctioned at Christie's for thousands of dollars: everybody is making money except the artist. Why should the professional management of a company be concerned with the price somebody is paying somebody else for its old shares? Management has to be concerned for both tangible and intangible reasons.

First, the intangible reasons. All employees, management particularly, like to work for a company whose stock is rising. People are proud of their company's stock and like to recommend it to others as an investment. For a top-management person, strong market performance is an "A" on the corporate report card; it also gives status in his intercompany peer group. Shareholders of a rising stock are not going to revolt.

Tangible reasons for management to want the stock price to rise can be classified under the headings of greed and good business. Most managers and directors own a lot of shares in their own company; in fact, the details of their ownership are often listed in prospectuses and annual reports to reassure other shareholders that management's heart is in the right place.

If share-holding management is going to be gung-ho to get the price up, why not get all the employees involved? Many companies do; they have an employee stock purchase plan to encourage share ownership by all workers. This is a fringe benefit, discussed in Chapter 13. As an incentive to productive and efficient work, it is less successful than management would like. Most employee-shareholders just hope that their stock and dividends will go up. They don't see much cause and effect between what they do and stock price. The numbers are against it: if a worker is smart enough to have an idea that will save the company several thousand dollars, he is smart enough to know that this won't affect the earnings per share enough to be noticed. He also sees much more money wasted or spent for government reporting, which nobody seems to be able to control. What the smart employee wants for his efforts is personal recognition and promotion—which are always his goals, with or without owning company stock.

So appealing is this concept of happy share-holding workers pulling together for the common good, improving productivity and the national welfare, that the federal government has got into the act. One of the silliest pieces of legislation to come out of Washington in a long time (which is saying a lot) is the Employee Stock Ownership Program (ESOP), which uses the taxing apparatus to transfer money to that group of citizens which probably needs it least. The government actually buys stock for employees in their own company at no apparent cost to the company. The workers are happy to get a new fringe benefit, and the other taxpayers, who are footing the bill, probably don't know what is going on. It is doubtful that this complicated program either improves worker productivity or gets votes for politicians. Most people just don't understand the program or don't know it exists.

The strongest incentive for higher management to get the stock price up is to cash in on the executive enrichment schemes which are usually based on stock options. (See "Perks" in Chapter 13.) A stock option is worth nothing—zero—if the stock price doesn't go up. If the price doesn't *continue* to rise or at least stay up, options can be fool's gold. Horror stories are still told of people who retired on stock option "paper profits" in the roaring fifties, only to have to go back to work when the market collapsed.

So much for greed. What about sound business reasons as incentives to increase stock prices? Most companies are large shareholders of their own stock—treasury stock on the balance sheet. A company doesn't pay itself dividends on these shares, which would be silly, but this treasury stock is a real asset whose value is tied to share price. (If the painter used earlier as an analogy had kept some of his old pictures, he would be happy to see their trading price increase.) Some companies like their own shares so much as an investment that they go into the open market and buy them to increase their holdings. The other shareholders like this action, because it reduces the number of shares outstanding and increases their share of ownership.

Corporate shares are the blue chips of the business game;*

---

* We have already identified millions of dollars as the white chips of the business game. The red chips must be people—the creative, competent people who make a business go. There is an open market in red chips too.

they are used as a medium of exchange in mergers and acquisitions. Treasury stock or new issues are used—which requires approval of the shareholders. There are often elaborate swaps involved: two and one-third shares of your stock equals one of mine. Obviously, if management wants to get into this kind of wheeling and dealing, it wants the value of its own blue chips, its stock price, to be high. More important, it wants the price–earnings ratio of its share price to be high—higher than that of the company it is dealing with. If the adventure is successful, the acquiring company will come out of it with more shares—shares which represent the asset value of the merged firm. If these new shares move up to the higher price–earnings ratio of the parent company, everybody makes money. On the other hand, if a company's stock price is depressed—if it has a low price–earnings ratio—it looks like a bargain to other hungry companies. A company with cheap stock is vulnerable to tender offers* and ultimately to painful negotiations to try to save some of the pieces. The changing values of these blue chips between companies are a bit like the changing exchange rates between national currencies in international trade and finance. If my dollars go up in value compared to your pounds, I am in the driver's seat. The converse is also true.

Another good reason to keep stock price up is that the company may wish to sell new shares—the painter is still painting pictures. Most companies don't like to issue new shares unless they are used for the acquisition of other companies or for new assets. The shareholders, including management, don't like to see the book value of their shares diluted. Sometimes there is no choice! Selling new shares is the only responsible way to raise money. A company can raise money only by borrowing or by selling off pieces of itself—new shares. Borrowed money, whether it be mortgage money (hocking assets) or from debentures (based on faith), must eventually be repaid, and interest has to be paid in the meantime. Rather than sticking the existing shareholders with new debt, it

---

* This has nothing to do with Loving Care. It is an offer to buy outstanding shares at above quoted value—a good way to get a lot of stock quickly.

may be better to bring in some new owners to share the burden.

A company may not be responsibly *able* to take on new debt. If it has to have new money, it must sell equity (shares). This is a discipline imposed by the financial community. The penalty of not complying is a lowering of the company's bond rating (Chapter 3), which could make the cost of borrowed money prohibitive.

It is relatively easy to compare the total shareholders' equity with the total indebtedness of any company by using data from the 10-K or from the annual report (ignoring convertible securities). The ratio of these two totals—the debt–equity ratio—is critical. There is an upper limit beyond which the financial community does not like to see a company go. This limit varies by type of industry: an 80 percent ratio may be tolerated in a stable industry like a public utility, while 40 percent may be considered high for a manufacturing company. If a given company is pushing its limit, it can't afford any more debt. If it needs outside money, it has to sell some kind of equity. The average investor doesn't know the reasonable ratio for a specific company, but his broker's representative can tell him.

Some investors may prefer to invest in shares of companies that have a relatively high debt–equity ratio. If all goes well, it means that the investor has other people's money working for him—like having a margin account with his broker. This is called high financial leverage, and such stocks are a bit risky, but the payoff may be good. A conservative investor will probably prefer a company with a low debt–equity ratio, or low leverage. Such a company can weather adversity better, but its gain will probably be less in a rising market. This is theory, which the market can and does violate regularly.

With all these incentives to boost stock prices, the small shareholder can be reasonably sure that the professional management of his companies is on his side. It is just as eager as he is to see his stock go up.

PART TWO

The Corporation

7

MACRO
ORGANIZATION

THE MEMBERS of any organization above a certain size can be divided into production workers and support personnel—line and staff. The army is an obvious example; combat troops as against support troops, and a higher level, which is actually called staff. In baseball, the split is between the players and the front office. At first glance, government bureaucracy looks like an all-staff organization, but if its mission is defined as *making* as well as enforcing regulations, then we can identify the few people involved in making design decisions as line people, different from the hordes who support them.

For a businessman, staff functions tend to be more interesting (at least more rewarding) than line operations. Staff functions tend to be self-justifying, to grow and multiply, and to skim the cream off the corporate pail. Staff cannot exist without line operations, just as an army must have some combat troops. Line likes to think it can do its job without staff help. (It can't, but it likes to think so.)

The creation and development of staff functions in business can be illustrated by a "historical" example.* Before the coming of the Industrial Revolution, there was a village blacksmith. He was a good worker, but he couldn't keep up with demand, so he hired an apprentice and a boy to operate the bellows. Now he had an organization—not yet a business but an organization, charted in Figure 7(a). Since everybody worked at the forge, this is an all-line organization.

Business continued to prosper, and the smith started to get orders from other counties and was required to maintain an inventory. None of the workers liked to handle paperwork (still typical of line workers), so he hired a clerk—the first staff job. Also, he hired an engineer (his son-in-law). Now his organization chart looked like Figure 7(b).

Things were looking up, but there were murmurs of dissent. The workers didn't like the clerk—he worked only eight to five, he wore a clean jerkin, and he talked funny. The clerk, on the other hand, didn't think much of the workers—they were crude, their jerkins were dirty, and they talked funny. By now nobody else could do the paperwork, so the clerk remained. Besides, the smith (now president) liked him.

One day the president made a historical decision; he decided he was tired of paying the men himself and would hire a new staff man (treasurer) to handle the money. From this day on, the staff/line competition was resolved. To control the money is to control the business, and although it may have moved slowly at first, from that day the staff started its takeover.

Now look at the organization chart in Figure 7(c), years after the Industrial Revolution has done its thing and the smith company has become a large steel maker and fabricator. Between the president and the line people (operations) there is now a whole pantheon of high-level staff people: vice presidents, directors, treasurer, controller, and their departments. These "executives"

* For a definitive history of the growth of American management, see Alfred D. Chandler, Jr., *The Visible Hand*, Cambridge, Mass.: Harvard University Press, 1977.

Figure 7. The growth of an organization staff.

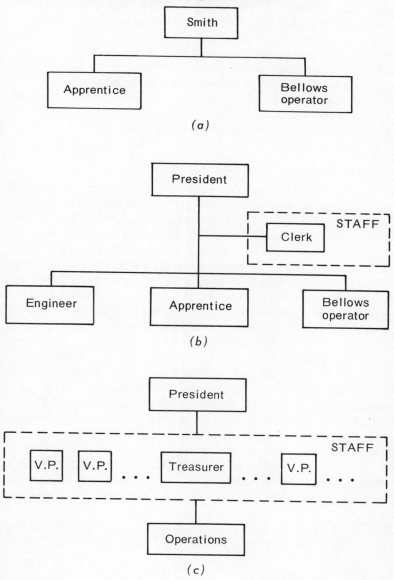

still work from nine to five (with a long lunch break), wear clean shirts and three-piece suits, and talk funny. The workers tend to work strange hours, wear blue jeans, chew tobacco, and talk funny. The line people have unfortunate titles like steel puddler and cat skinner. The staff people have invented classy titles for themselves, like "vice president—public relations." The staff pays the line and even writes their job descriptions. The victory is complete.

Any group as successful as corporate staff deserves a closer look, but before getting carried away, let us first take a look at the line. They may be losers, but they are far from dead.

THE LINE

According to the definition of the first chapter, production workers are not businessmen. Even plant managers are not businessmen if their main concern is production rather than money. Line operations like factories and mines are not businesses any more than engines are automobiles; their job is to implement plans and decisions made by businessmen in corporate headquarters. Even though this book is on businesses and businessmen, there are still good reasons to discuss the line and the line people. There would be no business without line functions—you can't have a baseball team without players. Another reason to discuss the line is the ambiguous position of top management, which is, of course, made up of businessmen. Is it line or is it staff?

Not all line workers are grunts by any means. Many are skilled craftsmen: welders, machinists, surveyors, and artists. In fact, it is not an exaggeration to say that the quality of their work largely determines the competitiveness of American goods in the world market. The prototype of the elite line worker is the engineer. Not all engineers are line people; those who work in research, planning, or design are staff. The line engineer is a builder. Perelman* recalls a Warner Baxter movie in which the hero (Baxter) enters his home wearing beautifully tailored breeches and cordovans and an-

* S. J. Perelman, *Hold That Christmas Tiger*, reprinted in *The Best of S. J. Perelman*, New York: The Modern Library, 1947.

nounces to his wife, while brushing dust off his shoulders, "Well, darling, I just finished Boulder Dam." This man was a line engineer.

Line people resent staff excursions to the "field" (plant, mine, drilling platform, farm) in much the same way that combat soldiers, doing their thing, resent visits of staff officers from the Communications Zone. A staff manager often feels uncomfortable on such junkets. He doesn't have the usual props of office—walnut desk, loyal secretary, carpeting. To carry a two-hundred-dollar dispatch case down a mine looks silly. There may also be a guilt feeling (these people are working harder for less money than he does).

I have known one manager who, to prove something, wore a pair of L. L. Bean engineer boots on field trips. This was a mistake. The best approach by visiting staff is the fairy godmother approach—spend money. Buy lunch, of course, but more important, buy booze after working hours. Field people will accept anything they can get. They have adopted a soldier's philosophy—"Don't look forward to your next leave, settle for the next ten-minute break." On the other hand, some field managers try to emulate the city slickers. They install a paneled office and require their secretary to wear a frock rather than the usual jeans and G.I. shoes. This is also a mistake. The best chance the field manager has to preserve a one-up position in his own domain is to come on as a horny-handed son of toil.

Some authorities consider top management to be staff. We don't. Top generals get combat ribbons without going near the front. A good general's first concern is the ground pounders; his job is in jeopardy along with their lives. Similarly, a top manager's sympathy must be with operations. He probably (not necessarily) graduated from a staff position, but now he has to look over the sea of paperwork to where the action is. Incidentally, if the staff managers are doing their jobs, he should be free of administrative problems. Apart from this empathy with the line, there is another reason to classify top management as line, not staff.

In the beginning of this chapter, we defined the critical decision makers even in a government bureaucracy as line people. This is also true for critical decision makers in a corporation. Critical decisions are those which will ultimately determine the character and future of a company: products to be made or abandoned, factories to be built or closed, major financial policy. These decisions are a different breed from those made by the vice president—personnel relations in setting new salary brackets, or the vice president—management services in bullying management into buying a computer it doesn't need. Critical decisions are operational decisions; they're the soul of the company—and pure line.

THE STAFF

The easiest way to define staff functions in a corporation is to fall back on a negative definition: staff functions are those which are not line. We can't use the usual supportive definition—the man-behind-the-man-behind-the-gun sort of thing—because, as we shall see, not all staff functions are supportive (some are even counterproductive). Just because the definition is wishy-washy, the staff is not to be despised; it is in fact the healthiest, fastest-growing part of a modern corporation. In the American Army, support troops outnumber combat troops two to one.* In most corporations, there are more staff people than line people, and together they make more money, even if top management is considered to be line. Unless one has a neurotic desire to get dirty hands or to build something, staff is the place to be.

In his autobiography, Bill Mauldin tells of a regimental commander who was relieved of his command in the field for following rather than leading his troops.† He then returned to a noncombat role in the States and was soon promoted. Mauldin (the dogface's friend) implies that this was unfair. Not at all. In businessese we would say that it took him a while to find a position where he could realize his total potential. He was a natural staff man.

Staff departments vary greatly. Without an organization chart, a description of their individual functions doesn't make much sense. More generally, there is a useful way to classify all staff departments. They are creative or bureaucratic, sometimes a mixture

---

* Department of Defense Annual Report, 1980 budget. There are as many civilian employees of the Army as there are combat troops.
† Bill Mauldin, *The Brass Ring*, New York: Norton, 1971, p. 13.

of both. Examples of creative departments are research, engineering design and development, and publicity. Typical bureaucratic departments are accounting and data processing. Mixed departments usually start out as creative but develop a bureaucratic infrastructure and start turning out an excessive amount of paper.

Creative staff departments are manned mostly by specialists: economists, engineers, mathematicians, artists—people who are not businessmen. The professional orientation of such groups tends to keep them honest, resisting the urge to grow and to turn out useless memoranda. No staff department works under discipline like that of line departments, which are tightly controlled by production schedules and unit cost control. There is a fixed limit to the tons of ore to be mined and the number of cars to be made (and sold), and it is easy to compute cost per ton or cost per assembly—costs which can be closely watched and controlled. There are no such uncompromising unit costs for the generation of reports and special studies.

The bureaucratic departments have certain common attributes and tendencies. Unless these are recognized and kept under control by top management people, the corporation (and its customers) will be supporting the same sort of bureaucratic apparatus within itself that it so justly deplores in government departments. The inclinations of any bureaucracy are to grow, to endure, to turn out excessive paper, to develop an image of importance. These tendencies are worth separate discussions.

Growth

Parkinson's laws* apply in business as well as in government. What these laws say is that the same amount of *real* work is done by more and more people as time passes. Parkinson's classic example was the continuing growth of the Colonial Office as the British Empire self-destructed. The irresistible tendency to grow is caused by an irrational rule of thumb and by human nature. The rule is

* C. Northcote Parkinson, *Parkinson's Law*, Boston: Houghton Mifflin, 1969.

that status and salary are a direct function of the number of people supervised. It is human nature to want increased status. This is an explosive situation, a chain reaction. In order for the incumbents to move up, additional people must be added at low levels—not to do work but to be supervised. These new employees soon become established and busy, and they in turn demand subordinates. When a department gets to be embarrassingly big, it may split, much as a stock splits when the price gets too high. Instead of a single accounting department we now have Tax Accounting, Cost Accounting, and so forth, with new department heads and staff and possibly a new vice president over the whole thing.

Modern technology has added a new wrinkle to the status equation. Not just the number of people but the amount of equipment (hardware) in the department determines the importance of the department head. This is particularly pernicious, since such status is largely extracorporate. At outside meetings, for example, the pecking order of the different attending data processing managers is determined by the size of the computer each operates. I have sat in many company conferences whose whole purpose was to plan strategy to convince management that the present hardware was dangerously loaded and it was time to move up to something bigger.

Most efforts to control this built-in growth tendency involve heavy-handed personnel or budget policy. A better approach might be to reward managers for making do with fewer people and less equipment rather than the existing more-is-better approach.

Endurance

A politician knows that the hardest thing to do is to eliminate an obsolete committee or institution. He also knows that if he tries, he is almost certain to lose some votes and is unlikely to gain any. A good example of endurance beyond reasonable need is the Army Veterinarian Corps. At one time this was a very important corps— the army needed healthy horses and mules as much as healthy men. The army did use mules in Italy in World War II, but it hasn't used them much since. The Veterinarian Corps still goes marching on. Not only does the army commission veterinarians, but until 1975 it paid them supplementary benefits to enlist; it *had* to, because civilian veterinarians were in short supply.

In corporations, durability of departments and of job positions depends mostly on their being listed on the organization chart. Until the chart changes (which usually means adding more boxes rather than deleting any), the job or department is safe. If an employee quits, is transferred, or retires and if his position appears on the organization chart, that position will be filled no matter how fatuous the job. The same is true of departments. In my company it took years, after billing and payroll were mechanized, to eliminate the comptometer department, which spent its declining years checking computed listings.

The department which should monitor this sort of thing—prune the corporate organization tree—is the personnel (employee relations) department. Since this is an almost prototypical bureaucratic department, it is usually a poor policeman. A discussion of the usual activities of the personnel department is left to the next chapter.

Output—Paperwork

Every staff department produces output, usually in the form of printed documents. This output is of three types: documents actually needed to run the company, reports prepared to satisfy government requests, and optional internal documents. The output of the first type, which fills legitimate needs, is at least finite. The forms used may be badly designed and the information redundant, but there is a limit to the amount of legitimate information required. By contrast, there seems to be no limit to government demands.

It is difficult to describe the magnitude and cost of government reporting; in fact, it seems impossible to exaggerate. The paper flowing annually into the federal agencies (1976 figures) fills 4.5 million cubic feet of space—the equivalent of ten forms for every person in the United States.* The estimated cost to business was

* Robert DeFina, *Public and Private Expenditure for Federal Regulation of Business,* Center for the Study of American Business, Washington University, St. Louis.

more than $24.48 *billion.* This cost is paid by consumers and tax-payers through higher cost of goods, higher taxes to pay for processing and storing the stuff, and most of all through inflation. Weidenbaum* states that government regulation is becoming one of the country's major growth industries.

Business has had to take a craven attitude toward government requests because, under existing law, the alternative may be an injunction, possibly incarceration. Discretion may be the better part of valor, but this compliance is made easier by the existence of computers in big companies. The data processing manager has a battery of 1,200-line-a-minute printers, and he is eager to turn out more paper. "Yes sir, we have that information in our data base. I'll put three programmers on it, and we will run an extra shift this weekend. I'll have the report on your desk on Monday morning. Can do, sir." Business does fight back, even suing the government for unjustified demands. Its case would be stronger if it *couldn't* comply.

This defensive approach contradicts the usual public image of business telling government what to do. Obviously, proper information cannot be withheld, but business must dig in its heels in the face of organized stupidity and unreasonable demands. For example, Exxon company is required to file more than 400 reports to 45 (count 'em) federal agencies. It submits over 50, largely redundant, reports relating to personnel, labor, and wages to 14 different agencies. As long as management has to comply with Washington's requests, the staff departments will have (and welcome) this extra load.

The third type of output, optional internal documents, may be more deadly, if only because someone within the company is expected to read them. Time and money are wasted both in preparation and in final processing. There are multitudes of these things in the average company: status reports, progress reports, special studies, newsletters. If staff departments grow without correspondingly increased duties, or if department missions become obsolete, some-

* Murray L. Weidenbaum, *Business, Government, and the Public,* Englewood Cliffs, N.J.: Prentice-Hall, 1977.

thing has to be done to keep people busy. In a business situation, unlike in the army, people can't be assigned to do pushups or paint rocks, but everybody has a desk and a pencil, so let's make a special study! This involves research, writing a draft, reviews and rewrites, and preparation and distribution of the final study report. Overtime may be involved.

Once a regular report is scheduled, it is almost impossible to stop it, particularly if it uses a special numbered form. We have both had the frustrating experience of trying to do something about document proliferation. The first finding of a survey to eliminate unnecessary paper is that there is *no* document that someone doesn't want and need. Another approach is to stop issuing certain reports and wait for reaction. If nobody beefs for several months, the company can probably live without them. This approach is a bit dangerous.

I don't think there is an easy solution to the paperwork problem as long as it is to staff departments' advantage to turn the stuff out. A brave top manager might require that internal paperwork be cut to no more than the number of sheets that all employees reading all day could possibly read. I wish him luck. Paperwork is the natural progeny of bureaucracy. The Department of Commerce even has a staff department to turn out paperwork about paperwork: the National Technical Information Service.

The largest cost of useless or redundant reports is the production and processing time, but the cost of paper itself is significant—it's one of the largest raw-material costs of doing business. There is an even more basic cost: the energy and raw materials wasted. Whole Canadian forests are dedicated to providing this raw material for American business. Instead of setting our thermostats back to 68°, we might do our descendants a bigger favor by saving paper.

The proliferation of paperwork may even be a threat to society. We could eventually spend our creative lives filling in forms—doing each other's income tax.* On the other hand, collec-

---

* We don't consider it aberrant that whole courses in business schools are devoted to filling tax forms. This is nonacademic pseudoknowledge.

tive wisdom may finally reject anything with a dotted line on it, in the same way that a frustrated laboratory rat finally stops pushing the colored button. This, of course, would end business (and government) as we now know it.

There have been a lot of sound effects proposed to accompany the decline of Western civilization, from the harlot's cry suggested by Blake to the whimper predicted by Eliot. A more likely sound may be the rustle of paper and the mindless yammering of computer-driven line printers.

Image

All departments strive for respectability, for recognized importance in the corporate family. The most obvious justification of a staff department is its support role—a vicarious validity borrowed from operations. "They couldn't build cars unless we bought the steel." This is true, just as true as the quartermaster's assertion that soldiers could not fight without food. Justification only by the reflected glory from operations tends to make staff people uneasy, and they try to establish an independent importance to their own function.

One way to improve image is to have an impressive name. The personnel department becomes Employee Relations, the typing pool becomes Word Processing, and the janitorial staff is now Maintenance Engineering. A better approach is to organize, to combine with opposite numbers in other companies to create or maintain a discipline. People like corporate planners and corporate security managers have their own national organizations complete with publications, meetings, and seminars. The ultimate way to improve image is to achieve certification of certain types of staff workers. The goal of certification is to control entry into the field, preferably to create a shortage of certified people and force management to respect them—the coercion of Chapter 5. There is something a bit incestuous about certification in that the group passes judgment on itself.

Sometimes the original need for a staff department disappears due to new technology or procedures. This is a real image threat. The counter is to change the departmental mission ("to enlarge its scope"). Remember what happened to the March of Dimes! When the army no longer needed veterinarians to tend to its mules, the ostensible corps mission was changed to that of inspecting meat (based, no doubt, on experience with animal cadavers in school). The real mission of the new corps is taking care of dependents' pets. A business example of the switch-and-survive technique is the conversion of a research department from basic research, which is often unsuccessful, to product development, using the same staff.

Failure is a dirty word. If a department is obviously unsuccessful, this is a signal not to quit but to "meet the challenge." A classic example is the public relations function in large oil companies. After millions of dollars were spent by big oil to sell its image, the general public has less faith in the companies than it has in an unshaved used-car salesman. The corporate response is predictable: Spend more money! Increase institutional advertising! This new effort may only increase the public's suspicion that there is something to hide. Contrary to accepted military doctrine, business does reinforce failure.

A DAY IN THE STAFF SALT MINE

Mr. Biggers gets to the office on time. He always does. His secretary knows this, and she is already there, pecking at some mysterious document on her typewriter. He unpacks his briefcase, adjusts the venetian blinds, and inspects the potted plants for overnight deterioration. His secretary comes in with a cup of coffee and *The Wall Street Journal* (he won't get *this* service much longer). "Thank you, Honoria, what have I got scheduled for today?" "There is a job applicant due here at three-thirty, nothing else. What distribution do you want for this memorandum on Article 10?" "Just section heads. You had better make six copies." (She will make ten.)

He settles down to *The Wall Street Journal*—there are his few speculations and his stock option value to check. He finds the editorial policy soothing. When he has finished ("finalized" in the current jargon) his coffee and the *Journal*, the mail comes. Today it seems to consist mostly of brochures from organizations that want to educate him in seminars and short courses. He is used to this and does not take it as an insult; in fact, he reads the folders to see where the courses are to be held and for how long. Finally he throws the whole batch away—he just got back from a trip and isn't ready to go again. With a clear agenda, he gets himself another cup of coffee and prepares to work on a new memorandum. The phone rings; it is the vice president for whom he works. "Jim, I'd like to have a meeting with you and the other department heads if you can make it. Say ten o'clock in the West conference room." Damn! There goes the morning. He knows what this conference will be about, and he is pretty sure it will be useless. He hates conferences—but he will go. The only thing worse than sitting in a meeting is not being asked—the kiss of death. He tells his secretary to cancel his usual lunch-hour bridge game and adds a good one: "If anyone calls, tell them I'm in conference."

The meeting is as bad as he feared, rehashing familiar ground. Today they even have some bright young people with Vu-Graph slides. Why are they always so hard to read? About noon, as he expected, the leader says that as they still have some points to cover, he suggests that they have lunch together at his club and reconvene at one-thirty. An hour and a half later the conference does reconvene, looking slightly worse for wear. The martini (three-martini lunches are largely a figment of editorial writers' imagination) and the red snapper Pontchartrain have done their deadly work. Although it has lost its zip, the meeting staggers on for over an hour. The closing benediction is typical: "I think this has been a useful meeting and we should all now have a better idea of just what is involved at this point in time."

Mr. Biggers returns to his office and another cup of coffee— black this time to wake him up. The interview with the job applicant does not go too well. The young lady is obviously disappointed because she did not get to see a vice president. Too bad. He would like to add another female to his staff to keep the feds happy. It is almost quitting time. Mr. Biggers cleans off his desk and packs some material in his dispatch case—he may have time to take a crack at it tonight. He feels unfulfilled and toys briefly with the idea of early retirement. When he gets home, he looks pooped. As his wife mixes him a drink, she remarks, "I wish you didn't have to work so hard at the office."

Mr. Biggers' day in the salt mine has cost the company more than $200 in salary and fringe benefits.

Now let us take a more sympathetic look at Mr. Biggers' day. We had better give him a job. He is head of an accounting department and in fact is a good manager. As we pointed out in Chapter 2, this means that he is a good accountant as well as a good organizer. He long ago organized his department to run smoothly and efficiently under normal conditions.

As a good manager and a person endowed with common sense, he largely ignores the management literature which tells him how to do his job. He pays his people the compliment of assuming that they are adult and qualified, and he ignores the injunctions to constantly direct, control, evaluate, and plan unless there is some sort of change or crisis. His routine job has become one of fine-tuning—keeping up with changes and making procedure revisions—and keeping his people satisfied. He could work up to an imposing 16-hour day by chivying his people and making special studies (this might even justify an assistant), but he prefers not to. Under normal conditions his job requries about two working hours a day. How to fill the rest of the time?

It takes a brave man indeed to read Civil War history on company time (I knew a man who did this and nobody complained, least of all his people). What is needed is some sort of activity which will occupy a lot of time and not cost the company money by producing more paperwork or leading to decisions which will require unnecessary procedural changes. The business conference satisfies this requirement almost perfectly. Not only does it fill up Mr. Biggers' day, but it keeps other department heads from stirring up the troops.

Of course, some conferences are necessary in the direct sense—a decision is required and will have to be implemented. Considering the number of meetings which go on in the staff areas of companies, it is obvious that if all resulted in definitive action, the whole balance and efficiency of staff work would be jeopardized. The contribution of most conferences is simply to occupy managers so the workers can get on with their work. The first thing to do when joining a meeting is to decide its significance and behave accordingly. Conference manners and behavior are discussed in Chapter 12.

Mr. Biggers had a guilt feeling at the end of the day; consciously or unconsciously he felt that he had not earned his pay. His guilt is unfounded. His name appears in a box on the organization chart; if he didn't have the job, someone else would—possibly an eager beaver type who would drive his people to distraction. The accounting department may be overly fractured into separate departments, due to past growth pressure, but that is not his fault. The job is there, and like bird watching, someone has to do it. In order to be content, he must get a vicarious satisfaction from the efficiency of his department's work and from his employee's job satisfaction.

A final note. As a businessman, Mr. Biggers doesn't have an ideal job. He doesn't have enough exposure, is not involved with large cash streams, and generally seems to be in a dead-end situation. He may feel the need to move on.

8

STAFF
FUNCTIONS

*. . . and never go to sea, and you all
may be rulers of the Queen's Navee.*
H.M.S. Pinafore

SINCE THE STAFF is the home of most businessmen, we had better
take a closer look at it. It is a house of many rooms; it is also a
shared residence—shared with professional and line people. Some
rooms are more interesting, more profitable for advancement, than
others.

A proper corporate organization chart shows many staff departments, so many, in fact, that it is useful to separate them into
groups for discussion. The grouping is based not on individual mission but on their general character and relation to the corporate
mission. We have identified seven groups: *operations, planning,
legal, bureaucratic, technical, housekeeping,* and *other* (see Figure
8). Some staff departments are members of more than one group;

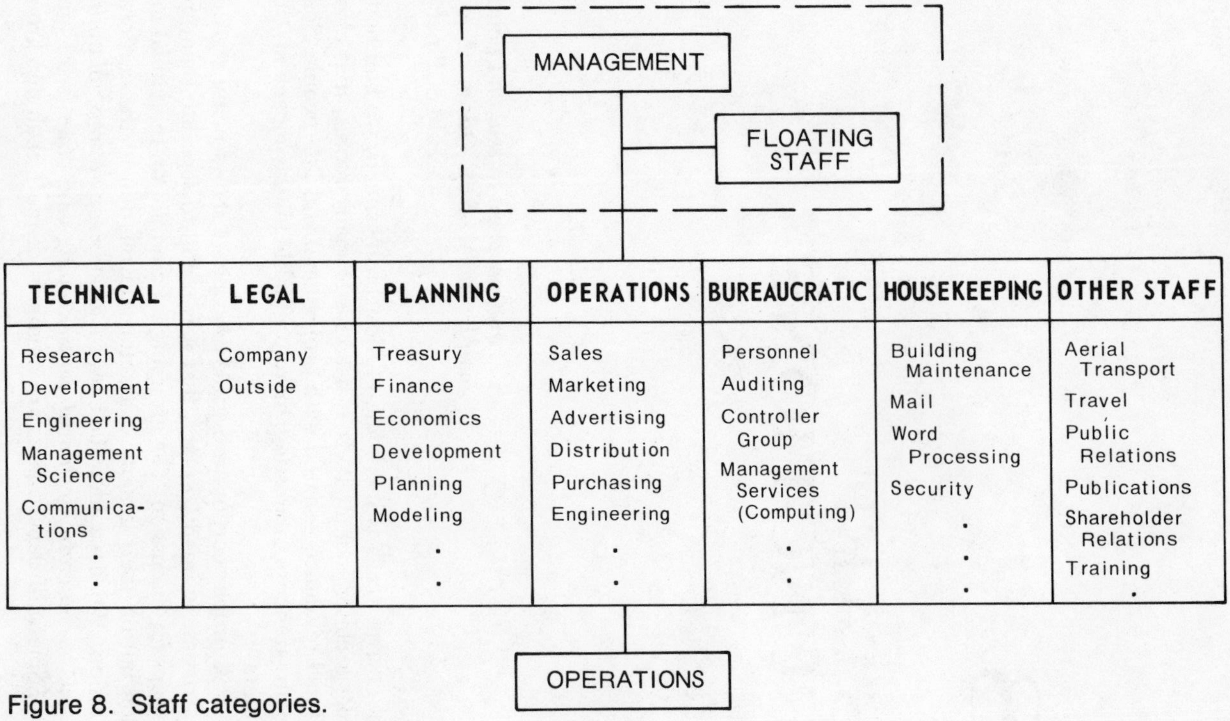

TECHNICAL	LEGAL	PLANNING	OPERATIONS	BUREAUCRATIC	HOUSEKEEPING	OTHER STAFF
Research	Company	Treasury	Sales	Personnel	Building	Aerial
Development	Outside	Finance	Marketing	Auditing	Maintenance	Transport
Engineering		Economics	Advertising	Controller	Mail	Travel
Management		Development	Distribution	Group	Word	Public
Science		Planning	Purchasing	Management	Processing	Relations
Communica-		Modeling	Engineering	Services	Security	Publications
tions				(Computing)		Shareholder
						Relations
						Training

MANAGEMENT

FLOATING STAFF

OPERATIONS

Figure 8. Staff categories.

engineering, for example, is shown as a member of the operations, the technical, and the planning groups. "Other" is an interesting collection of departments which seem to be self-justifying. Some staff people don't work in departments; we call them "floating staff."

In the next sections we consider each departmental staff group separately. The amount of space devoted to each is roughly equivalent to its relative importance to the businessman. Floating staff is discussed in the final section.

OPERATIONS STAFF

Operations staff departments provide direct support to line operations, over which they often have considerable control. A representative list of such departments is sales, marketing/advertising, distribution, engineering/development, and purchasing.

Operations staff is good training for the ambitious young businessman. In it he works closely with operations and learns what the company does for a living. He also has an opportunity to visit the field and to meet the line managers. There are professionals, such as engineers, as well as businessmen in operations staff. Working with these people can be rewarding.

Operations staff work is tough. The people in it work closely enough with line personnel to share their day-to-day crises—breakdowns, strikes, distribution problems, and customer complaints. It is to the operations staff that the line manager turns when he had problems—when he can't get material or when there are engineering problems in the plant or in the product. Sales and marketing, both business functions, are perhaps not quite so closely tied to line operations, but they have the problems of dealing with customers and with the public. The personnel department should be included in the operations staff department list only if it provides close, direct support to operations by recruiting and dealing with daily labor problems.

Operations staff people are usually overworked, enjoy their jobs, and are dedicated to corporate profit but even more to the line people they serve. They are cost-conscious. The job limitations, for the eager young businessman, are that he is too close to the line to be involved in big policy decisions, and too far from big money matters. On the other hand, operations staff jobs are good starting positions from which the holder can leave with a lot of useful friends and a collection of business "war stories" to last the rest of his business career.

PLANNING

Business planning is of two types: operational and financial. They are tied together by the fact that operational changes require money. Representative departments are treasury, finance, economics, engineering, development, and planning/planning models.

The treasury department is usually concerned with short-range decisions, such as paying the troops, and short-term investments, while the finance department deals with corporate financing. This is not always true; sometimes one department does both jobs, or their responsibilities overlap. Either area is an excellent home for the businessman. He is dealing with money, big money, and is exposed to top management. Another advantage is that he is doing exactly the sort of thing he was taught in business school. No tedious on-the-job training (say, how to make cement) is required.

Many companies have a separate, designated planning (or new projects, or whatever) department. This may be a real live item, or it may be misnamed and a dead end. The trouble with a central planning department is that to do its job it has to infringe on the received territories of older established departments such as finance, engineering, or even operations. Unless it is a creature of top management it will not be able to do any real planning. Sometimes such departments are set up and used as a final resting place for executives who somewhere missed the boat. The only one who doesn't know this is the vice president of planning. Like Thurber's midget* he wants to swing at the ball. He builds up an expensive staff and makes great plans—on paper.

Some companies have a new department which uses a new

* James Thurber, *My World—And Welcome to It,* in the famous story "You Could Look It Up."

planning method—corporate financial planning models.* These computer models simulate the movement of money in the corporation. The output is simulated financial reports, such as income statements and balance sheets which project corporate behavior into the future—two to twenty years, depending on the "horizon" of the model. The projection is based on planning data gathered from all levels of the corporation and on management strategy. Such models can be useful if they are well designed, make modest demands on other operations and staff people, and the output is trusted and used. This sort of model building is excellent training for a businessman.

The other planning departments—engineering, economics, and development—are staffed mostly by professionals and technicians. Of these only economics has a true business flavor. Business schools are increasingly emphasizing (micro)economics as the core discipline of business, and their graduates are well trained in the field.

LEGAL STAFF

Lawyers are still a problem. They are an integral part of the business world, but many of them are *in* rather than *of* it. Their interests are professional rather than company-oriented—the game they play is winning cases rather than the business game. They use an incomprehensible language.† Since legal education is narrow, lawyers need to work closely with businessmen (particularly with accountants and economists) and with technicians to prepare their briefs. Working on a legal team (see Chapter 9) can be a broadening experience for a young employee.

Lawyers may not need business (they could probably make a good living suing each other), but business needs lawyers—desper-

* Henry I. Meyer, *Corporate Financial Planning Models*, New York: Wiley, 1977.

† Years ago, when I was working with early computers, my director suggested a programming project: to use the computer to translate legalese into English. A few days later he returned: "Forget it. I have been reading some of the stuff; *it has no logical content.*"

ately. The whole climate in which business operates today is constrained by legal strictures. Lawyers are hired to keep the company operating within legal limits and to fight legal battles. Some lawyers eventually become more interested in the company itself than in its legal problems. Such converts can make very good top managers, and many of the top positions in American business are held by people with legal training. In fact, some students who have the time or the money (or both) get a law degree and a business degree before going to work. The businessman-lawyer is well equipped to handle today's problems.

BUREAUCRATIC STAFF

The bureaucratic staff departments are the businessman's home field. These are the departments that serve the whole company rather than special groups like operations or top management. Their input is data, and their output is paper. We have included the personnel department in this group, not because it ought to be (it probably should be closer to operations), but because this is its usual character. In most companies the other bureaucratic departments fall either under the controller or under the management systems director (data processing).

The personnel (employee relations) director has an impossible job (or, better, three almost impossible jobs): recruiting the right kind of people, administering salary levels and fringe benefits, and setting up career paths for promising people. These jobs have to be done within the constraints previously discussed. As far as recruiting goes, the personnel department handles the "walk-ons" and the paperwork. It does a lot of interviewing and screening. It fills low-level jobs such as clerks and typists. At higher levels, recruiting is usually left to other departments such as engineering, research, geology, and top management. It is asking too much of a personnel department to expect it to be able to evaluate and screen specialists and professionals.

Some large companies do have an effective executive training program—the fast track of Chapter 2. It is the job of personnel to set up, administer, and evaluate such a program and (almost impossible) to keep the other employees, who are not so favored, reasonably content. In this role, personnel has a decisive effect on the careers and advancement of others. Like all power situations, it can be used for corporate good or it can be abused.

As we have said before, the personnel department recommends the pay brackets for the rank classes. It also maintains job descriptions for different job titles and assigns these titles to pay ranks. This is a tough job: should a mathematician, for example, have the same rank as a senior accountant? It is hard to approach the thing objectively; after all, the personnel director and his people all have titles and ranks and mortgages to pay too. Fringe benefits are important for employee satisfaction. How important? What really motivates people? To put it kindly, this is a gray area. Management wants the personnel department to find a formula which gives maximum motivation at mimimum cost. The personnel department, on the other hand, usually acts as a people's advocate, trying to get the largest possible benefit for everyone.

In most companies the personnel department is a resident inflationary influence. Personnel directors swap (and publish) pay scales by job titles. If a director learns that any other company in a similar situation is paying its programmers, say, more than his company does, he may recommend raising the rank of his programmers or their pay bracket. This is often an automatic reaction; he does not question whether his people will actually leave the good old company for another fifty bucks or whether they may have other, valid reasons to stay where they are. The converse—because someone else pays *less*, we can hold the line or even reduce salaries—is never true.

All this is an argument that the personnel director (vice president—employee relations) should be a member of top management, whose remuneration is set by consensus rather than by title and rank. It doesn't seem fair to ask a man to show restraint when his own salary is at least indirectly affected by his recommendations for others.

The Controller's Empire

The controller has the responsibility for maintaining a practical and legal accounting system for the corporation. He is responsible for processing the entries (debits and credits) to the system and ultimately for the accuracy of the corporate financial reports. Except for bank transactions, which are the responsibility of the treasurer, and auditing, which is separated for control purposes, his people handle most of the business paperwork in the company.

It is of prime importance for any company to have a good accounting system. The reports that are produced are the fever chart of the business. If they are clear and well designed, they give top management a continuous picture of the state of the business—what is going well and what is going wrong. With this key role, the controller's group, particularly accounting, should be a good home for a businessman. In some companies it is; they're those where accounting plays an active role in management and decision making. In many companies it is not; they're the ones where accountants are considered super bookkeepers.

The accounting profession has allowed some really challenging opportunites to slip through its fingers. In most cases it has lost control of data processing (which used to be called machine accounting); it just couldn't stand up to the pushy technocrats who knew how to run the computers. Accountants are preoccupied with the past, with the data necessary to make the books balance. By not taking a longer view of their reporting responsibility as continuing in time, both past and future, they have opted out of the planning function. The new field of corporate financial model building should probably be an extension of the accounting system. It is usually done by other departments which do not have as much experience in data gathering and lack accounting discipline.

Accounting departments are usually well run—the field is an old one, and the managers know their jobs. The supervisors, from the controller on down, are usually Craftsmen (more on this later), which means they are as interested in doing a workmanlike job as in their career progress. They are cost-conscious. The empire may split into many departments under growth pressure, but it won't get out of hand. The leaders still remember when they worked for $300 a month. There are dead-end jobs in accounting—remember Mr. Biggers. Unless it is an unusual group in an unusual company, the controller's empire is no place for a swinger.

Computing

The marriage between business and computers has not been a smash hit. There have been success stories such as credit card processing and the airlines reservation system (which cost millions of dollars and thousands of man-years to make work). Most business applications have not been as successful. On the other hand, the marriage between technologists and computer systems *has* been a smash hit. Engineers and scientists are at home with mathematics and with machinery and can compete on even terms with the hardware salesmen.* Engineering problems are solved by using equations, whereas most business computation doesn't get much above $A + B = C$ or $A \times B = D$.

The obvious business applications—payroll, billing, accounting, accounts receivable—were mechanized years ago on what we now call second-generation computers. In most cases the promised cost savings were not realized—what used to be spent for clerical help went for computer rental and programmer salaries. Now the computing fraternity has moved up to third-generation computers. This means that they now have at least ten times the computing power and speed of the old machines. It also means they have at least four times the staff to man the monsters. The principal mission remains unchanged: to compute the payroll and take care of other business paperwork. To the outsider this is a mystery. How do the new big computers stay busy?

Computer output rises to meet computer capability. The government helps, of course, by demanding more and more reports. New internal company reports are developed—it is an unimaginative computer department that can't construct its own project-control and reporting system, which is one of the largest users of computer time in the shop. Computer time is also gobbled up by decreasing the efficiency of the throughput cycle in the name of efficiency. This requires some explanation.

Visual input/output terminals (television-type tubes) are convenient and showy; they are also a highly inefficient way to get data

* It is interesting that the suppliers who provide the bulk of the hardware for technical computing and control systems are a different set from those serving the business community.

in and reports out. Their installation requires a communication network and a sophisticated, resource-consuming computer program to support the "on-line" terminals. Data entry through terminals is much more error-prone and invokes more reruns than the old punch card system.

Another big item for using up computer resources is what is called the "operating system." An operating system is an internal computer program that schedules the computer load and assigns different hardware facilities. The computer talks to itself. The objective is efficient utilization, and from the computer's point of view the objective is realized: peripheral equipment is efficiently used and the central computer runs several programs at once by using one job's idle time to compute another (time sharing). Unfortunately, the care and feeding of such an operating system require inordinate resources, both people and computing. Modern operating systems could not even have been run on second-generation equipment, since they require more computing capability than the total of the old machines. A whole new type of specialist, the systems programmer, is required to keep the thing running. Formal documentation of an operating system takes more space than the *Encyclopedia Britannica*. The lastest threat to corporate solvency and management peace of mind is an extension of the operating system, called "data base management," which will require new large chunks of both hardware and software.

Using the leverage of exotic technology and the manufacturers' propaganda, the computer supervisor has done very well for himself. From being the humble manager of machine accounting (a section of the accounting department), he (or his successors) moved up to head a new computing department and now to vice president—management systems with several departments reporting to him. Management systems is the most expensive staff group in many companies. It has been estimated that by 1980, 8 percent of the GNP will be spent for computing.

Mechanization of data processing is an irreversible process. There is very little top management can do to control its increase. It is hard to control what you don't understand. Apart from ever-rising costs, the computer age has brought other, perhaps more critical problems, problems of dependence, security, and control. Companies are becoming dangerously dependent on their computers. For them to break down even for a day is an emergency. There is no effective backup except parallel hardware (which the airlines use). Simple arithmetic demonstrates this. Suppose an installation has ten high-speed printers, which is modest; then every hour of downtime represents a potential loss of about 600,000 printed lines—which could be a lot of paychecks. We don't know of any case where a computing staff has gone on strike, but if they did, they would win. Blackmail is a potent weapon.

Security for computing facilities is a nightmare. It may be possible to protect against outsiders, but not against insiders—the "little man with a magnet" who erases data on magnetic tape. Companies go to elaborate and expensive extremes to protect their data: cycling tapes daily from the shop to fireproof vaults, even putting the computer in its own fortress-like building. Companies have been wiped out by fire in their computer facility. Complete security is impossible.

Control of computer operations is now an act of faith. "Only computer people can audit computer programs." Very few auditors can read programs; in fact, it is difficult for one programmer to read another's program (I know of cases where it was easier to rewrite the thing). Program listings should not be the only documentation of computer systems, but in most cases they are. Formal intelligible documentation of systems is almost as hard to write as the programs themselves. It has to be done by a knowledgeable programmer, who probably doesn't like the job. Programs tend to change faster than they can be documented anyway.

The auditing department is usually pretty helpless to properly audit mechanized areas. Computers *do* make mistakes, though not often, and those mistakes are apt to be replicated thousands of times before being detected.* Computers are vulnerable to fraud.† What one man can program, another can manipulate to his own

* I still cherish a statement by an IBM salesman: "Our computers have never been detected in an undetected error."

† See a two-part report by Thomas Whiteside in *The New Yorker*, August 22 and August 29, 1977.

ends. In the early days of computing we used to speculate, in bull sessions, on ways to turn a dishonest buck. It is surprisingly easy.

With all this going for the computing function, and considering its explosive growth, it might seem to be a good home for a young businessman. Not so. People in this area have to be highly trained in what is now called computer science, just to know what the others are talking about. It is a good idea for them to be workoholics just to keep up. The average business school (or other school) graduate doesn't have a chance. His school may have insisted that he learn FORTRAN programming (business programs are usually written in COBOL); what he really needed was a course on "The Place of Computers in Business" or, better, "How to Defend Against Computers."

THE TECHNICAL GROUP

Technical departments are not the businessman's thing. There may be administrative jobs in a large research laboratory, for example, but research workers in such shops will head the pecking order as doctors do in hospitals. Management science may be an exception. Some business schools, Carnegie for example, give their students a good training in management science techniques, and some graduates with a technical leaning may like the work.

Typical technical departments are research, development, management science, and communications. "Research" is used here to mean *basic* research, while "development" refers to the implementation of scientific and engineering techniques, using pilot plants, for example. Back in the fifties, it was considered chic to have a research department; it was supposed to enhance the corporate image and impress the shareholders and the raters of corporate bonds. Business has since realized that only large technically oriented corporations such as IBM, Shell, General Motors, or Bell Telephone can effectively use a basic research department. There is so much published material from industry and from academia that a small department should properly spend all its time reading the literature. It is hard to hire and keep people to do this sort of thing. Development departments (often *called* research departments) are needed by most corporations to protect against costly mistakes and wasted capital expenditures. In some companies the engineering department does the development work.

Management science is relatively new. It used to be called operations research and still is in some companies. Practitioners are still trying to figure out whether management science is a separate discipline or whether it only provides specialized help to other departments to solve tricky problems. The second interpretation is more reasonable, if only because management science people actually do spend most of their time working for other departments. The management science people are familiar with mathematical algorithms such as dynamic programming and multivariate analysis and the appropriate computer programs (usually called a "bag of tricks"), and make these powerful methods available to others where they apply. They must resist the impulse to use sophisticated methods just because they learned them in school, and should first look for simple solutions.

Whether the management science department will be a permanent member of the corporate staff or not is moot. It may be that as engineers and economists become more knowledgeable, the special department will not be needed (refinery engineers can now handle their own blending problems). Before taking a job in a management science department, the applicant must determine its corporate stature. Is it well accepted and do other departments and management naturally turn to management science when they have a problem, or is it scrambling to sell its services?

Communications is new and growing. Like the computer department, the communications department uses new technology and the persuasiveness of hardware vendors to build an empire. Its road to corporate prominence is more difficult. There is well-established competition. Common carriers are eager to provide all kinds of communication links for a price: telephone, microwave, even satellite systems. The biggest obstacle, however, may be the computer department, which doesn't like to see anyone else playing the hardware game and which feels that *it* should be in control of any communications channel that ties in to a computer—and what doesn't these days? This is a family squabble the businessman should stay out of.

Housekeeping

Housekeeping departments come under the administrative vice president. Like the adjutant in the army (dog robber), he keeps things running. To mix metaphors, he keeps them shipshape (Chapter 2). The administrative vice president's job has been described as the worst job in the corporate hierarchy, but it is essential: someone has to see that the mail gets delivered and that burned-out light bulbs are replaced. One of his nastiest jobs is assigning space and facilities to other departments—everyone needs more space and new typewriters. It takes a lot of people to keep things running smoothly, and housekeeping activities are organized into many departments, most of which are of little interest to the businessman. We consider only two, word processing and security, as they are of particular interest at present.

Word Processing

Word processing is a new term; it includes the functions of the old typing pool and of duplication. As in other active areas, the key to sudden growth is the availability of new hardware. New duplicating equipment featuring high speed, color, copy size options, and relative ease of use is very attractive. It is tempting to equip a new department to handle large reproduction jobs. (The existing Xerox machines will stay on all floors.) It is more economical to do these jobs in-house than to send them to a job shop. The hazard is that as duplication and report preparation get easier and cheaper, there will be a corresponding increase in the amount of paper floating around the corporation. A compensating trend is the increasing use of microfilm and microfiche to reduce paper. This involves new hardware and creates new filing problems.

The humble typist has been upgraded to a machine operator, operating flashy equipment (made by computer manufacturers) which features internal memory, automatic registration, replication, and more. A whole battery of these machines is tied to a computer and to a communications network. A businessman can pick up his phone, dictate a letter, and have the finished copy on his desk quickly. Unfortunately, this runs counter to business tradition, and most managers prefer to use their own secretaries. Apart from the man–secretary relationship (Chapter 14), more letters than are usually admitted are joint efforts. "Did you really mean to say this, sir?" Such feedback is lost in electronic transcribing. Word processing is poised to take off, but is restrained by custom.

Security

Security is a growth industry. In business it takes two forms: invisible and highly visible. The invisible form is handled by undercover investigators who are hired in the usual way to do regular jobs but are there to investigate security problems in addition to their regular work.* Most cases involve theft (white-collar crime), mismanagement, and industrial espionage. There are a lot of these people hired, but they are known only to top security management and do not affect the business scene except in those cases where their role becomes public knowledge.

The other type of security is very obvious, since it amounts to control of people entering or moving about the business premises. The key words are "electronic surveillance," which refers to television cameras and to door locks which open only to the proper combination of magnetic code on a card and the employee's secret number entered in a keyboard. Somewhere in the building is a control console with television monitors and a dedicated computer. These space-age gadgets are manned by a security staff whose members may wear uniforms of gray slacks and neat blazers charged with the company logo—and look like members of a South African sporting club.

The hardware required for visible security is expensive: it is a poor salesman who can't move a half million dollars' worth to protect one building. The more the better, as far as the security man-

* See Studs Terkel, *Working*, New York: Avon, 1975. The pertinent chapter is "Anthony Ruggero, Industrial Investigator."

ager (director, vice president?) is concerned. The more expensive the system, the more important his job and the more people he can hire. In order to spend this kind of money, top management must be convinced that there is a threat to company property more serious than insurance would cover. A band of wild-eyed, hairy youths (a fairly exact description of Ivy League undergraduates) is going to storm the place. The rioters of the sixties may not have succeeded in their immediate objectives, but they succeeded in burdening business with a new expense.

Selective security in a business is required. Valuable data, competitive information, and computer tapes must be guarded; top strategic conferences must be kept confidential. Operating results such as quarterly earnings should be kept quiet until they are announced to the shareholders. If a stock goes up or down *before* official announcement of earnings, there is a leak somewhere. General building security, on the other hand, is a waste of money unless it is pushed to extremes like those in a jail—extremes which would make a civilized working environment impossible.

If management learned from history, it would know this. Before World War II, France spent billions of francs building the Maginot Line. French soldiers spent millions of man-years learning fortress warfare and gazing east looking for the Germans to come. They would have done better to have learned field tactics, and the government, to have spent its money on tanks and planes. The Germans never frontally attacked the Maginot Line, but that didn't keep them out of France.

The same principles are true in protecting a business building. Security people cannot look suspicious and inconvenience hundreds of people day after day without losing their zeal. The smart, dangerous intruder will not make a frontal attack on electronic devices, particularly as they are well marked. Against the insider— the disgruntled employee—there is no mechanical protection. The only real protection against internal sabotage is to have reasonably content, loyal employees and supervisors who are doing their jobs. Basic tactics suggest that defense against outside threat depends on flexibility and mobile reserves. Departments should police their own areas; only they know who has business there. Severe threat must be met by mobile reserves: police, the National Guard, and the Army, in that order.

OTHER STAFF DEPARTMENTS

There are well-defined staff departments in most companies which don't really fit in any functional group. Often they are optional or prestige items. In fact, if these departments have a common factor, it is that they are about as far removed from line operations, from making money for the company, as it is possible to get and still be corporate departments—pure overhead.

These other departments are of interest to the businessman, because some of them provide cosy corporate homes, and all of them contribute to the nature of the business community. Since some of them are optional, the departmental roster will vary from company to company. Usually, the larger the company, the more there will be. A representative list is aerial transportation (company planes), travel, public relations, publications, shareholder relations, and training. These odds and ends often report to the administrative vice president, but there is now a tendency to gather them up under a new hyphenated vice president—communications, for example.

Some companies *need* their own planes. Oil companies need light planes and helicoptors to get to offshore rigs and to other parts of the "oil patch"; other companies may have large operations, such as mines, in locations which are not served by commercial carriers. A few company planes can be economically justified to save executive time. The majority of the planes bought by business are for prestige and to provide a management perquisite—executive toys. A ride on a company plane can certainly impress an important visitor; free trips for politicians can cause raised eyebrows. Super Bowl and World Series cities have to make accommodations for the inevitable fleet of business jets. All this would be good clean fun if it didn't cost so much. Planes are expensive, pilots are paid more than most middle managers (and there are two in each plane, plus an engineer on big ones), and ground facilities and landing rights are not cheap.

Why companies set up their own travel bureau is a mystery. Here is a service that outsiders with experience and competent staff will compete to perform and which they will do *free*. Even with the agent discounts it must be hard to justify a resident department. It may be empire building or the "Please Mother, I'd rather do it myself" attitude.

The business role in society is so complex that big companies must have a public relations department. We don't live in a world where selling a good product at a fair price is enough to project a favorable corporate image. Someone has to filter the many requests for business support of community groups, give speeches at Rotary club meetings, and buy livestock at the State Fair. Public relations does these things, and it can provide some nice jobs for outgoing people who have strong stomachs. People in public relations must know their own company and the industry and work in close contact with top management. It is always a pleasure to be able to be generous with someone else's (the shareholders') money.

Company publications include newsletters and periodicals—house organs. These serve as a communications channel between management and other employees and are supposed to improve morale by making everybody feel part of a big organization. Most companies do have a good story to tell about the diversity of operations, the varied skills of employees, and of public responsibilities. People in publications are different from most business types: they are artists, writers, photographers. They are well paid for doing their own things, have interesting assignments, and, if the editorial policy is not repressed by management, do a professional job. Some house organs make good reading indeed.

The shareholder relations department is not concerned with mechanics such as the payment of dividends but rather with the promotion of corporate shares and with keeping the shareholders in line—making sure they vote with management. As we have seen, the only vestige of control left for most shareholders is to mark and return their proxy cards. The election is so rigged that, except in unusual circumstances, management can hardly fail to get a comfortable majority. This is not enough. The board doesn't want 60 percent support, it wants 90 or better, and so the shareholder relations hucksters hit the trail to line up the vote of large individual shareholders, often widows who couldn't care less. Companies want their stocks to go up. Good shares should sell themselves, and maybe they do, but many companies feel that they have to merchandise them. The main target of these efforts is institutional investors: mutual funds, pension funds, banks. With all the information available to the hard-headed fund managers (Chapter 3) it is difficult to see how personal selling by shareholder relations people can be very effective, but it is often done.

Another question that concerns management is the *type* of ownership of its shares—what percent is institutional, private, by women, by retirees, and so forth. Such statistical information can be maintained by shareholder relations, at least of those shares not held by brokers in street names.

The training department is yet another staff department which is riding the hardware hobbyhorse to bigger things. Every big company needs a training department, if only to orient new employees. With all the outside training available in short courses and seminars (Chapter 11), it is doubtful if it is economically reasonable to go much further. Opposed to common sense is the training department's bureaucratic need to grow. It has a couple of things going for it: new hardware and "canned" courses. In addition to improved traditional hardware such as Vu-Graph and other projectors and sound equipment, there are now tape-driven TV tubes for in-house viewing. Suppliers will provide tapes and do-it-yourself "programmed instruction" workbooks on almost *any* subject. It is possible to get the equivalent of college degree training while sitting in a darkened room looking at a TV screen. The quality of this teaching is high. Other departments, such as data processing, often set up their *own* training section to use these methods.

It is hard to fault in-house training and learning, but they are very expensive. In addition to the cost of the training staff and the hardware, there is the cost of productive hours lost by the trainees. It has to be soul-deadening to spend part of the working day looking at a canned program on a TV console, particularly after the usual hours spent watching at home. Older departments such as engineering, law, geology, and even research don't use this sort of training much. They may invite a guest lecturer to talk about a new and interesting topic, but mostly they pay their people the compliment of assuming that they know their jobs. It is still possible to give an employee a book and tell him to read it!

STAFF FLOATERS

In any large corporation there are staff people—specialists—who are not affiliated with any department on the organization chart. They have the best of both worlds: interesting work close to top management and no tedious supervisory details. Such jobs are not usually entry-level positions but are held by experienced people who have demonstrated ability in a particular field such as finance, economics, actuarial science, statistics, labor relations, or a legal specialty. Job titles vary and may be imaginative: senior staff analyst, vice president—special projects, assisistant to _____ . I had one friend whose specialty was keeping up with our pension fund managers who claimed he didn't know his proper title. That is real job security.

There are two main functions performed by staff floaters: they act as consultants to management (like the Scientific Advisor to the President of the United States), and they prepare special studies and reports, some of which are dignified as "position papers." Top management needs resident consultants who are not encumbered by supervisory problems and whose loyalty is to management rather than to their own staff empires. There are just too many aspects of running a business—government, labor, public relations, competition, business climate—for one man, or even a management team, to be expert in all. Management needs help from people who are on *its* side. It needs help to try to control staff growth and expense; it takes a staff man to know one. Management should have, for example, a technical person, probably a computer science type, on the floating staff to help control computing and communications or at least to tell management what it is getting for its money.

A current "in" job is that of econometrician. Econometrics (or macroeconomics) is the effort to quantify economic principles. Unfortunately, econometrics is still more of an academic exercise than a useful art. The really important determining factors, such as war, revolution, drought, and irrational human behavior, cannot be included in a mathematical model. The sudden oil price jump by the OPEC nations threw every econometric model prediction into a cocked hat. Management must still rely on intuition and experience and possibly on predictions such as those published in *Business Week*.

Other normally nonbusiness disciplines look hungrily at the business community and try to find a corporate spot for their specialties. If you want money, business (or the government) is an obvious place to go.* Occasionally, outsiders do find a staff home. For example, the Alaskan pipeline builders hired archaeologists to document the ancient living sites on the pipeline right-of-way. Psychologists have had some success in selling their services to business. They have promoted things like encounter sessions and T-group analysis, much to the embarrassment of middle management. More often, and more destructive, they administer tests to employees—personality and aptitude tests. Such tests are notoriously unfair. They favor people who are good at taking tests, particularly recent graduates. Since the tests are general, the questions are general, aimed at probing for common knowledge, and do not give fair weight to hard-learned special knowledge and experience. Test results are vulnerable to cheating. An employee who had prior access to an aptitude test could improve his score and his career chances. Fortunately, many companies have become disillusioned by aptitude and personality tests and no longer use them to screen employees. The tests which are now given are coldly objective. With the laws against discrimination on grounds of sex, color, class, age, handicap, and so forth, it is important to be able to document the reasons for employees' relative progress. Objective test results support the company policy.

Special studies and reports are made for top management;

---

* The usual transfer of funds between business and academia is by way of consultant fees. This is discussed in the next chapter.

more often than not they are made to satisfy government requests. Management needs confidential papers on conditions in its own organization, on the business and regulatory climate, and on other companies if mergers or aquisitions are being considered. There is a limit to what management can ask for and digest, but there seems to be no limit to what government wants and demands! A large, and expensive, part of the floating staff is engaged in making reports for the federal government. These people are actually working *for* the feds and being paid *by* business. A surprisingly large number of staff people owe their jobs to regulatory interference. When these people gather for a drink, their first toast should be, "To government bureaucracy," but it isn't. They adopt the official party line, which management rightfully takes, and bad-mouth the government at every opportunity—a case of biting the hand that feeds.

An implication of the preceding paragraphs is that floating staff people work alone. Often they do, but just as often they work with others on special project teams. A close look at such teams is the subject of the next chapter.

The Corporate Secretary

If this heading brings to mind a cute little typing machine, forget it; this is about the *Corporate* Secretary, possibly the best job around. Just as every club has a secretary to take notes and read the minutes of the last meeting, so a corporation has a Corporate Secretary. The duties are largely statutory: signing documents, presiding over the annual shareholders' meeting, keeping records. The Secretary often acts as the resident corporate master of ceremonies: setting up the directors' meetings (which can be pretty gaudy) and making travel arrangements.

The Secretary has the best of both worlds. As an officer of the company he (or she) gets the perquisites of top management without the responsibility; the level of decision making required is about that required of a good girl scout leader. The drawback of the job as a goal for a bright young man is that there is only one to a company. A job as good as this should probably be made hereditary, like having a box seat at the Montreal Canadiens hockey games or getting into medical school. In one case, when the job came open, management made the Secretary's secretary Secretary, which sounds complicated, but it worked out fine. The lady probably knew the work better than anyone else, and the company got a good-conduct star from the government for having a female officer.

9

PROJECT TEAMS, TASK FORCES, AND CONSULTANTS

BUSINESS WORK is mostly tedious and boring. Like a well-run household, or church, or college, things muddle along. with the employees doing their jobs well or poorly according to their nature. This comfortable pattern is broken when a special, knotty problem percolates up to the executive suite, when management has a bright idea, or when government or some other outside agency drops a procedural bomb. There is no provision in the organization to handle such special cases—management may not have the foggiest idea how to solve the problem. Set up a new, temporary group to take charge—punt! Such a group is called a special project team or, if management prefers the military idiom, a task force.

As business becomes more complex, technological, and increasingly harassed, the use of special teams is becoming common.

They may be set up by the chief executive officer (CEO) himself to solve a high-level problem; more often they are initiated by a lower-level vice president who has the responsibility to solve a problem and finds it over his head. He will usually have to work through the CEO in order to recruit the interdisciplinary, interdepartmental people he needs. This means good exposure for the team members.

The task force concept is good: use special people to solve special problems, and use them on a temporary basis. In a large company it is rare not to be able to assemble all the necessary talents: engineering, economics, legal, technical, and so forth. Still, companies do go outside and bring in consultants to beef up special project teams, which is not always a good idea.

For a company person, task force duty can be good or bad. To join means to give up something—a comfortable, structured job—in return for a share of the possible glory of a successful team effort. He may even have trouble getting back to his old job if the special assignment lasts too long and his colleagues have closed ranks. Before taking these chances the employee should have some assurance that the task force he is joining has a reasonable chance of success. For this he has to know something about the different types of task forces and their missions. A few general warning signals are valid for all such team efforts.

Unless a task force is headed by a member of senior management it will probably fail. Other employees often resent special groups, much as the regular army divisions resent elite forces. The outsider may be bitter because he wasn't chosen as a member; he may think the group unnecessary. Without the clout of management involvement, the team will work in an uncooperative environment and can fail. Avoid teams which are too large. A large group is almost psychologically incapable of making up its mind, and any credit will be splintered. Avoid teams which are set up as a buck-passing ploy by an incompetent manager.

Project teams are the natural progeny of Army-type management—their formation breaks fixed patterns. In Baseball-type organizations such special teams are rarely necessary, because management itself is one big task force. A project team set up by Baseball management may be a burying ground where people study a problem which has already been solved or which really isn't important.

The problem of evading duty on unpromising teams or of getting on promising ones must be left to the ingenuity of the individual. An implied threat of jury duty to decide a complicated case can be hinted, or an invented terminal illness in the family may get one off. Getting *on* a team involves office politics, which is too poorly defined a field for useful comment.

TASK FORCE MISSIONS

There are as many possible task force missions as there are serious corporate problems. For convenience, they can be grouped as operational, financial, regulatory, and legal. This is not an exhaustive list. Teams could be set up, for example, to deal with a crisis in the housekeeping or personnel area, but these four groups cover most project team activities.

Operational Missions

An operational task force is often the most rewarding type of project team, both for the company and for the team members. The problem to be solved is an operational one: build a new plant, expand the product line, install new technology, develop a new marketing area. Management is vitally interested and is willing to spend money on the basis of team recommendations. There may be glory and new job opportunities as a result. Team members will usually be engineers, technicians, economists, and marketing types recruited from the line and the operations staff, and they probably already know each other and work well together.

Outside consultants are often included on operational project teams, at the request of either management or the team members. This usually helps, but it can introduce problems, which we talk about later.

Financial Missions

Special financial problems call for a task force in order to bring together people from different functional areas such as treasury, the controller's department, and resident economists. In some cases other specialists such as engineers and management science people may be needed. Crisis problems involve things like refinancing, dividend policy, acquisitions and defense against them, and anything unusual which deals with balance sheet items.

Such a team is hog heaven for an MBA graduate, since it gives him an opportunity to apply some of the theory he learned at school. In fact, if he is both lucky and persuasive, he gets management to set up a team to investigate his ideas. A single person, unless he is at a high level, can hardly change company policy; a management-appointed task force can. There are examples of this sort of thing in most well-managed companies. The following example is one we know of.

Money raising (borrowing) in a particular large company was being done on an ad hoc basis by different divisions. For example, the marketing manager bought sites using mortgages to minimize cash requirements, whereas manufacturing financed its inventories with lines of credit from individual banks. There was no standard policy. At the suggestion (prodding) of a bright Harvard MBA, a task force was set up to see if things could be handled better. The team included representatives from treasury, the controller's department, marketing, manufacturing, and accounting.

The task force was given six months to do its work, but it was able to file its report much sooner. The point which the MBA made, and which the team members bought, was that lenders would prefer to have part of *all* the corporate action rather than just a piece of it. There is safety in numbers (the "law of large numbers" to a statistician), and the lenders could afford to charge lower interest rates. The ultimate extension of this approach—and the majority recommendation—was that money should be borrowed only by the parent company against its full faith and credit—that is, by issuing debentures. This was described by the task force as "hocking the company rather than its individual assets."

Management accepted and implemented the majority report. The corporation could then borrow more cheaply and have better purse-string control of its operations. I don't know the happy ending to this story—how far up, and with which company, the bright MBA went. The treasurer and the controller were undoubtedly rewarded for the improvement in their functions. This is proper. Any manager who does not resist change is helping his company.

There are other good ideas which can save companies money in the financial area: cash management and float management, for examples. Special project teams are probably the best way to get new procedures accepted and established.

Regulatory Missions

This term is used to identify task forces set up to help the company live with, or fight, new government regulations and interference. The federal government can and does throw legislative monkey wrenches into the corporate works. It often takes a special task force just to interpret new regulations and to evaluate their impact. Recent examples are the grotesque pricing and transfer payments required of the oil companies,* the safety standards imposed on the automobile manufacturers, and the environmental and pollution controls demanded of all companies. Laws can ruin some well-run companies and reward others. New laws and regulations can create classic cases where management doesn't know what to do. For one thing, there are usually no precedents. Punt! Set up a task force, and make it a good one.

Membership in a regulatory task force can be a rewarding experience if the problem is reasonably well defined and the time horizon for solution is limited. The danger is that such teams have a tendency to become permanent, to become an extension of government bureaucracy rather than a well-defined problem-solving group.

Legal Missions

Most law cases are fought by a legal task force rather than by lawyers alone. The reason is that most cases involve something beyond law alone. Lawyers need the support of specialists such as geologists or accountants. All the people who will be concerned in the case should be members of a team (perhaps not a full-time

---

* Under current law the way to make money in refining is to run small inefficient refineries. Large efficient plants are forced to subsidize such operations. See *Fortune*, August 14, 1978.

team) so that they can keep up with developments, support the lawyers, and tell the same story.

Shakespeare beefed about the law's delay. Dickens wrote a whole book about it. The delay has lengthened. A modern corporate legal case makes the Chancery process in *Bleak House* look like the express line in a supermarket. Lawyers come and lawyers go, judges come and judges go, appeal follows appeal, the very concept and meaning of the action changes, but the case goes on forever. If you like to spend hours in a courtroom waiting for something to happen or listening to pointless testimony, if you like to read legal jargon and to booze it up with lawyers after hours, join a legal task force. The glory is ephemeral, because most cases just drag on and on, and when they do end, most people have forgotten what they were about. If there is any glory left, it will all go to the prestigious New York law firm that represented the company. On the other hand, the job security is outstanding.

Even if you have a taste for this sort of thing, there is one type of case that is to be avoided at all cost: the class action suit.

THE CLASS ACTION SUIT

There is a new type of case on the American scene which has to be discussed somewhere in this book because it is malicious, its incidence is increasing, and it costs American business (and consumers) millions and millions of dollars—the class action suit. This is as good a place as any to discuss the unpleasant subject, because project teams are usually assembled to fight such suits. The best way to describe the working of a class action suit is to give a hypothetical example.

Dentist D tells patient P that her teeth are decayed, probably because of the sugar in the bubble gum she chewed as a child. Patient P, who has a certain amount of larceny in her heart (and a large dental bill in her hand), tells her troubles to her neighbor N, who happens to be a "plaintiff's lawyer" (the villain of the story).

The lawyer, N, therewith files a lawsuit against *all* manufacturers of bubble gum on behalf of *all* chewers of bubble gum, such as patient P, for a sum equal to all dental bills sustained by this class since 1950—*trebled*. He asks for a jury trial; he is entitled to one.

N's next ploy is to approach the larger defendants (which they now are) to remind them that their potential liabilities run into the hundreds of millions of dollars and that to avoid the chances of a jury trial, he is willing to settle for a lousy ten million today, cash in hand. In fact, because he is such a great guy, he will settle with the first bubble gum manufacturer, who agrees to get the ball rolling, for a trivial five million. (Plaintiff's lawyers get from one-fourth to one-third of the settlement, which keeps them going from case to case.)

Management, faced with potential damages of hundreds of millions, may be tempted to settle for a "trivial" five million. There is another incentive to take this "cheap" way out. The plaintiffs may legally turn to any single defendant for the total amount of damages awarded by a jury and leave it up to him to collect what he can from the other defendants.

The only thing unreal about the preceding hypothetical example is the nature of the target companies. Plaintiffs' lawyers are far too smart to attack bubble gum manufacturers. Like good con men they go where the money is: to big companies, particularly to ones who might be having public relations problems. Oil companies, automobile makers, and big food processors are favorite targets. Big companies have paid "modest" blood money to these public parasites rather than taking their chances on jury awards. But more and more companies are starting to fight the opportunists who use the law to enrich themselves (at the public's expense) and who rise in the esteem of the American Bar Association with every victory.

Corporations set up task forces to oppose class action suits. To serve on one of these teams is a bad trip. Not only do all the objections to service on any legal task force apply, but this type of assignment can be soul-shriveling. The avarice and opportunism of the plaintiff's lawyer can infect even the adversaries. "If you lie down with a dog, you are going to get up with fleas."

CONSULTANTS
There are two reasons why companies hire consultants, and there are two sources of these willing workers. Consultants are

hired to contribute special expertise to help solve problems; they are hired to provide authority and prestige to company arguments. They come from the academic community or from consulting organizations, which may themselves be big businesses.

Prestige consultants are usually hired as expert witnesses to support the company position in law cases and at hearings before regulatory boards. The rationale is that the jurist can hardly fail to be impressed when an international authority comes out strongly in favor of the company's arguments. The selection of a high-powered economist, for example, is straightforward. Find one who has a pro-business philosophy (no Marxist economists need apply) and who has written books and won prizes. If you can get him, pay him the going rate, which can be very high indeed. If the man is not familiar with your particular problem, send a company economist to brief him—it is authority, not originality, that you are buying.

Experienced jurists must know that such hired experts are often little more than expensive mouthpieces for the adversaries, but companies continue to have an almost pathetic belief that if they can get a big name to state their case, it will be believed. Companies even vie with each other. ("Our expert is more expert than yours.")* Whether these prestigious hirelings are helpful or not, they do provide a channel for the transfer of money from business to academia—a channel that rewards "right-thinking" academics.

Since project teams are set up to handle new, nonroutine problems, management may feel that it has to hire outside consultants to augment in-house talent. This hiring of outside experts is probably overdone. Management often underestimates the capabilities of its own people and overestimates those of outsiders. Often consultants help; sometimes their hiring is a tragic mistake.

Company members of a task force may be narrowly focused; their experience has been limited to one company rather than to

* In a recent hearing the judge stopped the proceedings and asked the competing experts how much money they were making. One was getting $400 a day and the other $1,400. The judge's comment was to the cheaper model: "You, sir, are obviously working for the wrong company."

the industry. An academic consultant may be overspecialized; he may have been rewriting the same paper for the last ten years. The typical consultant from a consulting firm, on the other hand, is likely to suffer in the other direction. He may be a "jack of all trades, master of none." Consulting firms advertise that they can handle any problem for a price; the employer is lucky if he gets one who has had experience in the particular problem he is hired to solve. The outside firm is not about to admit that its people are going to need on-the-job training when it can smell a $600,000 consulting fee in the offing.

Consultants suffer from an occupational disease: they believe they are smarter than their clients. This can lead to problems. The following cases are taken from our own experience.

A large corporation was considering the acquisition of a small company in an alien field to broaden its investment base and reduce risk (the "law of large numbers" again). A task force was set up to consider the deal. Since no one on the team had any idea what the new company was all about and the option was about to expire, a prestigious consulting firm was called in to make a crash study—for a fat fee.

The consultant did report back before the option expired. His conclusion was that while the outside company was a growth firm in a growth industry, it was too small to be a useful diversification (true), but that it was worth acquiring if only to get its vigorous, young management (wrong). The option was duly exercised and the firm picked up. The bright, young managers quit. As Baseball players, they were not about to join an Army-type organization. The consultant hadn't considered this possibility—he hadn't talked to these people. The acquisition's promise remained just that: a promise, an empty one. The consultants were the only winners.

In another case, a member of a consulting firm was called in to help make a marketing study in an unknown territory. In order to develop the determinants which characterize an ideal retail outlet, he fitted an equation with 25 variables to a sample of 20 observations! This sort of thing is just not done, but it *was* done, and the results were included in the final report. It was done even though most of the technical people in the consulting firm knew better. In the press to get the job finished—and the bill out—the work simply was not given adequate attention. In this case the client company paid for meaningless trash.

Consultants succeed more often than they fail. We chose to recall these horror stories as a warning against the careless use of consultants. The right people working on the right jobs can and do make valuable contributions. The problem is to select the right firm with the right personnel. Management is faced with the same sort of problem it has in selecting a new computer or a communications system—it doesn't understand what it is buying. This is a dangerous position for any consumer to be in; it is also the reason why consulting firms do a PR job. They publish glossy brochures with flattering pictures of their staff mambers and a listing of all their degrees and publications. The guys have *got* to be good. It is not apparent that a series of published papers on irreversible thermodynamics will be of little help in solving a refinery problem. Not all consultants are generalists like von Neuman.*

Consultants don't have to live with their mistakes; company specialists do. When the plant an outside firm designed will not meet its design capacity, when the overland conveyer breaks, when the pipeline slug catcher does not catch liquid slugs, the consultants who made the designs are off on other jobs. Of course, the consulting firm's reputation is at stake, but companies seem to be more forgiving of outsiders than of their own people; they keep hiring the same outfits again and again. Consultants can get sued (check the notes of their annual reports), but they don't seem to be hurting.

When a company or a task force hires consultants, it should monitor their work closely at every step of the way. At the onset it must make sure that the hired hands know what is expected of them, and it must find out how they plan to proceed. Periodic reports should be required to keep up with costs and progress. If it is obvious that you are going to have to train these people, do it. They

---

* The late John von Neuman, probably the greatest modern applied mathematician. He did some corporate consulting work after the war, possibly for his own amusement.

are smart enough to learn quickly, and the more they know about the company, the better help they will be. Don't settle the final bill until you are satisfied that the results are sound and that the contract terms are met.

It might not be a bad idea to hire *two* independent consulting firms to do the same job. Give them each the same data and the same objectives. After all, a wise man gets a second opinion before he agrees to major surgery. If the two reports agree, you have bought confidence. If they differ, you still have a problem.

There is another risk in adding a consultant to a project team: it can upset the company members. They consider it a vote of no confidence. They resent having a highly paid (or high-cost) star on their team, in the same way that stars or bonus babies can upset a baseball team. Some good company men may even get ideas: maybe they would be better off as glamorous consultants than working the way up the company ladder. At least try to pick a consultant the other team members will like.

Consultants are not necessarily outsiders. Large corporations usually have several in-house groups which operate much like outhouse consultants. These are groups like management science, corporate plannning, and economics. Captive groups can also be a disturbing element when serving on project teams, but at least the corporation has more control over its own people. Inside consultants can be used as a channel to outside consultants. They are better able to decide when outside help is really needed, because they are not impressed by glossy brochures and they speak the same language.

WHAT NEXT?

Special project teams are becoming an increasingly important part of the American business scene. As business gets more and more involved in sociological and technical change and is increasingly harassed by unpredictable government interference, crisis conditions will be more frequent. This will probably call for more multidisciplinary task forces. Legal problems will always be with us, but it is at least to be hoped that the current laws that encourage class action suits will be modified in the direction of common sense.

It is hard to predict what business's reaction to these increasing demands will be. The present trend to set up more and more task forces and hire more and more consultants may continue. Economics (special groups and consultants are expensive) could force companies to maintain permanent floating project teams, staffed and equipped to move from one crisis to another. As new and more technically oriented people move into top management, they will participate more closely in such groups. Business organization could split into two parts: an Army-style organization to keep things running smoothly in the right direction and a parallel Baseball-type "shadow" company that deals with crisis conditions and unforeseen changes. Such an organization would create a whole new batch of job titles and professional opportunities.

Things just may move in the other direction—toward fewer ad hoc project teams. As traditional departments become staffed with better-trained people, they are able to handle more of their own unusual situations. New accounting graduates are trained in computer science, and engineers in operations research, and MBAs (from some schools) are competent statisticians. Management might be surprised at the latent skills of its employees.

The best way for corporations to respond to outside perturbations is still an open question. There probably is no single optimum solution for all companies. Future books (and later editions of this book) will have to tell the story.

10

TOP MANAGEMENT

MOST BUSINESSMEN work in staff positions. Important exceptions are the members of the top management team, whom we have defined to be line people. Although relatively few in number, these business leaders are of critical importance, and in order to complete this discussion of business organization, we must take them into account. Where does top management fit into the organization? What sort of people are these leaders? How did they get there? Why?

THE MANAGEMENT TEAM

In a well-run organization, the top management group is small and it is established at corporate headquarters. Its members are a subset of the *real* vice presidents and other officers such as the general counsel. It may or may not have an official name such as "executive committee." Some high-ranking vice presidents may not be included; this is particularly true in multinational companies where some of them are (happily) concerned with a geographical region or with a particular product. Actually, titles don't mean much at this level.

The management team itself may be run as a cooperative effort (democracy) where each member has specific specialties such as engineering, operations, or law and major decisions are made on the basis of a pooling of knowledge and opinions. It may be run as a (possibly benevolent) dictatorship with the top man firmly in charge. The first type of management team is held together by mutual respect and ability and works well if its consensus decisions represent the best of individual thinking rather than a least common denominator. The second type of organization—dictatorship—puts a strain on the team members; the courtier–sovereign relationship brings out the worst in people. In addition to concentrating on the needs of the company, team members are also concerned with currying favor with the leader and with watching each other. ("Why did he send Jackson to Brussels instead of me?")

Jealousy is a wasting emotion. Dominant-leader management can be very effective if the leader is outstanding; it can be disastrous if the same man grows old and set in his ways—when he loses everything except his power. Some successful leaders solve the problem by delegating *their* power. Forrest N. Shumway, for example, who transformed the Signal Companies, turned the subsidiaries of the conglomerate over to chief executive officers and gave them free hands.

It is hard for an outsider to find out just how the top management of a company operates. The only organizational certainty is that there is such a policy-making group in every corporation.

THE PEOPLE

What sort of people make it all the way to the top? First, they are competent and intelligent. Luck alone as the route of promotions (discussed in Chapter 5) can only go so far; the man who goes all the way must also have ability. While it may be true that there are equally competent people who weren't as well situated and didn't make it, the ones that do are good. These winners are dedicated—in most cases the company comes first. They must be at least sufficiently personable to get along with their colleagues. Another absolute essential, one that is rarely mentioned, is physical stamina. A leader doesn't have to be able to do 20 pushups, but he must have the constitution and fortitude to keep going long after the rest of us would have said, "To hell with it, there has to be an easier way to make a living." Successful politicians have the same type of stamina.

These attributes—competence, dedication, personality, fortitude (the desire for money is assumed in all businessmen)—are necessary, but they are not enough. The leader must have the proper psychological approach to his life's work. Michael Maccoby* made a careful study of the psychology of businessmen and came to the conclusion that all *successful* leaders could be classified as what he calls Gamesmen. (He has other classifications of businessmen; we consider them later.) The essential characteristic of a Gamesman is that he deals with a business situation as with a game. Even more than personal enrichment, the goal is to *win*. The opponents in this game are competing companies, the government, and even public apathy. He plays for the exhilaration of winning; his scores and triumphs are recorded in financial statements and in annual reports. Money is a way of keeping score, much like the scrip used in the parlor game of Monopoly.

Incidentally, the Gamesman usually plays an honest game, and to do this he has to know the rules. One source of management frustration with the federal government is that it *will* change the rules. Sometimes a business leader feels like a baseball player who comes up to the plate expecting to be allowed three strikes and then finds out that today he gets only two.

It seems to us that Maccoby missed an important point, which may have been too obvious to show up on the answers to his questionnaires. The point is the sense of rightness, of almost crusading zeal, with which top management people view their jobs. What they are doing is a *good thing:* good for employees, good for the

---

* *The Gamesman,* New York: Simon & Schuster, 1976.

community, and good for the nation both now and in the future. You can usually pick up this evangelical note in the chairman's address to the shareholders in the annual meeting.

We mentioned earlier that company loyalty is an attribute of top management. It is easier to be loyal if the cause is just. Certain types of companies can easily be presented as public benefactors: oil companies provide the energy to keep Keep America Moving (forget the wasteful production practices of the early days), automobile companies provide essential transportation (forget the monsters of the sixties). Other companies may have more difficulty justifying their existence on moral grounds or on grounds of promoting the American way of life, but it can be done. There is probably not a product from pistols (self-defense) to pornography (light entertainment) which cannot be rationalized as a public beneficence. Top managers of such companies, good top managers, believe it.

REWARDS OF TOP MANAGEMENT

It should be fairly obvious by now that business leadership is not a comfy ride on a gravy train. Before taking a closer look at the frustrations at the top, let us consider the rewards.

The most obvious rewards are monetary—salary, bonus, stock options, and all the other perquisites which will be described later. It is enough here to say that whatever other people in the company get, top management will get more.* This is an old and honored tradition and satisfies most people's ideas of the fitness of things.

It is doubtful that money alone would attract the right sort of people to the responsibilities and frustrations of top management. Indeed, it is an article of faith in socialistic societies that money is not needed to attract the best talent to top jobs. Orders of Lenin

---

* This is not always true in all organizations. By a legal quirk, the mayor of Houston (1977) got much less than some of his subordinates. In the early computer boom some IBM salesmen, who were still on commission, had incomes dangerously close to that of top management. This has been corrected.

and Black Sea dachas suffice. The dacha and the limousine are thinly disguised capitalistic symbols. Western executives, on the other hand, are not insensitive to honors as rewards of service. East and West have more in common than we usually admit.

The greatest reward for getting to the top may be personal satisfaction. For a Gamesman, just to become a member of the management team is a victory. Most business leaders are nice people, not snobs. Few top managers enjoy power for its own sake, but this doesn't mean that they don't take pride and pleasure in personal achievement, in reaching their self-set goals. As leaders, they enjoy association with the other members of the management team in their own company and with their opposite numbers in other companies. These pleasures are enhanced, in most cases, by the missionary conviction that to be a member of top management is to be in a position to make the world a better place in which to live.

By becoming a member of top management, a man gets his player's card; he can now play the big business game which is his joy and his mission. Pete Rose is supposed to have said that he would play baseball for nothing if that were the only option. Most business leaders feel the same way. They are glad that so much money goes with the job, but the big reward is playing the game. This is their life, and any other way is hardly living at all.

Although it is usually not achieved, the ultimate reward for a business leader would be public recognition. Unfortunately, outside his own company and his own community, and away from his industry colleagues, he is apt to be unknown. How many people know who is the president of General Motors? of Exxon? These men had better have their names embossed on their American Express cards when they leave town. As far as the general public is concerned, big business is largely faceless.

There are attempts to promote business leaders. *Forbes* magazine, for example, has its businessman of the month, but mostly this amounts to preaching to the committed. More effective exposure is in guest spots on interview programs such as *Face the Nation*. A pleasant recent development is the appearance of the president of Eastern Airlines and the president of Chrysler Corp. doing their own television advertising. It would be nice if this were a taste of things to come, but these cases are not typical—their fame antedates their present jobs.

One reason for the lack of public recognition of business leaders may be that the title system that serves well inside the company is pretty meaningless to outsiders. Is the head man the president or the chairman of the board? (What board?) No reason to be impressed by the vice president who handed out the winner's check on a televised golf tournament when one recently got a $9,000 loan from a friendly vice president at the local bank.

Maybe businessmen *want* to be impersonal; anonymity may be a prudent policy or even a conditioned reflex. In some companies it is a good idea to keep a low profile if one wants to move ahead. It was not always this way. Early business leaders, covering a whole spectrum of respectability, were public figures. The names of Vanderbilt, Rockefeller, Carnegie, and Ford (the original) are better known today than those of our current business leaders. Personality visibility went even farther in Great Britain in the nineteenth century. Builders and engineers such as Rennie, Watts, Stevenson, and Brunel were national heroes and inspired later generations of engineers. Family names are often perpetuated in company names. We still have them with us: Mellon, Ford, Edison, Goodyear, Du Pont, and on and on. Today the trend is toward impersonal generic corporate names such as United Energy Resources or to meaningless acronyms like ARCO or Exxon, which was chosen to mean nothing in 47 contemporary languages. Even the "classless" Russians name their airplanes, like Ilyushins and Migs, after designers. We turn out better planes with catchy names like 747 and DC 10. It is hard to love an abstraction or an acronym.

The business world pays a penalty because its leaders are not well known to the public. In a democratic society, unknowns are not likely to hold elective office. The competence and leadership talent of the business community are almost totally missing in the legislative branch and have only token representation in the executive branch of the federal government. As long as Congress continues to be dominated by lawyers, the business community (and the general public) is not going to have a fair hearing.

FRUSTRATIONS OF TOP MANAGEMENT

Top management jobs can be frustrating. Business leaders usually take the long hours and hard work in stride, but they are also ridden by the two demons of isolation and threat.

Isolation is a usual penalty of leadership positions—"The captain dines alone."* Easy relations with subordinates are difficult to maintain; there is a tendency toward deference or opportunism. Most top management people do try hard to be democratic, at least when they first move up. ("My door is always open.") This policy usually attracts only drafts or the wrong kind of people. The danger is that top management will ultimately, unwillingly, lose touch with the thinking of the troops. Power does not always corrupt, but it almost always isolates.

While the penalty of isolation is largely psychological, threats to top managers are very real. There are threats both to the well-being of their companies and to their persons. Threats to the company come from both inside and outside the organization. Outside threats usually come from the federal government and occasionally from technological change. (The threat of competition is accepted as part of the game.) We have already discussed the *burdens* of federal intervention: irrational reporting requirements, irrational tax laws, and unrealistic environmental standards to be met. The *threat* is unpredicted change. It is frustrating to management to see its well-laid plans undone by new laws and regulations. Technological threat is less common but can be even more devastating, because whole industries can be casualties. Technological change is usually a distant threat. Good management tries to anticipate and even take advantage of it. Oil companies, for example, have large research commitments to alternative energy sources.

Internal threat—that is, by company people—may be even more painful to the top-management team. With its own personal commitment to the company welfare, anything less by employees seems almost to be treason. Management expects a self-serving attitude from labor; it hopes for, and doesn't often get, a more en-

---

* There are outstanding historical exceptions. Prince Hal fraternized with his troops on the eve of Agincourt. Napoleon was on familiar terms with his old soldiers.

lightened attitude from its professional and middle-management people. Employees look at top management as an inexhaustible source of funds, much as citizens look to their government. Seen from the top there must be times when the whole corporation looks like an organized raid on the treasury. The only things that stand between corporate chaos and ruin are the restraint and firmness of top management.

The (union) workers want more money. If they are sophisticated, they want it as a result of increased productivity and in forms not subject to income tax—for instance, in the form of larger pensions and better health care. Usually they just want more money. Justification by increased productivity is a specious argument. It states, for example, that the driver of a power-assisted 150-ton truck that moves dirt more cheaply is worth more than his fellow who is fighting an old manual 75-ton rig with an open cab. Increased productivity doesn't necessarily mean that a man is *worth* more, it just makes it possible to pay him more.° Top management wants to pay its workers well; its sympathy is usually with the line. Beyond a point it cannot go! Not beyond the point where it means taking money from capital improvements and jeopardizing the future of the company (as the Eastern railroads were forced to do) or beyond the point where its product or service is priced out of the competitive market (like the U.S. merchant marine, which exists only because the public is forced to subsidize it). It is top management which has to make the ultimate tough decisions: to accept a strike and then to end it when a possible settlement has been proposed.

The in-fighting between management and labor is relatively clean compared to that between management and staff—between bureaucracy and the executive branch. Part of the trauma is psychological. The Gamesmen at the top put the welfare of the company first; they long ago gave up on labor, but they do hope that

° Few employees realize how much they cost a company. It is good business for a company to spend upward of $150,000 in capital improvements to eliminate a single employee. The joker is that now the remaining employees consider themselves worth more. Sometimes it is cheaper to shut down an inefficient plant and build a new one.

the businessmen who work for them have the same priorities. This is not generally true. The first priority of staff management (with the exception of a few natural Gamesmen) is to preserve the system. Staff people have a good thing going for them—they have tenure, and they want to keep it.

As we have already seen, bureaucratic staff departments tend to grow in size and expense whether their work load increases or not. At budget time, then, the staff department requests which come up to the top are based not on need but on individual empire building and ambition. Top management is not always well equipped to sort the wheat from the chaff. Unless the president is a lawyer himself and understands the legal mind, the legal budget request must seem outrageous to him. Data processing (which was once supposed to save the company money) says it needs a new and bigger computer, and unless someone on the management team knows something about computer science, it is hard to say no. None of these requested staff increases contributes to income. What it means is more overhead. Under the harsh realities of Kirchoff's law, something has to give.

It is at the top level where these difficult decisions and allocations are made, where a small management team holds the line against threats from the outside and from its own employees. Sometimes the fight is lost. Sometimes wages get out of line, and sometimes the staff gets to be too big a load to carry. American steel makers pay such high wages that they cannot compete in their own backyard with Japanese makers, who must not only import their raw materials but ship the final heavy product many thousands of miles. The construction of the Alaskan pipeline was a special case where labor costs got out of line. Since some skilled workers were able to demand premium wages to work under Alaskan conditions, everybody got premium wages. Timekeepers wound up earning at a $60,000-a-year rate. The job was not even well done, and parts had to be rewelded at even higher rates. The public and the shareholders will pick up the tab.

Of the cost threats, unproductive staff growth is probably the most difficult to counter. One counter is the "finger in the dike" approach, which usually involves a crash program to reduce overhead. This may be effective in the short run, but it is hard to maintain year after year.* A better strategy is expansion. Accepting that staff is going to grow in any event, the best way to keep overhead down to a reasonable ratio is for the company to grow at least as fast.

Excessive growth of staff costs is a wasting disease. It is endemic in government agencies and in socialized industries. Top managements of such organizations are not subject to the discipline of the annual report. As their own salaries are tied by a ranking structure to those of their employees (unlike business management, whose remuneration is set by consensus), they have little incentive to keep wages down. Horrible examples abound: the Post Office; British Leyland, which has parlayed its natural advantage of being the only large indigenous auto maker into huge losses; Canadian National Railways, which costs the taxpayers money while Canadian Pacific (private) pays dividends and taxes. There is our own New York City.

Prospective employees or shareholders would like to be able to diagnose this wasting disease in a company. The symptoms are not always obvious. A lower-than-industry-average return on sales or a rate of increase of sales expense that is higher than that of sales may be warnings. A strong statement in the annual report that the company has initiated a cost control program indicates (a) that things are pretty bad and (b) that they may get better. The best insurance is to affiliate only with companies that have a high growth rate so that management has room to control the problem. There may be truth in the old stock market superstition that companies either grow or die. Staff-ridden companies are sick; sometimes, like Railway Express, they just fade away.

The ultimate threat to top management is personal: the safety of its members. We haven't come to the point in this country where business leaders need bodyguards as they do in Italy and Argentina, but there is a threat. Kidnappers rarely waste time on paupers.

* The original Henry Ford controlled accounting costs by severely limiting the space allowed for accountants. He overdid it. When Ford went public and the books were examined, it was almost impossible to tell where the company was making or losing money.

Many business leaders find it prudent to install elaborate security measures in their own homes. Few, for security and other reasons, care to make a show of their wealth. Most prefer to stay in safe enclaves: office, home, and company transportation. A very real threat does exist for those management people who are assigned to combat zones overseas.

THE BALANCE

Ultimately, the weighing of the advantages and disadvantages of elevation to corporate leadership must be made by the individual candidate. Is the flame worth the candle? Some leaders thrive in the unfriendly environment. Like a good relief pitcher coming in with the bases loaded, they enjoy the challenge and rise to it when called. Some accept it less enthusiastically and tend to withdraw from the common stream. Some quit.

Try to visit a top executive of a large company. Come as a shareholder, say, for a friendly visit. If the headquarters building has modern equipment, you can't get through doors without a magnetic pass card, and it takes a special code to enter the executive suite. Building security will come to your aid. Following its usual policy of maximum reaction to minimum exposure, it will assign you a guide. The executive suite is on its own floor and is served by its own elevator.

Having passed through all the inanimate barriers you come to the ultimate animate one—a hard-faced secretary. She will ask you, politely of course, what the hell your business is and, finally, frisking you only with her eyes, will send a message to the inner sanctum. Mr. Noster is in conference. Your best chance of talking to the man is that he just might wander into the reception area when you are talking to Aunt Agatha.* If he sees you and finds out why you are there, he will probably take you back to show you his office, have a pleasant chat, and even offer a drink. Behind the security shield is a nice guy.

* Not to be confused with Bertie Wooster's good and deserving Aunt Dahlia; this is the one who eats broken bottles. P. G. Wodehouse, *The Code of the Woosters.*

In some companies, particularly those which boast a new building and which employed an interior designer, the executive suite is an enclave. In addition to offices and conference rooms, it may include a private dining room and even an attended gymnasium, all maintained under tight security. In such cases it is hard to know where prudence ends and paranoia begins.

Some leaders drop out. The easiest cop-out is through alcohol. There is probably no higher incidence of alcoholism on the executive floor than on other floors, but it is still the only socially acceptable response to threat. Drugs, crying, or temper tantrums are frowned upon. It takes a special personality to put up with the stresses and frustrations of leadership (in any field) and to still lead a balanced existence with a satisfying home life and outside interests. The surprising thing is not that people drop out but that most do not.

The ultimate cop-out is to quit—to pick up one's winnings and leave. Often these "exes" start a new and quite different career: photography, writing, or just gardening or sailing.* This seems like rational behavior for a man who doesn't need any more money. According to case histories, however, the withdrawal pains from power can be severe. To go from being a top frog in any pond (political, business, athletic) to being just another rich citizen is a tough transition. This seems to be particularly true if the decision was a voluntary one; after all, the man did not have to quit. Mandatory retirement at a certain age is probably the kindest solution to the problem; then the decision to leave is impersonal and made without prejudice.

* See interviews with Wheelock Whitney and William G. Damroth in the *Harvard Business Review*, September–October 1975.

PART THREE

People
in Business

11

TRAINING FOR BUSINESS

ALL BUSINESSMEN need training to be successful: background training before entering, on-the-job training, and continuing refreshers throughout their career just to keep up. Background training is both specific and general. Specific subjects are obvious: accounting, economics, computer usage, tax law, and the list goes on. General background can be very general indeed; almost any subject will be useful: political science, mathematics, even such despised humanities as history and languages (English preferred).

Is business sufficiently different that a special curriculum of training is appropriate, or is it better to have a more general background which will be augmented by on-the-job training? This question is still unresolved. The special-discipline school of thought favors business school training, with the seal of approval being the MBA (Master of Business Administration). Some companies make a point of hiring MBAs to fill their managerial vacancies. Other companies avoid them as being overpaid and underexperienced. Neither policy seems to lead automatically to corporate success or failure.

Business schools are a twentieth-century phenomenon. There were highly successful businesses before MBAs. The most successful management operation in history was probably the Indian Civil Service, which ran the Indian subcontinent efficiently with fewer than a thousand English staff. The only deviation from a classical education for these managers (both at Haileybury and at Oxbridge) was the learning of Hindustani. Practical education came through experience in the field. Even today, British Petroleum (BP) shows a preference for hiring Oxbridge classics wranglers over technicians.

Business school graduates do get good jobs—in fact, this is the business school's own measure of success—but do they rise to top management? This depends on the individual and on the company. Many companies which hire MBAs to fill managerial staff positions traditionally look to operations or to a specific discipline such as engineering to fill the top spots. The ambitious entering employee may want to check.

Business schools are a peculiarly American institution.° They were founded on the optimistic nineteenth-century concept that with a proper curriculum you can train bright people to do anything well, even to run a business or save society. Teaching methods vary, but the goal of all business schools is the same: to move graduates into well-paying, responsible positions. Using this goal as the criterion of ranking, the Harvard Business School is the odds-on leader. This school has become such a part of the American business scene that it deserves a separate discussion.† The following comments are not written by an alumnus; they are based on visits to the school and on talks with its graduates.

° There are now business schools in Western Europe, but they are modeled after American prototypes.

† For a complete story see Melvin T. Copeland, *And Mark an Era: The Story of the Harvard Business School,* Boston: Little, Brown, 1958.

THE HARVARD BUSINESS SCHOOL

It is a pleasant stroll across the Walking Bridge from Cambridge to Boston over the Charles River. On a nice day, the Harvard and MIT crews are rowing up and down the river and a lot of largely naked bodies are lying on the banks in the sun. It is nice, too, to leave behind the untidiness and bustle of Harvard and Brattle squares in Cambridge. Here on the Boston side is a different world. Impressive, orderly New England–style red-brick buildings with enough domes and finials to form a pleasing skyline; neatly cut lawns and broad streets. The students look better, too—you see less hair and fewer rags—and the women seem to be wearing underpinning. (The difference is comparative—if you want to see really neat students, you must go further inland, to Northwestern Business School, for example.) There were no riots *here* in the roaring sixties. Even the faculty parking lots look different; where in Cambridge there would be rows of Volvos and Rabbits, here there are modest Fords, Chevrolets, and Dodges.

This is the Harvard Business School—as wonderful in its way as Disneyland. Here students enter as ordinary people, spend two years, and leave as graduates with an MBA* and a claim on American business for over a million dollars each in their working life. The outsider feels like an NCO assigned to duty at an officer's candidate school where he sees grunts come in and officers and gentlemen go out. There is magic here.

To some extent, the Harvard Business School is self-justifying. Business *believes* in the "B-school" and supports it. To deny its graduates their piece of the action would be sacrilege. There are enough alumni in high positions that the old-school-tie business is effective. This sentimental loyalty would not last beyond a single generation if the graduates were not good. They are good. The most important contribution to this excellence is the quality of the applicants for admission. Only good students or already successful business people need apply, and of these only the most promis-

---

* Harvard and other business schools also prepare students for doctor's degrees in business. Since these degrees usually lead to a teaching rather than a business career, we don't discuss them.

ing—less than a fifth—are chosen. As the director of the office of career development told me, "We could lock them up for two years and they would still be good employees." Along with their opposite numbers at medical schools, the admission people at the B-school come closer to playing God than most of us do on this earth. The school doesn't lock up its students for two years; it trains them, using a technique which is a pedagogical sport, a method developed at Harvard—the case method.

The Case Method

Some subjects, like accounting or welding, are learned; others, like mathematics, history, and theology, are studied. The case method is an approach in which problems are talked to death. The rationale behind the case method (originally called the problem method) is that the important contribution of a businessman is to make decisions which are necessarily based on historical, subjective, and even conflicting data. His job is not to gather these data (such as accounting reports and statistical analyses) but to evaluate them and make a constructive decision. Ordinary teaching methods are not appropriate to this open-ended sort of problem or case study.

The case method presents a problem as a sort of skit or scenario. The characters in the skit have a problem, and they talk about it. If the case is well written, the dialog does a good job of defining the problem and its history and presents different points of view.* Supporting documents, the sort of thing that would be available, are provided. The students read the case, study it, request more information if they need it, talk about it in conferences or workshops, and finally make a decision. The job of the instructor is to monitor the discussion, but not to direct it. *There is no correct answer to a case.* However, the student may have to live with his decision, since the next case may be based on his solution to the last. If he decides to build a plant, for example, he now has the problem of building the thing.

Critics of the case method claim that it turns out too many de-

---

* An illustrative case is presented in Appendix I to this chapter.

cision makers and not enough Craftsmen. The graduate's first job is more likely to involve learning a staff function than making important decisions. Harvard doesn't buy this. It claims that *any* business subject can be taught by the case method and that the tiresome details should be delegated anyway. Ninety percent of the teaching at Harvard uses the case method (they cheat a little by requiring entering students to have read a standard accounting text). This approach puts a burden on the faculty, who are constantly writing new cases after scouring the literature and discussing problems with corporations. Harvard is committed to the case method and even makes its cases available to other schools at nominal cost.

It is hard to argue with success.

The Score

What happens to the hungry graduates? (Even the Dean admitted to me that they tend to be "impatient.") What kind of jobs do they take? The B-school can answer these questions; it keeps careful records on its alumni. (Businessese creeps even into the vocabulary of a distinguished faculty. Placing graduates and contacting possible employers is called "marketing.") The school maintains a computer program to match candidates with job opportunities and vice versa. This seems more like computer dating, but it is exactly the sort of thing business likes to do with its computers.

The first choice of graduates is finance, which normally involves the study of companies to evaluate loan or investment opportunities. Harvard graduates are reasonably well equipped to step immediately into such jobs and do useful work, because the case method makes them critical. Some graduates are hired by large companies to go into an executive development program (the fast-track Baseball players of Chapter 2). Some go into accounting, as a second choice or fall-back position, but this isn't too bad. As the director of career development said, "The partners in an accounting firm *do* make a hundred to a hundred-and-fifty thousand."

A few graduates go into "standard" staff jobs where the criteria for advancement are knowledge and experience. This may be a mistake. They can be a trial to their department head. I had one who made a novel appeal* for a raise: "I am not moving as fast as my classmates." The easiest solution is to move the man to a more congenial environment. There is little interest in personnnel work either by faculty or by students. This is a shame, as personnel direction seems to us to be the most challenging and needed skill in business today.

These people do succeed. Eighty of the exclusive *Fortune* 500 companies are led by B-school alumni. Even more significant, some ten thousand graduates are the chief officers of their own small businesses. With all this positive evidence, plus the documented fact that Harvard graduates start at a higher level and move faster than the graduates of other business schools, it seems silly to question the success of the school. Still, there are a couple of nagging questions.

Is American business, and the country, better off because of the efforts of the Harvard Business School? The B-school has been on the scene since 1907. This period has seen wars, booms, depressions, the depletion of natural resources, scandals, and riots. Have the Harvard graduates been a stabilizing and ameliorating influence, or have they mostly worked to move money—from the earth, from others—into the hands of a select few? What are their relative values? Admitting that Harvard graduates play an important role in business leadership, that international business affects our foreign policy, and that American business managers have an increasing responsibility for spending taxpayers' money both at home and abroad, what are their priorities? How do they equate national welfare with the profit motive? We don't know; it is hard to measure these things and dangerous to generalize. Harvard doesn't know either, but it does know exactly how much money its people make.

Before going back over the Walking Bridge to Cambridge, look around you at one of the most remarkable panoramas in the nation. Looking down the Charles, you can just see the ugly silhouette of Massachusetts Institute of Technology on the Cambridge skyline—MIT, where they are training the engineers and scientists

---

* There are two usual appeals for a raise: "Joe is making more money than I am" and "I need the money." Both are, of course, non sequiturs.

who will design the planes, the processes, and the electronics on which our nation's prosperity, image, and even survival depends. Look straight across the river to Old Harvard, where scholarship still reigns. Its graduates may never see a lousy $100,000 in one piece, but some of them may write treatises on transfinite numbers, Indic philology, or literary criticism which will fire the imagination of a select few. Some may even win Nobel prizes. Behind you is the Business School whose graduates will put together the deals and supply the funds to make dreams a reality (and who will skim a lot of cream in the process). It is a nice walk back across the Charles to Cambridge.

THE OTHERS

Harvard isn't the only business school. With about 45,000 MBAs graduated a year, Harvard's 800 looks like small beer. Some of the others are very good; some are not. It doesn't take much to start a business school. In addition to classroom space you need some aggressive accounting and finance teachers, a second-rate economist, a part-time psychologist (personnel relations) to titillate the troops by describing the importance of early toilet training, and a few specialists to handle added attractions like tax law, econometrics, computer usage, and, for light entertainment, stock market behavior. You can even get ready-made cases (cheap) from Harvard. Xerox copies of *Harvard Business Review* articles can form much of the reading material.

Good schools, of course, do a responsible job. There are a lot of them. Many state schools have sound departments. Some private schools—Stanford, Carnegie, Wharton, Northwestern, Chicago, and the Sloan School come to mind—are highly respected in the business community. We choose to discuss only two of these, Chicago and the Sloan School, not because they are necessarily better, but because they offer pedagogical approaches that compete with the Harvard way.

Chicago

Chicago University is a private university, and one of the best. Its home is a beautiful campus on the near south side of Chicago which looks like, and was built to look like, a transplanted Oxbridge college. Unfortunately it is located in a now-depressed part of the city and is not known to many Chicagoans, let alone to tourists. The business school has been around for a long time—it was founded in 1898 and is the second oldest in the country. (Wharton, at the University of Pennsylvania, was founded in 1881.)

The Chicago approach is different from that at Harvard. To quote Dean Rosett, "We believe in the scientific analysis of decision making and of decision rules but . . . also analyze the structure and function of business organizations and examine the total environment. . . ."* The key word here is analysis. Chicago believes that most business problems *can* be analyzed and solved. The decision process is objective rather than subjective. The key subjects on which this analysis rests are accounting and economics. This is a happy choice for Chicago, which has top-ranking accountants on its staff (the outer reaches of accounting, which involve such things as inflation accounting and replacement cost analysis, are far from dull) and which is supported by the university economics staff, arguably the best in the country.

There seems to be good cooperation between the university and the business school. Both use the Regenstein Library, for example, but the business school maintains its own resident mathematics and economics professors. Students† are required to take a core of hard subjects—accounting, economics, statistics, calculus (let's see you teach *that* by the case method)—but have a wide selection of electives in areas of marketing, finance, policy, and even in hospital management.‡ Behavioral science (personnel) is available but is not popular. The case method *is* used in some Chicago courses, but only on a small scale and where it is considered appropriate.

* From *Business Education at Chicago*, an excellent, concise description available from the Graduate School of Business of the University of Chicago.

† Chicago has both full-time and part-time students. This section is written with full-time students in mind, although there isn't much difference. See the section on continuing education later in this chapter.

‡ Appendix II to this chapter is a list of the subjects in the Chicago curriculum (1977).

Chicago has long had a fascination with stock market behavior and, supported by Merrill Lynch, Pierce, Fenner & Smith, has done definitive work in this area. Unfortunately, the results of these researches have been negative in the sense that they indicate that you can select winning stocks as well by throwing darts at *The Wall Street Journal* as by analysis.

The Chicago approach then is academic and analytical rather than academic and discursive as at Harvard. What sort of students does Chicago attract, and what happens to them? Chicago gets good students, perhaps not quite the caliber of the Harvard novices but plenty good enough. Many of them* are "retreads"—people with degrees, advanced degrees, in other fields who found the job market in their old field too crowded and who turned to business to find a "rewarding and challenging" career (read: "to make a living"). Like all converts they tend to be very committed to their new persuasion. In answer to my question on the most valuable thing he had learned, one imminent graduate replied, "To be able to read and understand *The Wall Street Journal*." Strange words from a retreaded anthropologist and Peace Corps worker!

In declining order of frequency, Chicago graduates go into the following fields: finance, accounting, marketing, international business, and none of the above. With their analytical and statistical training they are particularly well suited for investment banking and for work as loan officers. Operations research training serves well in marketing.

Even more than at Harvard, where the students must feel privileged just by having been admitted, I got the feeling that I was at an officers' candidate school. These bright students, many of whom have abandoned other careers, lying around the commons room (and leaving their trash behind), were going out into the business world after two years' residence to make more money than I ever did. They seemed contented with the prospect. Perhaps a few, a very few, may look back someday and wonder if somewhere along the line they hadn't sold a little piece of their scholastic souls.

---

* The full-time students, that is. Most of the part-time students are already in business.

The Sloan School

Massachusetts Institute of Technology, *mirabile dictu*, has a graduate business school: the Sloan School. It shares the Sloan building, facing the Charles, with the MIT faculty club, which used to have the distinction of supporting possibly the worst restaurant and the best bar in the Boston-Cambridge area. Martinis came in Erlenmeyer flasks, and from far above the bustle, one could gloat over the traffic jams on Memorial Drive and watch the dinghys sailing and capsizing on the river.

But back to business. The Sloan School is different. It does not try to accommodate business by turning out clones who will fit smoothly into the management team. Quite the opposite! The Sloan School claims to have solved the business environment and to be able to simulate it with mathematical models. No job too big: multinational companies, city planning, even world ecology (the Club of Rome study used an MIT type model). The moving figure behind this approach is Jay Forrester, who calls it systems dynamics.*

While Harvard considers decisions to be arrived at from enlightened discussion and Chicago looks for the optimum solution, in the MIT models the decision process is represented as a control function in a feedback loop. This sounds obscure, but it is reasonable. *If* the corporation can be successfully modeled, then its future behavior must be a function of ongoing decisions made at all levels. Most important, decisions (more properly, policy) can be tried out first using the computer model before taking expensive business risks.

Armed with their mathematical equations and computer programs, then, the MIT graduate is prepared to model and optimize the future of any business. If the popular image of Harvard Business School students is a group in conference discussing a case and that of the Chicago student is a lonely figure clutching his textbooks to his bosom as he struggles through the snow, a reasonable picture of the MIT student is a man sitting in front of a computer terminal watching the wiggles on a cathode-ray tube. MIT students do

---

* *Principles of Systems*, Cambridge, Mass.: Wright-Allen, 1968.

spend a lot of time at terminals, but this is a warped picture. In order to model something, you have to understand it. The business model builder must have an intimate knowledge of business—supply, demand, marketing, accounting, the whole thing.

A criticism of the systems dynamics approach is that if the practitioner has to have this knowledge of business, why model it? Why not settle for running it as other business school graduates do? The answer involves the time dimension. Forrester sees a business (or any system) as a living, changing thing over time: decisions made today will effect changes years from now and will be affected by other interim decisions, by exogenous factors, and by built-in time lags in the system itself. Only a model can investigate this sort of thing. He may be right. Every business leader has been frustrated by the cyclic nature of things—for instance, when he contracted operations during a recession instead of expanding his plant to anticipate the next boom, or, conversely, when he made unneeded capital investments at the start of a recession.

It is not quite fair to characterize the Sloan School as completely dedicated to model building and systems dynamics. Basic business subjects must be, and are, taught. MIT probably does a better job than most in interesting its students in personnel problems (behavioral science). There is even a conservative faction in the school which favors a more traditional approach to business teaching. It is model building and systems dynamics, however, that set the Sloan School apart as something different.

How do Sloan School graduates get on? Individually, quite well, since they are smart, well trained people. As apostles of a new management method, not too well. Management, which may have had previous painful experience with computer solutions, is not quite ready to put its house in the hands of a computer model and to have its decisions simulated in Z-space. To gain wider acceptance, systems dynamics models need more field testing (a vicious circle), and they need to be refined and tied in more closely to traditional reporting formats.

Dedicated graduates keep trying. Some do get to use their methods in a business, some teach, and some set up consulting firms to propagate the faith. We wish them well. American business can use an approach that stresses policy and planning rather than profits and rate of return—particularly an approach that considers the global impact of business decisions.

The Sloan School is a fun place to visit.

OTHER ROUTES TO THE TOP

Business school training is not the only way to prepare for top management jobs. In fact, some large organizations won't touch a business school graduate with a fork. These companies have to look for top management people among their own middle management—staff or operations—or they must hire from the outside. Hiring from outside shifts the training responsibility to another company.

People enter business corporations with diverse training: accounting, science, engineering, law, even liberal arts. Many of these people will never be businessmen as we have defined the term; they will have useful careers as research workers, builders, or writers. A few—those who're natural Gamesmen—will eventually move into business management, for which they were only partially trained in school. The knowledge gaps are filled by on-the-job and off-the-job training. Although employees can rise to corporate leadership from any training background, three professions are most productive: engineering, accounting, and law.

Engineers should make good top managers. Their schooling teaches them to break problems into component parts, to identify the important parts, and to look for a simple, practical solution. High-technology companies such as tractor manufacturers and oil companies often prefer engineers—mechanical and chemical, respectively—in their top spots. Geologists are also preferred by oil companies, but for this discussion they can be lumped together with engineers. Engineers are line-oriented, which helps them fit well into top management.

A glance at the business school curriculum in Appendix II shows how much new training a technologist needs to move up. He has a lot to learn. Most scientists and engineers are Craftsmen by nature and may not have the incentive of the Gamesman to accept all this new training to enter the frustrating world of big-business leadership.

With the increasing preoccupation of corporations with reporting and paperwork, accounting is becoming an appropriate background for management. An accountant needs additional training, particularly in areas of operations and technology. A good in-house executive development program which moves people through operational staff jobs can fill these gaps. If the company *is* an accounting company, even this is not necessary. Possible problems in recruiting top management from accountants are the change in loyalty required (from staff to line) and the difficulty of gaining confidence on the part of the operating people.

Legal problems in a company are so important that at least one member of the top management team—usually the general counsel, but occasionally even the chief executive—has to be a lawyer. Some lawyers are natural Gamesmen, and close proximity with top management makes them want to play the business game even though they don't have the financial incentive of other professionals to change roles. Some of the most successful top managers are lawyers; their training in confrontation situations may help.

Lawyers are apt to be more comfortable and effective in dealing with government people—they understand each other. Outsiders have the uncomfortable feeling that some lawyers *use* the law (to obtain government money, for example) rather than respect it. The public may be afraid of the law taking over business as it long ago took over Washington. The ghosts of Watergate die hard.

Engineering, accounting, law—these are the more common routes to the top. But the list is not exhaustive; anyone can play the management game. Except in those companies that are so bogged down in Army-type management that all promotions are based on seniority rather than ability, management is looking for bright people wherever they are. An employee may be eliminated by chance or circumstances, but not by his particular academic degree (or lack of it). With the opportunities for continuing education in the cities in which big business is at home, the capable, personable employee who is willing to make the sacrifice can pass even his coworker with an MBA (if he wants to, he can get his own).

Some other disciplines seem to be emerging as new logical candidates. Eggheads—economists and researchers—may have claims, particularly in high-technology companies. Even the once-despised personnel director (vice president—employee relations) may have his day as management is forced to acknowledge the importance of its employees. A good personnel man can have a lot of unpaid debts to help him up the ladder.

CONTINUING EDUCATION

Whether they are business school graduates or not, all rising managers need continuing education. The MBA needs to learn operations, and the line managers need to learn pure business subjects. On-the-job training is the most important, but it must be supported by outside contacts. Continuing outside education is of three types: formal schooling, informal or ad hoc courses, and on-going reading.

Formal Schooling

The classic example of formal continuing education is the full-time employee going to night school to learn new skills or to get a degree. Most universities and many business schools offer part-time instruction. Chicago does a good job. Its business evening courses are taught in downtown Chicago rather than on the main campus, but the programs, the requirements, and the faculty are the same. An MBA degree from Chicago got the hard way in night school is equal in value and prestige to that earned by full-time students. Most large companies pay the tuition to accredited night-school courses.

There is a growing trend to offer educational leaves or even sabbatical leaves, with pay, to middle-management people. This is an expensive perk for management to offer, but it may be a good investment. Thinking businessmen need an opportunity to regroup just as much as college professors do; in fact, their job requirements probably change more rapidly. After an educational leave, the returnee should be assigned to a new job which uses his new skills.

Graduate schools of business like to offer short refresher

courses—informal education. A few offer long-term formal training programs. Some of them work with a company to fill an educational leave for as much as a year. The Sloan School has such a program. These long-term programs are prestige items; the student is obviously a marked man in his company. The most prestigious of all is the Harvard Advanced Management Program (AMP), also known as the "charm school."

The Harvard AMP is business's answer to the Army General Staff School. The typical student has 20 years' experience and is already in a high-level position. The course lasts 13 weeks. Just to be selected to attend is a high honor. There may be some question whether three months of intensive schooling can really change a middle-aged man, but there is no question that it is a good deal for all concerned.

It is a good deal for the manager/student. He has been singled out by his company. The honor may not be quite equivalent to that of being made a vice president (he probably is that already), but it is close—on a level perhaps with a Wilson peerage. It is an earnest of better things. On his return he is forever an alumnus of the Harvard Business School, and he has a diploma to prove it. At the school he has an opportunity to make friends with, and exchange notes with, his opposite numbers from all over the world (there are 160 students in a class). The work is hard, but he wouldn't have it any other way—most managers equate hard work with value in the same way that people formerly judged the efficacy of patent medicine by how bad it tasted. Harvard cooperates by making the learning experience rigorous, almost a retreat, but the end justifies the means. For graduation all the stops are pulled out: wives and friends fly in from all parts of the country on company planes, the ceremony is impressive and the speeches are reassuring, the parties are fun—now that the pressure is off—and everybody goes home with a feeling of purpose and self-satisfaction.

The AMP is a good deal for the school. It gives it a new batch of 160 loyal alumni who will improve its image as a creator of business leaders. Since this program, and other executive education programs, is expensive, it is a means by which business supports the Harvard Business School.

It is a good deal for the professors. It gives them a chance to mingle with high-achieving, experienced managers. It keeps them on their toes. Business school professors are quite different from those in other graduate schools. For one thing, they like their students and treat them a lot better than serfs. (The converse is true: the students leave with an affection for their teachers.) For another thing, they are good teachers. No unprepared lectures, mumbling, or speaking in unknown tongues. They are so sold on their calling that they really admire business leaders to the point of name dropping. "I had lunch today with Mark Zindler." (Unfortunately they usually have to qualify this for an outsider. "He is president of _____, you know.") In any event, at the AMP the professors make new business friends, which will help them in their work by providing useful high-level contacts and material for new cases.

Informal Courses

There are literally thousands of short courses, both in-house and outside, available to upgrade the businessman. In Chapter 7, Mr. Biggers got several brochures on one day offering seminars and short courses. This is typical; a middle manager can expect to get at least ten of these a week. Most of them look alike—little 4" × 10" folders, designed to fit a pocket but sure to distort a standard file folder.

Everybody wants to get into the teaching act. Any university worth the name has a series of one- and two-week summer courses. The American Management Associations conducts a floating series of well-regarded short courses in key cities. Technical manufacturers and software houses run continuous series of courses on their products. The IBM company has a larger teaching load than many colleges. Professional organizations promote seminars and workshops. There are an increasing number of organizations which are set up only to teach businessmen. If all this teaching were effective, the American businessman would be the smartest man in the world. It isn't, and he isn't.

Some of these courses are very good; some are bad. Some are necessary; for example, if IBM comes out with a new operating system, it has to be explained to the users. Even a good course is effective only if it teaches the right subject to the right person. With this limitation, university courses are usually good, but there is tremendous duplication. Such seemingly obscure subjects as linear programming (for the businessman) and multivariate analysis (for the businessman) are available from dozens of institutions. The obvious thing for a student to do is to choose a nice location. Business schools also offer short courses—it is too good a thing to pass up. Harvard keeps a whole series going, usually two-week courses, each aimed at a specific problem. Typical subject: Program for Health Management. This sort of thing is very useful for the right students.

Informal teaching comes closest to being a racket where a small team of self-proclaimed specialists moves into a company to teach a select group of managers a poorly defined subject like management theory or leadership. We have doubts that management is a separate discipline or that it can successfully be taught—not in two weeks anyway! If such a team can sell its act to a high-level manager, the stage is set. All *his* managers drop their regular work for a week or two and listen to outsiders telling them how to do their job. It does break the monotony for these people, and after the course is over and they have caught up again, they can get back to what they were doing before. A businessman will accept an amazing amount of trivia if it is presented in a classroom format and may even congratulate the teacher at the end for doing a good job! He has spent so many years of his life as a student in a student–teacher relationship that he accepts anything given out in this format as a good thing. If the teachers are smart, they give out high marks and impressive-looking diplomas to all participants; the student's cup runneth over. This is regression.

Ongoing Training

Ongoing training, as we use the term, refers to the reading that a businessman does on his own. For an ambitious, or even intellectually curious, businessman, this is a constant activity.

The heaviest outside reading is textbooks. There are many available in all fields. A good sample of business subjects is the Chicago Business School curriculum in Appendix II to this chapter.

Business books, printed by reputable publishers, are meaty and authoritative. Special book clubs exist to help particular specialists such as accountants keep abreast of current publications. Every discipline develops its own writing style. Mathematics, for example, is compression—saying as much as possible in few words.* The characteristic of most business books is that they are dull. The readers expect this. Employing the "patent medicine syndrome," they mistrust easy or pleasant reading.

Monthly or quarterly business publications are usually very good and vary in interest from highly technical journals such as *Management Science* and *The Journal of World Business* to *Business Week*, which has popular appeal. Professional societies publish their own journals. Particular industries are served by publications like the *Oil and Gas Journal* and *Engineering News Record*. Popular monthlies like *Forbes, Fortune,* and *Dun's Review* are almost pan-business house organs which enable top management to keep up with the business climate and with what others are doing. *Barron's* weekly is widely read by investors, particularly by common-stock investors. There are many respected business periodicals. By far the most respected, so much so that to be a subscriber is a status symbol, is the *Harvard Business Review.*

The Harvard MBA, or the AMP graduate, naturally keeps a copy of the *Harvard Business Review* on his coffee table to impress visitors. Middle managers like to get a subscription approved in their budget without being accused of being presumptuous. Apart from the prestige of its name, is the *HBR* really that good? Possibly. Its closest counterpart in the publishing business may be the *Scientific American.*† The *Scientific American* does a good job of making the latest advances in science available to the educated layman. The *HBR* does the same thing for business topics, with articles written by the best people in their fields. It also serves as a forum

* "Obviously" means that the next equation can be derived by the reader after an evening's analysis. "One readily sees that . . ." means that only a specialist has any hope of figuring the thing out.

† These two magazines share an excellence in editing, format, and graphics well above the norm. Sometimes the text in the *HBR* articles seems overwhelmed by the multicolored pie charts and other graphics.

for presenting new business ideas, particularly those developed by the staff of the Harvard Business School, in nontechnical form.

The most "businessy" of all business publications is a daily (work days only): *The Wall Street Journal*. Its receipt is also a status symbol, but more widespread than the *HBR*. It is a lowly manager indeed who doesn't get his daily copy (he may have to share with others, but his secretary can smooth it out to make it look fresh). The *WSJ* is one of the best newspapers in the country (in the world, in fact—in addition to regional editions in different parts of this country, editions are published in Europe and in the Far East). It does carry complete stock market and commodity market quotations and it does serve as the bulletin board of business where offerings and earnings reports are advertised, but it is also a good *news*paper. The covering of general news is concise, compared to *The New York Times*, for example, but it is selective, well written, and sometimes even amusing. The editorial policy is surprisingly tolerant. An archenemy of business, such as Ted Kennedy, may even be allowed to present his side of a controversial question on the editorial page. The *WSJ* is the daily bible reading of the businessman; he could do a lot worse.

EDUCATION PROBLEMS

With all this business education going on, formal, informal, and ongoing, it seems snide to suggest that it is not enough. Special training may be in order for the American businessman who is going to work abroad, but even the domestic businessman is often too weak in some areas. These weaknesses not only can slow his own progress, but the cumulative effect may be a general business infirmity which can hurt business and cost society. The problem areas are the humanities: history, ethics, political science, and language, both written and spoken. With the increasingly job-oriented, philistine trend of higher education in America, we may be turning out not only domestic but world business leaders who are not sensitive to the cultural systems in which they will exercise their power.

Before continuing this criticism we had better make a disclaimer. There are many businessmen, at all levels—including readers of this book—who are well rounded, literate, informed, and perceptive. We are not talking about them.

Communications—Businessese

Colleges and universities assume that the students matriculated in their technical and business schools have already learned how to read and to write, and they may make no particular efforts to teach language skills. Unless the student was lucky enough to have gone to a good public high school or to a private school, this assumption is not justified. As a result, many technical and business students graduate from college with only a primitive knowledge of their own language. They have done little writing (tests are increasingly true–false or fill-in-the-blanks for mechanical scoring) or public speaking, and their reading has been confined to textbooks.*

Consciously or unconsciously, the graduate resents this deficiency. He wants to be able to write effectively, in a style that is accepted and sounds important. Following the example of his associates, he soon picks up a working knowledge of *businessese*. The common language of business is ostentatious, sounds important, and is inefficient. An example:

July 2, 1978

To: All Managers and Directors
From: J. Doakes, Director of Security

In order to effect the conversion of improved electrical capability for the Management Systems Department, power in the Headquarters Building will be degraded over the holiday weekend extending from 5:30 P.M. Friday July 2 to 8:30 A.M. Tuesday July 6. This implementation will necessitate minimal air-conditioning capability. Please plan your work to not use the premises in this interim.

As you may know, Management Systems has upgraded its facility to a larger computer to increase throughput and enhance service to the corporation. The inconvenience of a

---

* Even in the humanities, there is a trend to second-hand knowledge. In many college bookstores you will find more books *about* Shakespeare's plays, by obscure professors, than the plays themselves.

temporary shutdown is justified as the price of enhanced future productivity.

If these arrangements are incompatible with your mission we will try to accommodate you with limited access. In this event, call the Director of Security and make arrangements. Only the Northwest doors, facing on Grokum street, will be open. They will be manned throughout the period by a uniformed attendant.

JD/bss.

This is a fairly mild example, written off the top of my head. It does show some characteristics of businessese: it is wordy, shows a love of long words, contains gratuitous information, and boosts the company. A reasonable translation is:

The office will be closed this weekend from Friday night to Tuesday morning. If you *must* get in, call me.

Winston Churchill used to request a *one-page* report on, for example, the situation in the Middle East. This would be impossible in businessese.

Spoken businessese (used in conferences) is more colorful than the written version, as it uses more invented words, vogue words, and catch phrases. There is a strong tendency to mutate existing words by adding endings: "-ize," "-ed," "-ly." "Ize" is used to make a new action verb from a noun—typical examples, "computerize" and "jumboize." The closing statement of a conference could be, "I don't think we can concretize this concept today. I suggest we tablize it until our next meeting and try to finalize it then." "Ed" is also used to make verbs, as in "we jumboed into Dallas." "Ly" is the favorite. There is something irresistible about turning a correct adjective into an incorrect adverb: "firstly," "secondly," and, most importantly, "importantly." If kids still play the old street game of Kick the Can, they probably yell, "Readily or not, here I come!"

Vogue words have a strong businesslike sound: concept, implement, promote, terminate. Possibly the favorites today are "total" and "totally." To be committed is good; to be totally committed is better. There is nothing wishy-washy about a proposition that is totally unique. Catch phrases come and go. They might add welcome variety to conversation if the current ones weren't used *ad nauseam*. The latest batch has a pseudo-scientific flavor (for which we, possibly unfairly, blame the computer people): "at this point in time," "the current state of the art," even the unnecessary use of the impersonal pronoun "one," as favored by the academic community. ("One loves one's baby, One's baby loves one.")

The use of businessese increases paperwork and impedes communication. Business has enough inherent inefficiency without being conducted in a confusing language.

The Humanities

If a businessman could confine his work to the manufacture of (say) trucks and the selling of them on the domestic market, he wouldn't need to know any history or political science. Such a primitive state no longer exists. Even if he does not export his products, he must fight imports; whether he likes it or not, government is a partner in the enterprise. He would be more tolerant of, or at least better able to defend himself against, his own and other governments if he knew something of their problems and history. With the increasing responsibility of business leaders to spend public money at home and abroad, they owe it to the taxpayers to know something about the people they serve.

Foreign businessmen are apt to place a higher value on things cultural than we do, and they may prefer to do business with people who share their interests. An Arab expects to make friends with a man *before* he does business with him. If the only subject a man can talk about fluently is business, he is going to have a tough time getting started.

APPENDIX I

A Sample Case: Changing Values

This sample is not from the Harvard files. It does at least show the character of a case: dialog format, statement of a problem, fair presentation of different approaches. A good case should leave the readers with the information and inclination to continue the debate.

The scene is a business office. It belongs to Norman Miles, chief accountant, middle-aged. He is sitting behind his desk. A cadaverous-looking middle-aged man, Harry Reed, manager of data processing and a friend of Miles, enters.

Harry: What's the matter, Norman? If you tell me the computer goofed, I'll scream. (He sits down.)

Norman: No, Harry. Strange as it seems, I just want your questionable advice. I have a problem.

Harry: Well, this is a nice change. What's the scoop?

Norman: I asked Dave Foster from personnel—employee relations, that is—to join us. This is a personnel problem.

Harry: Kiss of death! Look, I've got a book overdue at the library. (He makes a motion to leave, but as he does, Mr. Foster enters. He is obviously a "bright young man.")

Norman: Come in, Dave, we need your advice. Also, keep an eye on Harry. He is trying to chicken out. (He gets up and rather pointedly closes the door.) This thing is kind of unusual. I'd like you guys to keep it quiet. I particularly don't want it to get higher in the organization.

Dave: No sweat.

Harry: That book is way overdue!

Norman: Well, here it is. One of the girls in my department has been selling marijuana to the other employees.

Harry: This makes my day. How did you find out?

Norman: It's kind of embarrassing, really. My daughter came here to meet me for lunch one day last week, and when she came into my office, she was laughing like a young idiot. She said, "Daddy, did you know your people are smoking pot?" I thought she was kidding—asked her how she knew. She said the bull pen smelled like a dorm before finals, and then she said what got to me: "You are always lecturing us, Daddy, and you don't even know what it smells like." She thought it was funny!

Harry (interested): What does it smell like?

Dave: Sort of sweet.

Norman (continues): I got one of my men, a clerk, to check it out on the QT. It seems one of the girls is selling the stuff.

Harry: Fire her! Now can I go, Daddy?

Dave: Wait a minute! Is she black?

Norman: Oh yes.

Dave: Well, don't do anything rash. Can you prove the case?

Norman: I don't know, it's difficult. That is why I wanted you here.

Dave (leans back and makes a small tepee with his fingers): Check this scenario. You fire the girl, she sues us under Fair Employment. You lose the case, the company loses a lot of money, and our management looks slightly ridiculous.

Harry: Our management *is* slightly ridiculous.

Dave (continues): You know, from a legal point of view, you should call in the police. Let them handle it. There is a law against selling pot.

Norman: I was afraid you'd say that. Great publicity for the company! We'd wind up on the front page.

Dave: I just said that is what you *should* do.

Norman (doubtfully): I suppose I could discipline her. . . .

Harry: A real brilliant textbook solution. Daddy Miles is going to scare hell out of a black girl who undoubtedly grew up in a tougher situation than we can imagine. She probably actually thinks she is doing the other girls a favor. How do you "discipline," anyway? We gave up flogging some time ago.

Norman: I guess it wouldn't work. (He thinks.) Is there a *company* rule against selling on company time?

Harry: Lord no! Dad, do you realize how much stuff is moved around here? Lottery tickets, Girl Scout cookies, Avon products, you name it. I wouldn't be surprised if they were selling their bodies.

Dave: That does give me an idea, though. Employee relations could put out a strong memorandum against all selling on company property. Then she would be breaking our rules.

Harry: A typical cowardly company solution. I say fire the wench, or call in the cops.

Since there is no correct solution to a case, the reader is on his own. I have tried this example on groups of friends. It invoked positions ranging from bringing back flogging to doing nothing at all. Such is the instinctive loyalty of the upper middle class that nobody put the finger on the one I consider the real culprit: Daddy Miles, who didn't know what was going on in his own department.

APPENDIX II

Business School Curriculum

The following course list is taken from the 1977 announcements of the University of Chicago Graduate School of Business. It shows the richness of the curriculum in a good business school. In addition to the courses listed here, the catalog mentions more than a dozen seminars and workshops.

Microeconomics
Applied Microeconomic Analysis I & II
Macroeconomics
Industrial Organization
The Economics of Regulation
International Commercial Policy
The Public Control of Economic Activity
The Economics of Public Management
Managerial Accounting I & II
Accounting Managerial Decision Making
Accounting for Income Determinants and Interpretation
Statistics
Statistical Inference and Decision I & II
Applied Business Forecasting
Introduction to Econometrics
Applied Econometrics I & II
Financial Management
Money and Banking
Investment
Corporation Finance
International Financial Policy
Applications of Financial Theory
Financial Markets and Institutions I & II

Selected Topics in Investments
Public Finance
Introduction to Industrial Relations
Management, Unions, and Collective Bargaining
Wage Determination and Labor Market Analysis
Policies and Problems in Personnel Management
The Government and Industrial Relations
Industrial Relations and Public Management
Industrial Relations and International Business
Special Topics in Industrial Relations
Market Organization and Price Policies
Marketing Research for Marketing Managers
Market Communication
Industrial Marketing
Marketing Strategy: Analytic Approaches
Forecasting Consumer Markets
Consumer Behavior
Special Topics in Marketing Management

Business Policies/INTOP
Development of New Businesses
Production Management
Mathematical Models for Production Management I & II
Introduction to Computers and Programming
Mathematics for Business Analysis
Introduction to Management Science
Linear Algebra for Business Applications
Digital Computers and Applications
Formal Models in Business I & II
Information Structures
Digital System Simulation
Computer Systems
Managerial Systems Analysis
Law and Business
Public Policies Toward Business
Legal Aspects of International Investment and Finance
Health Services Organization and Management
Introduction to the Health Services System
Sociology of Health and Illness
Public Policy in Health Care
Medical Economics
Behavioral Decision Making
Cognitive Models of Judgment
Risky Decision Making
Small-Group Processes
Work Motivation and Performance
Organizational Structure and Process
Group Decision Making

Behavioral Aspects of Public Management
Job Stress, Health, and Performance
Special Topics in Behavioral Science
Special Topics in Microeconomics
Macroeconomic Analysis and Forecasting
Public Financial Management
Urban Economics
The Economic Analysis of Urban Policies
Federal Income Taxation
Audits by Public Accountants
Income Taxes and Management Decisions
Accounting for Diverse Equities
Readings in Accounting Theory
Statistical Inference and Decision
Applied Multivariate Analysis
Sample Surveys
Bayesian Inference in Econometrics
Time-Series Analysis for Forecasting and Model Building
Econometrics I & II
Special Topics in Econometrics
Analysis of Financial Statements
Theory of Financial Decisions
The Economics of Foreign Investment
Theory of Financial Decisions III
Seminar: Management, Unions, and Collective Bargaining
Wage Determination and Labor Market Analysis II
Organization Improvement and Management Development

Seminar: The Government and Industrial Relations

Advanced Marketing Management

Marketing Research Methodology I & II

Quantitative Models in Marketing

Marketing for Nonprofit Organizations

Seminar: Retail Management

Policy Problems of Public and Nonprofit Institutions

The Firm in International Business

Seminar: Small-Business Problems

Special Topics in Business Policy

Theory of Scheduling

Extensions of Linear Programming

Nonlinear Programming I & II

Mathematical Inventory Theory

Selected Topics in Management Science

Introduction to Queuing Theory

Integer Programming and Network Flow

Information Systems Management

Resource Management in

Hospitals

Hospital Management Policies

Organization and Delivery of Physicians' Services

Hospital Administration Practicum

Health Care Organizations and Institutions

Quantitative Methods in International Economics

Data Analysis

Statistics and Public Decision Making

Seminar: Advanced Topics in Banking

Seminar: Conflict Resolution

Advanced Topics in Management Science I, II, III

Contemporary Questions of Public Policy and Health Services

Demography of Health and Illness

Regulation of the Health Industry

The Financial Environment of Hospitals

Evaluation Problems and Techniques in Health Service

Individual Study in Business

12

PEOPLE

PEOPLE ENTER the American business world, or any new world, carrying a lot of different psychological baggage. Their social, ethnic, economic, and cultural backgrounds are about as diverse as is possible in a communicating society; training, religious beliefs, and values are dissimilar. Time served in the business world tends to moderate these differences and to create what has been called the "Organization Man"*—the identifiable businessman.

The transformation of people into business managers is a proper study for anthropologists and psychologists, but this subject has been largely neglected by them. Anthropologists prefer to spend their time in real, rather than business, jungles. Recently, an anthropologist and psychologist, Michael Maccoby, did turn from studying Mexican villagers to American managers and published his findings in a book, *The Gamesman.*† His conclusion was that business managers are best classified into four identifiable personal-

* William H. Whyte, Jr., *The Organization Man*, New York: Simon & Schuster, 1956.
† New York: Simon & Schuster, 1976.

ity types, which he calls the Craftsman, the Jungle Fighter, the Company Man, and the Gamesman. We have no argument with the conclusions of his very readable book. We accept his four types but add one more on the basis of observation and experience rather than of psychoanalytical tests.

The methods of psychoanalysis are embarrassing to a layman. Maccoby and his helpers relied heavily on Rorschach tests and on dream symbolism. To be expected to tell a stranger what one sees in an ink blot and to describe one's dreams seems like an invasion of privacy. (A completely honest answer—"Looks like a dirty old ink blot to me"—would probably call for a straitjacket.) In any event, all but two of the 250 managers approached were willing to submit to this type of inquisition and also to fill out a long questionnaire. From analysis of these test results, Maccoby defined his four proto-type character, or personality, types.

We are not only concerned with the *personality* of a businessman; we are also interested in his *image*, which involves behavior and communications. We want to identify characteristic behavior patterns, particularly in the confrontation situation in business conferences. Everyday supervisor–subordinate confrontations have already been discussed. Off-duty behavior and social conventions are subjects of a later chapter.

THE MACCOBY CLASSIFICATION

Few businessmen are pure examples of the Maccoby character types; in fact, some seem to change under different conditions. His definitions are clever enough, and real enough, that it usually is possible to classify an associate (or oneself) as being predominantly of one class or another. The following description of the Maccoby personality types is not definitive. It is a layman's interpretation of what a psychoanalyst is trying to tell us. To do more would be improper, like practicing medicine without a Mercedes. If the reader is sufficiently interested, he should consult the original reference.

Personality is what a person *is*; he is stuck with it. Even psychologists cannot change a person's personality. They can teach him to live with what he is; they can change his behavior, but not his personality. If the man you know as a genial, easygoing guy is really a Jungle Fighter in disguise, he is going to lie awake nights working up an enemies list.

The Craftsman

The Craftsman takes pride in the quality of his work; traditional examples are builders, farmers, and artisans. The business Craftsman inherits the values of a long line of self-employed Americans who opened the West, ground corn, made farm equipment, and built furniture—men who took pride in work itself and in a job well done. The businessman-Craftsman no longer makes horseshoes; he assembles income statements, builds buildings, conducts research. He likes working for a large company because it takes care of him and gives him the opportunity to pursue his specialty. His first priority is his work, not the company; he would say "I am a physicist" rather than "I am a manager in the Gulf research department."

Of all the Maccoby personality types, the Craftsman is probably best adjusted to modern business life. As long as he gets his main satisfaction from work well done, he has it in his own hands to fulfill himself. He does not live in the competitive environment of the Jungle Fighter or the Gamesman or in the slightly neurotic world of the Company Man. Being content and not demanding, he is apt to be easy to get along with and likely to be popular with other employees. Secure in his own competence, he is willing to help his subordinates.

The private life of the typical Craftsman is tranquil, even boring by other standards. Not a competitive person, he is less concerned with outdoing his neighbors than with building a really good barbecue pit. People take advantage of him; he fixes the neighbor's lawn mowers, serves on the vestry at church, and coaches Little League. Ideologically he is as likely to be liberal as conservative. Since he never expects to be rich, he won't feel cheated if he never is.

Business needs Craftsmen; somebody has to do something right. On the other hand, a company whose managers were all Craftsmen would have difficulty competing in a competitive society. The density of Craftsmen is highest in the line functions, although there will be some in exacting staff positions such as accounting and management science. If you want someone to do a job for you, from fixing the air conditioner to doing your income tax, get a Craftsman.

The Jungle Fighter

The Jungle Fighter sees the business world as a battleground—"Dog eat dog" and "Every man for himself." He sees it as an adult version of the childhood game of "King of the Hill." He expects every man's hand to be against him, not for any personal reason (he is not necessarily paranoid), but because he assumes that the other actors in the arena play by the same rules. The object is to gain power, to get ahead by any (legal?) means. If this involves stabbing an ostensible friend in the back, so be it; he should have kept himself covered.

This sketch sounds harsh, but it is not meant to be derogatory. The mark of the Jungle Fighter is stamped on American business history by the robber barons of the post–Civil War era and by the moguls who built the giant (now largely paternalistic) corporations of today.* The cardinal sin of the Jungle Fighter is not that he is ruthless and self-seeking but that he is now an anachronism. There isn't much room for him in today's business. He may move well for a while if he plays his cards right, but in most companies he will run into something he cannot fight: the fact that he "is not the sort of person we want on the management team." A Jungle Fighter needs enemies; if he doesn't have them, he will invent them. In the face of organized complacency he is helpless.

There is no really happy place for a Jungle Fighter in most companies. For his own good (he can't stand failure) he should go into a highly competitive, Baseball-type business such as advertising where he will meet foemen worthy of his steel, or he should set up his own business or go into politics (and stay out of jail.).

The Company Man

The prototype Company Man is a company man: he is loyal to the company, and, just as important, he expects the company to do

* Stewart H. Holbrook, *The Age of the Moguls*, New York: Doubleday, 1954.

the right thing by him. He is neither venturesome nor brilliant, but he does his job according to the rules (job description). The more rules, the better. He wants to work in an Army type of organization, where promotion is based on loyalty and on time in grade. Bureaucracy, business or government, is his natural environment. He is conservative in deportment and politics. A majority of businessmen *are* Company Men, and they set the popular image of the businessman.

The Company Man personality is needed by the corporation as a moderating factor to counter the occasional excesses of the Gamesman and the Jungle Fighter and to attend to the messy details the Craftsman is not interested in. It is the Company Man who arranges the compromises that are necessary to keep management from falling apart. The loyalty and reliability of the Company Man managers also ensure that the housekeeping and bureaucratic chores will be properly done.

The loyalty of a Company Man to his company is a bit like the loyalty of a rather plain wife to a handsome and successful husband. By making one fateful, fortunate decision—to join the company (to get married)—he assured himself a comfortable, improving life. If he doesn't rock the boat and "keeps his nose clean," he will steadily move up the corporate ladder—not to the top, but high enough. The rewards are out of all proportion to his usually modest contribution.

If loyalty is an expression of gratitude, this is to his credit—it is much more seemly than the attitude of the Jungle Fighter or the Gamesman, who assume that they are doing the company a favor. As the plain but loyal wife has bad moments when she questions her husband's loyalty, so the Company Man has his occasional fears. Will the company continue to play fair according to his cherished rules? When a person's career or life depends on an outside agency, it can create tensions.

Maccoby takes a dim view of Company Men. His first example of the breed is of a failure. The man had three goals: to be a vice president, to have a good relationship with his wife, and to become a warm human being (whatever that means). The wife goal depended on promotion; he (possibly rightly) assumed that she would despise him if he didn't become a vice president. When the company didn't come through for him, in spite of his loyal work, he cracked and wound up in the hands of a therapist, which probably added poverty to his other problems.

To balance the picture, Maccoby discusses a successful Company Man who was competent, had done valuable work for the company, and had reached a high executive position. *But* he developed psychosomatic symptoms: depression, anxiety, restlessness, obsessive doubt, back troubles, and serious gastrointestinal difficulties. This is success? Not all Company Men get ulcers.

The Gamesman

The Gamesman is Maccoby's proudest creation—the business leader of today and tomorrow. The Gamesman is intelligent, creative, courteous, kind, a great guy. Above all, he is willing to take risks and play the business game to win. He is the Dink Stover of the Harvard Business School.

The Gamesman is ambitious, but unlike the Company Man, who is content with promotion based on loyalty and service, he is eager to make it on his own merits, measured by how well he plays the business game. The elements of this game are money, people, and ideas rather than the physical constructs of the Craftsman. The Jungle Fighter needs enemies; the Gamesman needs competition, because competition defines the game. The competition may be other employees, business rivals, and, always, the government. Every game is different, but the goals and the winners are usually clearly defined.

The true Gamesman gets his satisfaction from contributing ideas (plays) to the game, from controlling the action, and most of all from winning. He can work alone, but, unlike the Jungle Fighter, who is a loner, he is more effective working on a team which can develop strategy and devise a "game plan." To play and to win is more important than the personal fortune and titles which will follow.

Maccoby says that to be successful in today's technological business world, a company must have Gamesmen in key management positions. This is equivalent to saying that the top management team must operate with a Baseball philosophy and its members should be free of administrative details. The Gamesman at the top is then in his element. The Gamesman on the way up, on the other hand, may be a bit of a misfit. At lower levels of the company the prime requisites have to be quality of work (Craftsmen), attention to detail (Company Men), and cost-consciousness. For the lower-level Gamesman, the only game in town may not amount to much. The threat to a Gamesman's emotional well-being is that he may lose too many games; for him, loss is humiliation. He may not be as good a player as he thinks he is.

ANOTHER PERSONALITY TYPE

There is at least one more personality type found in the business world that Maccoby did not catalog: the Son of a Bitch. We chose the name not to shock but because it is the term commonly used, not always unkindly, to describe such a person: "Joe is a good old boy, but he must be a son of a bitch to work for." In order to keep this text from looking like that of a modern novel we will use the acronym SOB to refer to this personality type.

The SOB wants power, not for its own sake as the Jungle Fighter does, but to establish a secure and well-defined base from which he can bully people, both his own employees and outsiders such as salesmen. He may be satisfied with a modest operation as long as he is the boss; on the other hand, he may be in a high, responsible position. Nonbusiness organizations provide familiar examples of this personality type: the government clerk who dispenses forms, the unfriendly worker in the post office. The Army is infamous for providing examples at all ranks. The memory of his first sergeant or supply sergeant will serve as a good example for the former serviceman. The SOB is jealous of his* power; he does not want to share it and so is reluctant to instruct his subordinates or to delegate authority.

* We use the masculine pronoun, but this is not always appropriate. I still remember the mess officer looking at her watch and closing the hospital dining-room door as I approached in my wheelchair. She qualified.

While the SOB can be found at all levels in business, he is most likely to be head of an isolated or independent department such as transportation or reproduction or manager of an outlying district. He knows the rules, he knows exactly what he can get away with, and he isn't going to let anyone else get away with anything. "The bastard wanted first-class tickets to Baltimore. For Christ's sake, who the hell does he think he is?" (SOBs tend to use strong language).

All of this is very negative, but there is a positive side to the SOB as a business manager. He may even be indispensable in some companies. The successful, or even moderately successful, SOB is extremely competent. He has to be; he isn't selling charm. ("I don't know how Mace does it, but we've got to have the best reproduction department in the industry.") He is cost-conscious for the simple reason that he considers his people to be underworked and overpaid ("The Los Angeles office always has the lowest unit costs.") He may bully his people, but he will stick up for them and may even generate *esprit de corps*.

SOBs are natural for certain types of jobs such as purchasing agents—no salesman is going to sweet-talk *him*—and trouble shooting. If major surgery is indicated in a corporate operation, send an SOB as hatchet man. There may well be at least one SOB on the top management team. If it were composed only of Gamesmen concerned with their own careers and with winning the game and of Company Men trying to preserve the status quo, there would be no one at the top whose "property it is" to cut costs, to represent the shareholders, and to prevent the staff from taking over.

Maccoby didn't identify the SOB. This is not surprising, since most of his research involved managers in two large, modern, highly technical corporations and he analyzed only those managers who were willing to cooperate. Such go-go companies are not as good breeding grounds for SOBs, at least in managerial positions, as are older, more rigid organizations. It is unlikely that any SOB would permit himself to be psychoanalyzed or would fill out the questionnaires; he would consider it damn foolishness. If Maccoby *did* find this personality type, he could not have reported it anyway if he followed his own rules. He used only type names that were acceptable to the people typed. Any SOB who would admit to being a son of a bitch belongs in a higher league.

These are five character types found in business. With the possible exception of the Jungle Fighter, they are all needed. In fact, they have to monitor each other (John Kenneth Galbraith's counteracting power?). A company without Gamesmen in top management would probably lack the verve to compete in today's business world. A management of nothing *but* Gamesmen might throw the dice too often—to them it means losing a game, whereas to the Company Man it means losing his way of life. There are even times when the Craftsman needs to be heard. It must have been Gamesmen who decided that what the American public wanted in automobiles was power, chromium, and tail fins; it is the Craftsmen who are going to have to do the solid engineering to compete with foreign imports.

BEHAVIOR TYPES

Whereas personality is innate, behavior is to some extent assumed; it is the part we play for our fellows. If you analyze closely enough, there must be almost as many behavior types as there are people, but there are some recognizable general patterns that are usually found in the business world.

The Stuffed Shirt is a famous character. Actually, this is a defensive and protective behavior role: to defend against inconvenient intimacy and to protect the status of position. The difficulty of Stuffedshirtmanship* is that it is hard to be consistent; it is easy to be pompous toward a secretary but difficult and inadvisable when dealing with equals or with superiors. The Company Man, particularly the frustrated Company Man, may use this pattern to protect his ego. The SOB is more likely to adopt a Hard-boiled Egg or Old Campaigner approach. Both of these designations are self-

---

* A neologism following the tradition of Stephen Potter, introduced in *Gamesmanship*. There is a pertinent chapter in his later book *One-Upmanship*, called "Businessmanship." (New York: Holt, Rinehart & Winston, 1952.)

explanatory. Secure managers, top management particularly, don't need to be Stuffed Shirts.

The Egghead title is as often thrust on its unwilling subject as it is cultivated. Some businessmen, particularly those with higher degrees from lesser universities, encourage the designation; the ambitious person will avoid it. Non-eggheads use the term in a patronizing sense that implies that the person, though smart enough, isn't very practical. To label a man an Egghead is to limit his effectiveness. He is listened to politely, even respectfully, but nobody really takes him seriously. If a smart young economist (say) has the disturbing habit of disagreeing with his betters and of usually being right, it is easy to emasculate him by marking him as an Egghead.

The safest, and most common, behavior pattern, is that of the Cautious Man. The Cautious Man behaves correctly, he carefully observes the mores and taboos of the business world, he is friendly and polite, and, above all, he tries never to be put in a position where he has to make a decision. This is a negative posture that the Gamesman or the Jungle Fighter is psychologically incapable of assuming. For most businessmen it is the best approach. The businessman has tenure—if he does his job and doesn't make waves, he can expect to get regular "merit" raises and promotions when jobs become vacant, just because he has seniority and nobody can think of anything against him. I have seen employees who based their whole careers on the policy of letting other people stick their necks out rise steadily through the ranks and eventually be knighted as hyphenated vice presidents for their loyal service.

Good Old Boys (and Gals)

A common, and very American, behavior pattern is the Good Old Boy. Actually this is a subpattern; a businessman may be a Hard-boiled Egg or a Cautious Man on company time and a Good Old Boy when he is out with the lads. I have even seen Eggheads grab their guns on the opening day of hunting season as enthusiastically as if there were a rumor that the establishment was trying to integrate the local high school.

The Good Old Boy is a man's man. He likes football better than baseball, poker better than bridge, hard liquor better than wine, and, of course, likes beer.* His politics are simple: "Throw the rascals out." He likes *things* better than ideas: cars, boats, CB radios. If his wife were to drag him on a cultural European trip, he would be more interested in his camera and in taking clear pictures than in the beauty of Salisbury cathedral. Actually, he would rather be home with his buddies.

He is a sports fan but not necessarily a connoisseur; he would almost as soon drink beer at a high school game as at a professional one. His really big sport items are hunting and fishing. He yearns for an earlier, simpler world where there was more room and men fought the elements. He doesn't necessarily want to commune with nature (he may do that too); he wants to kill little pieces of it. He loves guns. ("They'll have to pry my gun from my cold, dead hand.") On the subject of hunting he sounds like bad Hemingway (not Bad Hemingway, who plays center on the company basketball team).

The ultimate goal of many Good Old Boys is to get a ranch or farm for weekend use. This is such a status symbol among higher-level managers that land around cities like Dallas, Houston, or Kansas City, and even in "dude" country, is being bought up and is sprouting its brick-veneer split levels. This pushes up land values, much to the consternation of the natives.† In the Southwest at any rate, cattle is the thing; it is more *macho* to raise cattle than soybeans.

As a city boy I could never see anything noble about spending a weekend castrating cows (may have something wrong there), but there is. Not just any kind of cow will do; they must be the right kind of cows—White Face, Angus, Brahma, Charlerois, Hereford. Having a ranch is good for the soul and for the kids ("teaches them to do a day's work"); it is also a good investment. Following the sound policy of keeping the eye on the balance sheet and the tax

* Billy Carter is everybody's Good Old Boy. He may belong to a subset of the genre: the Smart Good Old Boy.
† This is not a contradiction. Farmers and ranchers, real farmers and ranchers, prefer land to money. If the price of land goes beyond its economic value (rent), the farm family must sell some of it in estate settlements.

collector rather than on the income statement, part-time ranching is about the best thing going.

The Good Old Boy's attitude toward women is simple but double-valued. On the one hand he wants women to be pioneer wives—to keep house, to raise children, to help their husbands in their struggle up the corporate ladder. To such women he is polite and respectful. On the other hand he likes women who are young, about nineteen, who are pretty, obviously unmarried, have big breasts, and wear tight clothes. Take a line through the Dallas Cowboys cheerleaders. To such women he may not be as polite or respectful. He is a natural male chauvinist: he just can't see what women have to complain about.

How do the wives of Good Old Boys react? Some of them try to civilize their men; they drag them off to concerts, museums, and other cultural diversions. Some husbands even enjoy this change and become only part-time Good Old Boys. Very few will object as long as the little woman lets them off the hook occasionally to play poker or go hunting with the boys. Other wives join the act, poker games, hunting trips, and all; they become Good Old Gals.

You can spot a Good Old Gal at a party. She has an outdoorsy look, often skirt and blouse and a practical hairdo. The Southwestern version wears a neckerchief (from Neiman's) knotted under one ear in a style made popular by the late Judge Roy Bean. She greets you with a handshake that approaches the pain threshold and has a hearty laugh that sends the domestic pets scurrying for cover. She is glad you could come and is having a wonderful time, but somehow she gives the impression that she would really rather be out on the range driving a pickup truck or shoveling manure—the right kind of manure.

I like Good Old Boys as long as the density isn't too high. They are friendly, are fast with a drink, are good husbands, neighbors, and churchmen, and are patriotic in a flag-waving sort of way. Good Old Boys fight our country's battles. They are morally honest; they not only enjoy but believe in their philosophy of life. I have some reservation about Good Old Gals. I don't mind—in fact, I rather like—their inclination to freeze in duck blinds or to drive hot dusty tractors, but I don't think it quite fair for them to automatically accept their husbands' values, including male chauvinism. They do accept it; some even imply that their man might beat the stuffing out of them if they didn't (from the matchups I've seen I wouldn't give odds). It doesn't seem fair to their sisters, who are trying to make it in what is still pretty much of a man's world, to repeat their husband's line, "I don't see what women have to complain about," when their own future was secured back in the sophomore year of college. What they really mean is, "I don't see what women like me have to complain about"—which isn't the same thing at all.

CONFERENCE BEHAVIOR

Every businessman plays three roles: as a partner in everyday confrontation situations between equals and between higher- and lower-ranking people, as a member of business social groups, and as a participant in business meetings or conferences. All roles are important, and to play any one poorly is a liability, but conference behavior may be the most critical. Perhaps this is why the Harvard case method, which uses a conference format, has been so successful in training businessmen.

Most business decisions are made on the basis of prior conference activity (the exceptions are emergency on-the-spot decisions and those made at the top by a dominant leader). The usual sequence is: problem identified; conference to analyze it and to assign tasks to working parties; conference to evaluate the results of studies; recommendations; and, finally, a decision made at a higher level (often in another conference). This is the straightforward routine; usually there is a good deal of feedback and extra conferences before a recommendation is made.

Conferences which are a part of this decision-making program may be called Type I conferences; they have a well-defined goal. Most meetings, which may be called Type II, do not have this sort of orientation; they are concerned with progress reporting, budgeting, planning, and so forth. A lot of Type II conferences are high-level make-work activities. It is a good idea to decide early in the proceedings if a meeting is important or not—there is no point in taking a strong position in an unimportant conference. It is also a good idea to *act* as though every conference is critical; it may turn out to be important after all, and, anyway, the man who called it thinks it is.

In any meeting there is a leader, the one who called it, and the others—the members. There are two possible stances for a member or a leader to take: active or passive. The active member has ideas; he presents them and defends his positions. The passive member is a listener; he doesn't present any ideas of his own, and he doesn't really knock anybody else's proposals. He doesn't really support any proposals either. He becomes a master of the equivocal statement, "There is a lot in what you say, but I think we ought to look at some other aspects of the problem," or, "You certainly have expressed yourself well on this point and given us all something to think about."

For conference members, the passive position is much better. Consider the odds. If you take an active position and win—sell the concept, have it implemented, and it is a success—the chances are that the leader will take credit for it. At best, you have to share the glory with all the other conference members. If an activist fails—if he doesn't sell his good idea or if he gets the committee to make the wrong decision—he takes the blame alone. Winning is a shared honor, losing is lonely. The pacifist has it both ways. During the course of discussion he has probably both mildly supported and mildly opposed every proposal; whatever happens, a convenient memory will put him in a winning position. If you *have* to provide positive input to the debate—a special report or study, for example—make it factual and statistical and don't editorialize. Activists may even get the reputation for being troublemakers, in which case they will not be invited to many conferences.

The leader should be active or passive depending on his goal. If he has called a meeting only to legitimize a prior decision, he can come on strong. Unless he is a sadist and likes to watch people make fools of themselves, he should, in such cases, tip his hand. "I think we ought to drill here, don't you?" If he doesn't know what he wants to do and really wants input, he should adopt a passive position and encourage ideas from the members. Again, it is nice to clue the people. "This is a brainstorming session, men. I'd like to get your honest opinions." Like the leader of a case study discussion he refrains from taking sides. Somebody might come up with a good idea.

With the obvious advantages of passive meeting behavior, it might seem that most meetings would resolve into a situation where the members sit around looking at each other and waiting for someone to make a move, like two counterpunchers waiting for the other to throw a punch. This does not happen; the members do mix it up. Any Gamesmen or Jungle Fighters in the group have to get in the act. Craftsmen will get aroused if an unworkmanlike proposal is made. Even the Company Man will get involved if his territory is threatened. A lot of people just can't sit still in a conference, even though they know better. They feel they have to give the company the benefit of their knowledge and opinions. Be a good conference man if you can. Be an activist when it would be cowardly to be passive. Above all, keep your cool.

13

BENEFITS, PERQUISITES, AND STATUS SYMBOLS

Man shall not live by bread alone
Matthew 4:4

THERE IS MORE to the business world than take-home pay. Economists have long maundered over the concept of "psychic income," as a passing acknowledgment that there are values in this world that are not preceded by dollar signs. The concept is dear to capitalists and to commissars who take the position that an Order of Lenin (with a kiss on each cheek) is as rewarding to the worker as is an incentive bonus in our society. The English do it better. A knighthood has more psychic value than anything we or the Russians have to offer. Even the commissars are coming to the view that a dollar (or ruble) sign had better be involved in an award or it will have little effect. Nobel prizes include walking-around money.

In this chapter we are concerned with employee remuneration

beyond simple salary. Most of these extras carry dollar signs, some do not. We work our way from the familiar to the unfamiliar: from fringe benefits to executive compensation to mild larceny to psychological perquisites. Many of these benefits are so familiar that we can almost take them as read; others are not well known or understood outside the business community and need some explanation. The underlying question to be answered is, "Why do corporations resort to such strange devices to reward their people rather than just paying them more money?" It is an interesting story.

FRINGE BENEFITS

We define fringe benefits as those extras which are given to *all* employees of a large corporation. Most of these might be called "general" fringes, because they are not confined to the business community. There are a few "special" fringes which are peculiar to the business world and which are often under attack by outsiders.

Fringe benefits today are taken for granted, so much so that we have forgotten the struggles to institute them, their reasons for being, and their impact on society. Few employees appreciate how much these things cost their company. Fringe benefits in a typical company amount to 25 to 30 percent of payroll costs. A $15,000-a-year person costs the company about $20,000. The "fringe" has become a "zone."

Fringe benefits in preference to straight salary were fought for by union members and other employees because they didn't trust themselves to handle their own money. There are few normal fringe benefits, except vacations, which cannot be bought on the open market (tax advantages and inflation protection became apparent only later). The demands came from a craving for security. Once an employee signed up, the company or the government (Big Brother) would protect him against disaster and his own foolishness. Governments were quick to follow the business lead. In fact, normal fringe benefits for government workers are often better than those of business—civil service workers get sick time off whether they are sick or not.

Fringe benefits divide our society into two parts: those that have them and those that don't. The corporate or government worker is sheltered and protected. The small-business man, the self-employed craftsman, farmer, writer, or plumber are not. These people have to pay for their own insurance, hospitalization, and retirement annuity out of income. Some of them, of course, do very well (most do not), but they don't have the security of the corporate or government worker. We are divided into a society of "innies" and "outies."

The cost of security fringes has a heavy impact on nongovernment, nonbusiness organizations which have to compete for competent workers. Churches, private colleges, service organizations such as the Girl Scouts or the YMCA may barely be able to meet going salary rates; they may founder on the rock of fringe benefit costs. Let us take a look at some of the more common fringe benefits.

The retirement plan is the best-known fringe benefit. All big companies have one, although the details vary. Under the new law the employee even carries his accumulated benefits from one company to another; this is called "vesting."

If the employee makes the entire contribution to his retirement fund, there is no benefit except protecting the employee against his own thoughtlessness. Increasingly, employers pay part or all of the annuity costs. A related fringe is Social Security. Currently the employer pays half the contributions to this plan, although there is continuing pressure to increase his share.

Social Security, as it has been manipulated by the social tinkerers in Washington, is now the world's greatest con game. Each generation places a larger and larger burden on its successor generation so that, sooner or later, the whole thing must collapse under its own weight. In the meantime it is a fringe benefit.

Life insurance is closely related to retirement. It takes care of those cases where the employee doesn't make it to retirement. Companies pay all or part of the premiums. Security is thus extended even to the next generation. When the level of insurance gets above a certain point, the IRS (killjoy) takes a dim view and requires that a portion of the company contribution be treated as taxable income.

The most reassuring benefit for the average employee is medical insurance. He knows that without it he is living dangerously. If he has a serious sickness, the doctors and hospitals will cheerfully bleed him white while restoring him to health (not an easy thing to do). Modern corporate packages cover doctors' fees, hospitalization, dental work, and pregnancy. Even Bubba's teeth braces are covered. Companies pay most of the premium cost. Who needs socialized medicine? The outies do, and don't you forget it.

Paid vacations are an important fringe benefit which most people today take as a *right* rather than a privilege. Not too many years ago such a benefit was rare. Today the employee's discretionary vacation increases with service time from one week to four or five. Extra holidays such as San Jacinto Day and Patriots Day are getting more common. Some companies even give their employees their own birthdays off.

There are all sorts of other normal fringe benefits—corporate credit unions, travel expenses to and from work, company cars for certain kinds of jobs, and so on. The aim of all these is to protect the employee from unusual expense which would probably strain his precarious budget. A good example of the problems which sometimes arise in trying to meet this aim is the attempt to reimburse employee moving expenses.

Large companies want to be able to tell their people to pack up and move to a new location at a moment's notice, and they try to make the process as painless as possible. The employee and spouse usually fly to the new location, put up at a first-class hotel, hire a car, and have a week or so to find a new home—all at company expense. The mechanics of the move are covered: selling and buying expenses, the actual move, and temporary accommodations. Even new draperies may be thrown in. All this costs a lot of money, but the employee should be spared the extra expense; all he should have is the inconvenience of moving.

The IRS takes a different view of the whole movement (perhaps it considers it subversive) and considers the moving expense reimbursement as regular income for the mover. To counter, the company reimburses the employee for the extra tax on this "income," but *this* is also taxable, so the company must reimburse the tax on the tax, and so on ad infinitum. Without boring the reader with the algebra, the result is that a $2,400 move costs the company $4,000 and may elevate the poor mover into a higher income tax bracket.

The employee stock purchase plan (or savings or thrift plan, or whatever name it goes under) is a special or business benefit rather than a normal one. Its purpose is to encourage employees to save for the future and to build up a vested interest in company stock. It is also a tax break. The details of these plans vary from company to company. In some flexible plans the participant may say how his money is to be invested—in company stock, in a mutual fund, or in some other income-earning asset. In most plans the only investment allowed is company stock. The employee may invest up to a certain specified percent of his salary in the plan when he is eligible to join. For each dollar he puts in, the company adds more, usually ranging from 50 cents to a dollar, the amount being based on some service time formula.

Such plans are real cash benefits for employees, but they have delayed fuses, since the participant typically can't get his money (easily) until he leaves the plan or retires. He will probably forfeit the company contributions if he withdraws. If he stays in, on the other hand, principal and interest build up over the years and it is remarkable how much money even a relatively low-paid employee can pile up.

The beauty of these purchase plans is that they are tax shelters; income on the investment and the company contributions are not taxed until the employee retires, dies, or resigns (it is not quite that simple, but this is not a treatise on tax law). The money he would have paid out sooner in taxes is itself tax-sheltered. Eventually, the taxes are going to have to be paid, but at a lower rate— unless the employee makes the vulgar error of retiring with a high taxable income or new tax laws come along to hurt him.

Recently, the federal government has been questioning these plans—not the IRS, which is satisfied with its bite, but the sociologists, who worry about discrimination. Is the benefit fairly distributed over all employees, or does it favor the higher level, mostly WASP, people? Since joining the plan is voluntary, as it must be, there *is* a higher incidence of higher-paid members. Lower grades, particularly minority groups, don't think they can afford to join (it seems like throwing money away); they want their money now. If this is discrimination, it is a strange form.

Some fringe benefits are fun benefits. When a secretary finally has to take maternity leave, when someone retires or gets promoted, when 25-year-service pins or watches are handed out, when some brass from the parent company comes to town, it is customary to throw a party—technically known as a "fringe binge." Any minor corporate feast day provides an excuse. It is even proper to take the girls out to lunch during National Secretary's Week. These social gatherings run the gamut from a quiet luncheon where the girls drink "wine coolers" to something approaching a Babylonian orgy for more important occasions. The fringe binge offers opportunities to increase one's connections—or one's waistline.

The final fringe benefit doesn't show up on the payroll stub or on the company books, but it is probably the most expensive of all. It does more than anything to separate the innies from the outies of this world. This rather recent benefit is the implicit granting of tenure to all employees—the fact is that once a person has been working for a company for a relatively brief time, it is considered bad form to fire him.* Even SOBs, whose natural instinct is to boot out incompetents, are likely to transfer their problem children to some other department rather than fire them. Short of being caught making out in the stock room (which might not be enough reason at that) or criminal activity, it is almost impossible today to get rudely fired. This is particularly true at middle and lower levels; management can't afford to be quite so considerate of its top people.

Tenure is a concept that business has borrowed from the civil service, where it is called "job security"—a feature of the recent postal settlement. Business and government agencies seem to adopt

---

* People do get fired ("laid off" is the preferred term) when, for example, production lines are shut down or when an airframe company loses a government contract. The separations are not for incompetence, and the leavers are all eligible to be rehired. In the world of the businessman in staff jobs such firings are rare.

the worst aspects of each other's personnel policies.* All levels of government got so carried away over fringe benefits that many civil servants retire at more money than they ever made on the job. The taxpayer picks up the tab if he can; if he can't, we get a replay of the New York scenario.

EXECUTIVE COMPENSATION

Executive compensation, as it is now called, is different from fringe benefits in that it has a different goal. The goal of fringe benefits is security—cradle-to-grave security. This goal has been largely achieved by big corporations. There are many workers whose entry into the world was paid for by their fathers' company medical plan and whose burial will be paid for by their own company insurance. The goal of an executive compensation package is to allow top corporate managers to become wealthy men.

Wealth and high income are not the same thing. As we pointed out earlier, most take-home pay is spent (expenditures rise to meet income) even by highly paid people. Wealth consists of old money, assets safely socked away as certificates in vaults or as real estate. Executive compensation packages are designed to enable the recipients to accumulate old money, an estate, while they are working.

There are frequent articles in the *Harvard Business Review* comparing current actual executive compensation with what it was a generation ago. The conclusions are always that the old-timers were better off. The average reader, still drooling over the six- and seven-figure numbers, could hardly care less, but business is worried. In the good old days business leadership was *the* way to wealth. (There were a few exceptions, but the film stars kept pretty well to their own Hollywood playpen, and who could object to

* There seems to be a love–hate relationship, at least on the government side. It is a reasonable theory that the recent GSA scandals involving false contracts and kickbacks resulted from an attempt to copy business practice—a wrongheaded attempt since business, big business particularly, runs a straight game.

Babe Ruth?) Now the old executive suburbs of our cities are being invaded by a new elite: writers of trashy best-sellers, airline pilots, plaintiffs' lawyers, rectal surgeons, orthodontists, basketball players. Business fights back. The problem is to get important money in the hands of its leaders; the hazard is the tax collector; the mechanism is the executive compensation package.

Many forms of executive compensation are well documented, for instance in recent *HBR* articles. Some, such as interest-free (or low-interest) loans and deferred compensation, are too specialized for this discussion. We confine ourselves to the two important elements of most compensation packages: bonuses and stock options.

Bonuses

I must start by saying that I have a prejudice against bonuses. My father's company had a bonus system. In the Depression years it was a survival policy that enabled a company to underpay (but keep) its people. If by any chance the outfit made money during the year, it could make it up to them in the form of bonuses. They were (and most still are) handed out near Christmas (which may violate the spirit of the First Amendment). If Dad got a bonus, we had a good Christmas. If not, he consoled himself with bootleg whisky. (Dad could remember when bonuses were paid in hard money—$5 and $10 gold pieces, which were then turned in at the bank for real money!)

A lot of bonus money is handed out. In 1977 Ford paid $111 million, General Motors paid more, Chrysler paid none. There are two ways to handle the transfer of all this money. One is a sort of profit-sharing to executives. A fixed, known percentage goes with each high-ranking job. This is the method automobile companies use. The other way is a "merit" system, where bonuses are supposed to be a reward for superior work. In some companies this merit system is quite pervasive and extends down to middle management. In others it is a quiet little melon cutting by top management that most employees are not even aware of.

Since the actual transfer of bonus money has to be one of the most moving ceremonies in the business world, let us eavesdrop on a typical event.

Mr. Biggers enters his boss's office. The vice president is sitting behind his reasonably clean desk, on which there is a pregnant-looking brown envelope. He is trying to look as much like Santa Claus as possible (which is easy when you are handing out someone else's money). The vice president asks Mr. Biggers to sit down and then tells him what a fine job he has been doing, while Mr. Biggers tries to X-ray the envelope with his eyes. With the encomium over, the vice president smiles and hands the envelope to Mr. Biggers. "This is a reward for all that hard work last year, and I hope you earn another next year."

Etiquette demands that the envelope be opened casually. Mr. Biggers sees that he has been awarded a $10,000 bonus, $5,000 payable this year and $5,000 next, that $2,500 has been deducted for taxes, and that a check for $2,500 is enclosed. He thanks his boss nicely, rises, does an about-face, and leaves the room wondering how $10,000 can shrink to $2,500 so quickly (his wife has already redecorated the living room on speculation).

Back in his own office, Mr. Biggers reads the fine print. Next year's bonus is waived if he leaves the company other than by death or retirement—the "fur-lined mouse trap" at work. Twenty-five hundred dollars is not likely to keep Mr. Biggers in a dead-end job if something better turns up, but deferred bonuses (and options) can pile up and be a major deterrent to change.*

The administration of a merit bonus system is delicate. The idea is to reward only the high performers—the top 10 or 15 percent in their peer groups. In a well-run system, each supervisor ranks those below him, and these rankings are reviewed for consistency. In middle management, then, the job title is not as important as what your boss thinks of you. At top management no such problem exists, since all members are, by definition, outstanding. It has not been unusual for the chairman or CEO to set his own compensation or for a group of officers just below him to do the job. This sort of arrangement has led to criticism, much of it justified. Today, the executive compensation committee is usually staffed in the majority by outside directors in an effort to see that top man-

* See "Golden Handcuffs," *The Wall Street Journal,* August 31, 1978.

agement compensation has some relation to performance and going practice.

Stock Options

The stock option, or stock appreciation right, is the most common form of executive compensation. In its original form the stock option is simplicity itself: it is the right, or option, to buy a certain number of shares of company stock at a stated price at any time during a fixed period. If the price of the stock went up during this period, the optionee could buy his shares at the stated lower price, sell the shares on the open market, and take his profit as a capital gain. If the price goes down, the option expires unexercised and no one is better or worse off.

A company might seem to have the right to sell pieces of itself—shares—at any price it chooses. Years ago, options were granted at prices below their open market value. The feds quickly closed this loophole by ruling that the instant paper profit on such an option was ordinary taxable income. Most options today are issued at the market price at time of issue.

The next "reform" by the government was to rule that in order for the profit on a stock option to be taxed at the favorable capital-gains rate rather than as regular income, the optionee must hold the purchased stock for a certain period of time before selling the shares. This can put the employee who exercises a qualified option in a sticky position. He can sell his new shares immediately, take his profit, and pay taxes on it as regular income, or he can elect to sweat out the waiting period and take the risk that the price goes down and his profit evaporates. Because of this, and due to other, more subtle regulatory and tax restraints, companies are issuing more nonqualified options, which do not allow capital-gains treatment.* Let us take a look at a typical stock option transaction.

A rising young executive in the $50,000 range, with one kid in college, another soon to be there, a large mortgage, and a large bar bill at the country club, needs ready cash. He has a qualified option

* This is not a simple subject. Refer to a tax lawyer or accountant. See also Louis J. Brindisi, Jr., "Comeback for Restricted Stock Plans," *Harvard Business Review,* November–December 1977.

to buy 250 shares of his company's stock at 40, issued four years ago. The stock is now selling at 70, and his option expires next year. He would like to nail down his profit before it gets away; to do so he must cough up $10,000 cash on the barrelhead ($40 each for the 250 shares). Where does he get this kind of money? From the bank. He shows them his option, and they work out the details.

Now comes decision time. He can exercise the option, sell the shares, pay off the bank, and wind up with a $7,500 profit—taxable as ordinary income. The net, $3,750, will just about pay for one semester at an Ivy League college.

If he is a daring gambler, he would like to hold the shares until the profit is taxable at the lower (half) capital-gains rate. This means taking the chance that the price stays up and paying interest to the bank in the meantime. *If he can!* There is an untidy federal regulation that limits the amount of money a bank may lend for the purpose of buying stock. Unless the current price is far above the option price, he will not be able to buy and hold the shares as he would like. The executive's lot is not a simple one!

Many corporations now recognize that their younger managers have a cash flow problem (Kirchoff's law) and cannot exercise their options and hold out for capital gains. To meet this problem the stock appreciation right, or SAR, has been introduced.

The purpose of the SAR is to give the employee his profit without his having to raise money. If the young executive in the previous example had had an SAR instead of an option, things would have been different. On surrendering his SAR, the company gives our young man a check for $3,750 to pay his taxes (he is in the 50 percent bracket) and the other half in company shares and money to round off a fractional share. The check goes to the government with his next quarterly tax declaration or he faces the threat of going to the local equivalent of Sing Sing.

The best thing that can happen to our hero is to get a bonus *and* an option at the same time. Now he has the cash precisely when he needs it to exercise his option and hold out for capital gains—it's like winning the daily double.

A couple of comments on executive compensation are in order before we leave this subject. It is obvious from our examples that bonuses, stock options, and SARs don't do much at middle-manage-ment levels to create old money or estates. It is only at the top, where the bonuses run into six figures and the options into tens of thousands of shares, that this desirable end is achieved. If an em-ployee (or anyone else, for that matter) *knew* that certain shares were going to go up, and he had the ready cash, he wouldn't need an option. He would be better off buying at the market price, put-ting the certificates in a safe-deposit box, and thumbing his nose at the IRS. This is old money at work.

THE PUBLICANS

These last sections on fringe benefits and executive compensa-tion dealt with the outward visible signs of a continuing ideological battle between corporate employee relations departments and the tax collector or publican. The employee relations departments are trying to find legal ways to get remuneration into the hand of the employees and executives beyond the reach of the tax collector. It is no coincidence that most of the devices and stratagems we have discussed have appeared after the passage of the Sixteenth Amendment.

By making fringe benefits such as retirement, hospitalization, and insurance an integral part of the pay package, the employer ensures that the employees have security and will probably not be lobbying for more federal programs and socialized medicine. It also saves the employee 20 to 30 percent which he would have to pay in taxes if he got money instead of benefits. More important these days is the inflation protection; benefits rise as costs rise.

The tax collector has no objection to normal fringe benefits—he gets them too—but his attitude toward business fringes and ex-ecutive compensation is similar to that of a hard-line Baptist to having fun: he is afraid that somebody, somewhere is getting some-thing insufficiently taxed. The goal of the publican is to tax all forms of compensation (even the three-martini lunches) as regular income. The goal of management, which is already in the 50 per-cent tax bracket, is to wind up with something left over. The fight goes on.

PERQUISITES (PERKS)

Perquisites, or perks, are usually noncash items, so we can now leave the tax men happily auditing 1040s. The most graphic definition of perks was Mauldin's cartoon of World War II vintage. A major general has had his jeep driver stop to admire the sun setting on the snow-covered Alps. "What a beautiful view! Is there one for the enlisted men?" If the Fifth Army in Italy had been a large multinational corporation, the answer would probably have been "No."

Perks vary from company to company, and they can have weird manifestations. In the old United Gas Company, an important perk was a spittoon. If you reached a certain level, you got a green enamel model; only the top brass got a genuine brass spittoon (polished daily). The executive wrath against anyone who brought his own would have been terrible to see.

Little things, subtle gradations, are the mark of many perks—the key to the executive washroom, the right to stay in the company suite in a Washington hotel, or, more important, access to the key to the liquor cabinet in the suite. Other perks are more rational.

The expense account is not technically a perk: it is a way to reimburse legitimate expenses. It *becomes* a perk in the auditing process. While a $7 dinner entered by a low-ranking employee might be challenged, a senior manager can safely put down $50 for "entertainment." Club memberships are perks, as is access to the executive dining room if there is one. This can be a humbling perk: when a meeting breaks up for lunch, some members take the elevator up to the executive dining room or go to eating clubs while the others go down to pig it in the employees' cafeteria.

Size and furnishing of, and view from (remember the Alps), the businessman's office are important perks. Employees used to be able to add homey touches to their offices—pictures, desk sets, and so forth (I once sneaked in an Oriental rug)—but these days are over. With today's functional architecture and modular interior design, everything is reduced to formula. Using the "open concept"—no walls but enough potted plants to make the place look like the Tropical House at Kew Gardens—and expensive, shoddy, modular furniture, a modern overpaid interior designer can turn any building floor into an almost impossible working environment.

Status is measured in inches and numbers. Your desk is three inches wider than mine; I have one more chair than my section heads and 10.4 more square feet of floor space. Accessories are strictly company issue, the only allowed exception being family pictures—no cheesecake allowed. Desk sets are graded; my ash trays are gold colored while my people's are plain black (whether or not either of us smokes is immaterial). Gold contact paper is peeling from my wastebasket, black from those of the other ranks.

This conformity is forgotten in the executive suite on the top floors. Good wood furniture, rugs, and pictures are provided, often to suit the taste of the occupant. The executive suite at Chase Manhattan Bank is tourist country. Visitors ooh and ah over the offices of absent top brass; in fact, these art objects and antiques represent a wise investment by the bank.

First-class rather than tourist-class plane tickets, travel on company planes, and limousines are perks. Sometimes these advantages are part of an elaborate published code; more often they follow unwritten custom.

What might be called "business vacations" are becoming common. Instead of just going to the local clinic for his annual physical checkup—which is another perk—the executive goes to White Sulphur Springs, where the testing is scheduled so that it will not interfere with daily golf. Most industries have a top-level meeting once a year at a plush spot like The Broadmoor where top management from different companies can play and socialize. "Bring your wife." For many companies the annual board meeting is a high-class binge.

To be selected to go to "charm school"—to the Advanced Management Program at Harvard or at Stanford or MIT or even to Texas A and M—is an important perk for the rising executive.

The variety of perks is limited only by man's imagination; the list could be extended almost indefinitely. Their purpose is to extend a nonmonetary consideration to the executive—a consideration which costs the company heavily. The number and degree of perquisites rise with rank and reinforce the pecking order. Rank has its privilege in the army; rank has its perks in business. Some perks such as junkets are "hard" and visible, others are "soft" and psychological. The psychological perquisites that go with business success are so important that they are considered separately in a later section.

The less important money is as a class determinant in a society, the more important perks become. In Russia, Sweden, and England they are more significant than in this country, where a person can still earn enough money to buy status. The English tax system is so confiscatory that high salaries are meaningless and more and more of top management's compensation is in perks— graded perks. Middle management drives a company Consul and moves up to a Rover, to a Jaguar, and finally, at the top, to a Rolls Royce. The ultimate English perquisite is knighthood. In Sweden, where income leveling has gone further than it has here, perks and status symbols are so important that businessmen's titles are listed in the telephone books. The Russians keep giving out their dreary Orders of Lenin and wishing that other countries would take the honor seriously. Our government gives out presidential medals too, but few people have ever heard of them. What this country needs is a good budget knighthood system.

FIDDLING

We chose to use the English term "fiddle" to name the next kind of benefit rather than the closest American equivalents, "rip-off" or "steal," because our own words have an unpleasant sound and imply an unwilling victim who probably doesn't exist. Fiddles involve the appropriation of company goods or services (not money—that is embezzling) for private purposes. As long as these misdemeanors are tacitly approved by management, or are at least accepted as a cost of doing business, they must be considered to be a fringe benefit. The higher in the corporate organization, the more this sort of thing goes on. The real victims, as usual, are the shareholders, but they either don't know about it or don't care. If someone told them that the employees systematically misused company resources, they would probably be neither surprised nor shocked.

Fiddling is not an official policy in any company, but there are often fairly well understood limits beyond which one cannot go. These limits expand with increasing rank. One of my first jobs as a young engineer, after taking a civilian job, was to build a natural-gas metering installation and a building to serve a power plant. I made careful estimates and drew up a bill of material; everything was approved by my superior except for the brick estimate, to which he added some 10 percent. I was too new to know that I was also supplying material for a couple of barbecue pits. The benefactors were already queued up, presumably also the ones who would benefit from the next meter house. This is fiddling.

Employees soon develop the attitude that minor, commonly used items around the office or shop—paper, erasers, tape, pens, and so forth—have no real value. It comes as a shock, after retiring, to find that people make an honest living *selling* office supplies. I knew a research director who decided that the only way to keep a complete set of hand tools in the shop was to have enough spares for all the research workers. He was wrong; he still came up short. It is a rare automobile mechanic who buys his own spark plugs or motor oil.

The fact is that keeping a close control of minor items costs more than the inevitable "shrinkage." Accounting practices often depreciate the book value of durable goods like typewriters, drafting equipment, and furniture far below their real or market value. The company can, with a clear conscience, sell such items to favored employees at the low, unrealistic book values. This is fiddling.

At higher levels of the organization the emphasis shifts from things to time and service. The manager who has his secretary write his personal Christmas cards or buy his wife's anniversary gift on company time is fiddling. A top manager may even have a private secretary on the payroll whose only duties are to take care of his personal affairs and investments. He may get his mother-in-law a free ride on a company plane to meet her package tour to the Loire valley. The availability of modern copying and duplicating equipment is an almost irresistible invitation to use company services. It *seems* free to run off copies. I once used company people, equipment, and time to turn out an annual report for my church, complete with nifty illustrated covers. I didn't feel the least guilty, and we were all proud of the outcome, but—this is fiddling.

With the exception of petty theft and possibly the mother-in-law trip, most fiddles can be justified, or at least rationalized. If the secretary isn't busy and if she doesn't mind, she may as well do her boss's Christmas cards; a top executive may really be too busy doing company work to take care of his personal business. A lot of outside services are marketed in such a way that it is hard to put a unit cost on, for example, making copies or using the company WATS line for personal telephone calls (the commonest fiddle of them all). Even computer time, although fiendishly expensive, is often leased on a "shift" basis. If the machine isn't busy, why shouldn't I run some multiple correlations for my daughter's dissertation? The costs are hidden, but they are real. If all secretaries stuck only to company business, we might not need as many. If the use of all facilities were carefully controlled, we could reduce copying, computing, and communication costs.

The net result of fiddling is that it makes the company scene a nicer place in which to work. If even a low-ranking employee knows that he can make "free" copies of his income tax return or call his sister about her new baby, he is going to feel just a little bit more important—the company takes care of him. Fiddling is so common that it is taken for granted. It shouldn't be; it is a true fringe benefit. Unfortunately, unofficial benefits, particularly if they are not quite proper, encourage hypocrisy. The same man who fiddles a ride for a friend on a company plane rises up in righteous wrath when he hears that an elected official takes a city car home. We don't see how fiddling can ever be codified or legalized, or done away with for that matter. It is best to admit that, like tipping, it exists, it goes with the job, and it makes life easier for some people.

PSYCHOLOGICAL PERQUISITES

The most important perk for management people may not even be a tangible one: the personal satisfaction and comfort of *being* a member of management and enjoying the life-style this entails.

For many men, the most congenial working environment is that which is associated with war—not battle, where people get killed, but war. Wartime duty gives the serviceman a sense of importance and of rightness. It also provides comradeship and the joy of working together for a just cause. Even the advertised hardships of field life are welcome—they make the occasional leaves or liberties that much more gratifying. All this provides day-to-day emotional gratification.

Many human endeavors succeed or fail depending on how closely they simulate wartime conditions. The most successful, closest parallel is found in team sports, which offer unity of purpose, fellowship, a just cause, and even an enemy. For the Yale players, to beat Harvard becomes almost as important as life itself. There are dozens of heroic sports stories to support this position. Even such ritual sports activities as bull fighting and fox hunting pit good against evil (the bull, the fox) in the minds of the players and the spectators. As Jorrocks said of hunting, "the image of war without its guilt and only five-and-twenty percent of its danger."* Business does a pretty good job of simulating wartime conditions, at least for people in higher management.

There are two types of officers in the services and two types of managers in business: line and staff. Each type is particularly gratified by its own peculiar set of stimuli or perquisites, but both equally demand and find (in business or in service) a sense of right purpose and comradeship. Well-adjusted managers identify with their company and its goals. They honestly believe that these goals are just and are worth fighting for. Military terms are used: we "fight" competition, we "battle" the regulatory boards. If hardship is not really called for, many managers will court it voluntarily: they will work late, take material home, make unnecessary and inconvenient trips. When they tell their disappointed wives that they have to take another trip to the Coast this weekend, they may secretly enjoy making the sacrifice and proving their loyalty.

* Robert S. Surtees, *Handley Cross,* published in England in 1843.

The higher in the company hierarchy, the more a manager is expected to subjugate his own interests to those of the company. To accept an outside code and to be supported in this doctrine by his comrades provides a soldier's satisfaction—"my country, right or wrong." It can be gratifying for a businessman to be able to substitute "company" for "country" and arrange his priorities accordingly, sure of his virtue and supported by his associates (though not necessarily by his wife, who may even commit the heresy of suggesting that he "forget the dumb company for a few days and relax"). This identification with the company is the final fringe benefit for management.

In addition to fellowship and a sense of purpose, the field officer enjoys a lot of little things—sights and smells mostly. Business can provide a close approximation for its line managers. The smells of gasoline and diesel fuel from tanks and personnel carriers come equally well from construction equipment. The sun which rose over the Libyan desert and over the convoy at sea still rises over remote mines and offshore drilling rigs which work a 24-hour day. The thrill of improvisation, of making-do, in emergencies is still there. The triumph of completing a new plant or of getting it onstream compares with that of completing a military mission. Celebrating with friends and a few cans of cold beer at a remote tavern comes close to the joy of leave after danger. The higher he is in the line organization, the more a manager can savor these things; it is a perk of management. All ranks, on the other hand, get to wear hard hats in the field, which are about as similar to a soldier's helmet as it is possible to make them.

Staff officers don't get their kicks from shaving with cold water from a helmet or smelling 10-in-1 ration bacon frying in a mess kit; they enjoy status and privilege. As we have seen, business does a pretty good job of providing impressive "outward visible signs" and company-time luxury for its leaders, but it can't quite match the privileges enjoyed by Flag and General grade officers (only Congress can do that for its members). Business can never approach the gaudy spectacle of Patton, wearing cavalry breeches and six-shooters, being convoyed up the main drag of Heidelberg, or even the pomp of a finance corps major being driven in a staff car by a WAC sergeant to Paris headquarters, where the guard presents arms as he enters. The businessman has to make do with the black company limousine and chauffeur and possibly a private elevator to the executive floor, but he can think big. Business conferences do map "strategy" and make "tactical" decisions. The Duquesne Club or the Coronado Club or the executive dining room serve as adequate substitutes for the ward room on a ship. If there is no sentry at the door to salute him, his fellow managers treat him with respect and the working stiffs with awe (if they recognize him, that is—there is no substitute for shoulder stars).

This psychological, or *milieu*, perk is male-oriented—it doesn't do a thing for female managers who don't have the ancient and honorable tradition of slaughtering each other. Women managers are thus a subtle threat to the preferred way of life of current business management. Women's priorities are different; they may well treat business as a game, but not as mortal combat. As more women enter higher management (they will), the form of this psychological, way-of-life perk will change: the desiderata will no longer be the war room or the ward room.

It is too early to predict what the new management style will be. Perhaps the luncheon clubs will do away with the captain's chairs and fumed oak tables and look more like a country club with a "sensible" menu. The impending change of the mores of the male world of privilege is a threat which may keep top managers from welcoming women to their level—not because of prejudice, which is senseless discrimination, but in a logical defense of the existing order. When a woman joins a poker game, the subsequent play is still a card game (it may be a better game), it still observes the same rules, but it is no longer poker.

Another threat to maintaining a simulated war environment in the executive suite is that we are running out of people who know the rules. Businessmen who served as officers in World War II (the last noble war) are getting to retirement age, and a new war on such a scale is now too horrible to contemplate. There will soon be nobody left to set the tone, to tell war stories (which isn't boasting, as is usually assumed, but a way to create a congenial atmosphere). Management will have to find a new model for its chosen world. It may be one imposed by the new women members; it may be a horror emanating from the Stanford Business School in which people will actually enjoy sitting around and discussing the "Implications of Arbitrage on International Transactions." We don't know what it will be, but we do know that if this book is revised in future years, this section will have to be rewritten.

14

TRIBAL MORES
AND TABOOS

WITH SOME NOTABLE exceptions, businessmen look like businessmen, act like businessmen, and think like businessmen. The general public accepts this almost intuitively. When, for example, a man is running for a political office or is proposed for a church vestry or as a member of a Girl Scout Council and is described as (or describes himself as) a businessman, the public forms a mental image of the man, which is often quite correct: gray suit, short, graying hair, glasses, slightly overweight. He is assumed to be honest, conservative, and a sincere if rather ineffective speaker.

What sort of process produces this conformity? Considering the diversity of creatures that enter the business world—white, black, other ethnic, big-town, small-town, even foreign—it must be effective. There must be environmental forces at work in the business world to reduce its members to canonical form.

The image of the businesswoman is less clear. For one thing, not enough women have been in responsible business positions long enough to establish precedent. Novels, theater, and the media seem to suggest two formats: the "hard case" and the "piece of fluff." The hard case has a severe hairdo, wears tailored suits, sensible shoes, and black-rimmed glasses, and eats junior vice presidents for lunch. The piece of fluff is feminine and uses her charm as a business asset. She may not be very smart, but what she does always seems to turn out right (woman's intuition to the rescue). All the people who work for her love her dearly. Whom she loves is nobody's business.

To make generalization more difficult, the women in business don't seem to have a consistent *self*-image. Not having many precedents (Hetty Green?), they prefer to be themselves or to play a part of their own choosing. Women who have succeeded in business are often exceptionally talented—they have had to be to overcome the traditional discrimination and prejudice. Outstanding people are less likely to conform; they don't have to, and they usually don't want to. This is true for both men and women. In fact, this chapter concerns average run-of-the-mill businessmen and not the exceptions, who aren't interested in reading about conformity.

It seems safe to say that businessmen conform to a pattern because they want to. Which only raises the next question: why do they *want* to conform? Without getting into deep psychological waters and Rorschach tests, it seems that there are three good reasons to join the crowd: safety, self-esteem, and convenience.

To be safe is to be protected against criticism, even if it's only in the form of raised eyebrows, and against innuendo, which could hurt when promotions are considered. The careful businessman—Craftsman or Company Man—observes the received dress code, interests, and ideology and swims in the safe water of conformity. It is a peculiarity of human behavior that if we do anything often enough, for whatever motive, we come to believe it to be proper. Safe behavior becomes proper behavior.

Most people have models, if not heroes, to emulate. The rising businessman wants to look and act like his superiors. The private soldier wants to look like an officer (in consideration of dog-face morale, the dress difference between officers and men is now slight). It is good for the ego, the self-esteem, to conform to a desired norm and, more important, to be accepted in the role.

There is a danger of moving too quickly. The mail clerk wearing a three-piece flannel suit is an object of ridicule, not respect. To be able, confidently, to dress and act like a manager can give satisfaction to a businessman and to his wife. ("You *do* look nice today, Dear.")

The last reason to conform is honorable and uncomplicated. To know the rules of the game and to follow them is convenient and time-saving. It eliminates petty decisions. The soldier in wartime knows when he is well dressed, he doesn't have to think about it. After years of wearing nothing but uniforms, I remember my distress contemplating my old college wardrobe, which seemed to consist mainly of sport coats made of material which had obviously been designed for padding under rugs. I sympathize with nuns who discard their habits and change to mufti for field work; the switch must be a culture shock. To conform is efficient; it leaves the conformer to save his energy for more important decisions. The only problem is to determine just what is normal dress and behavior. The rest of this chapter is a guide.

THE DRESS CODE—GENERAL

John Molloy has written a book on dressing for business, in fact two books, a "ladies" and a "gents."* This may be overkill. The rules are not too complicated. There are general rules, and there are regional and occupational deviations. This discussion is for men only—we are not as brave as Mr. Molloy.

The English are usually cited as models for business dress. This is a bit impractical for most of us and can be confusing to any American who has spent some time in London pubs. We have a more available and reliable guide: the Ivy League look. Gents' haberdasheries like J. Press and Brooks Brothers in the Boston–Cambridge metroplex set the tone. General operative rules are: don't innovate; be behind rather than ahead of fashion; and buy good clothes. The last rule is just common sense. It is actually cheaper to spend more for clothes and wear them longer. A man looks better and is more acceptable in a good worn suit than in a

---

* John T. Molloy, *Dress for Success*, New York: McKay, 1975, and *The Woman's Dress for Success Book*, Chicago: Follett, 1977.

cheap new one; at least people don't have to waste time commenting on the new threads. With these general rules in mind, let us take up a garment-by-garment inventory of what the well-dressed businessman is wearing.

Suits

Grays and blues are preferred. Stick to conservative patterns: plain, herringbone, chalk- or pinstripe (a bit formal), or a subdued plaid. Remember, you are going to wear the outfit for several years, so get something you can live with. The weight of the suit depends on climate. For most of the country, with efficient heating and air conditioning, the same medium-weight suits can be worn year round. The material should be a worsted or flannel. Double-knit suits are *out*. For one thing, they don't meet the general criteria for quality and durability.

Style is Ivy League, single-breasted, two-button with medium lapels. Avoid double-breasted suits; they tend to look too stuffy even for businessmen, and they can (painfully) remind some of the senior members of Dewey's debacle. The vested suit is almost an exception to the rule of staying slightly behind the times. It looks as if it is here to stay. For one thing women like it (it makes their man look like Gregory Peck). If a vest is worn, it *must* match the suit. Gambler's vests are a no-no.

These details and the general rules are all you need to select suits for most business situations. To emphasize some pitfalls: don't wear a so-called leisure suit, don't buy one with an extreme cut—bell bottoms, nipped waist, wide lapels, the European cut. Most Americans prefer a center-vented jacket, while most English wear side vents. The choice doesn't seem important. Cuffs are also optional.

Conservative sports jackets and contrasting slacks are permissible as an occasional alternative to the suit. The safest selection is a plain blue blazer (without pocket ornament) worn with gray flannel slacks. This is a comfortable choice for traveling.

Shirts

White shirts are always acceptable but tend to look a bit formal. Light plain colors—blue, gray, cream—look more friendly. A very conservative stripe pattern is allowed as a change, but collars must match the shirt. Don't go for monogrammed shirts (unless they are covered by a vest); they tend to make a man look slightly affected or dominated by his wife. Shirting should be cotton or a mixture, not silk or even shiny.

The real Ivy League look is Oxford cloth shirts with button-down collars, usually wrinkled. It is better to leave these items to people who actually went to Ivy League schools and feel at home in them (the shirts). It is too easy for the uninitiated to look like slobs.

Do not wear flowered or patterned shirts or even white-on-white (which has a Mafia or gambler look). Avoid details such as extra pockets and military-looking tabs on the shoulders. Shirts are an easy item so long as they fit.

Ties

We had better cover ties next, having just done shirts. There isn't a lot to say except keep them quiet. It is not a bad idea to wear a tie that matches the suit, although very few people will notice. The usual advice is to wear club-stripe ties or small patterns. Club stripes have no special meaning for American wearers, but they do have a neat look if they are not too bold.* By now you should know to avoid anything loud or different. We don't particularly approve of ties with the initials of spurious royalty sewn in them, but they do seem to be accepted on this side of the Atlantic. Better leave them at home on your next English trip.

Bow ties are great if you can wear them. A tall, well-built man with a neat bow tie on a good shirt has class. On the other hand, a short stocky man wearing one tends to look like a small-time bookie. Wear them if you like them and if you can, but wear the kind you have to knot yourself. To use the clip-on kind seems a bit like cheating; besides, people respect the unusual ability to tie a bow tie properly.

Ties do offer a chance to express personality, within limits—

---

* A conversation point: the stripes on American-made ties usually point over the right shoulder, whereas English ones point over the left.

the bow-tie wearer, the Scotsman who always wears a quiet plaid, the man who always wears red ties. There are possibilities.

Socks

Sock rules are simple. They should match the suit, they *must* cover the calf of the leg, and they must not wrinkle. Don't wear white socks except for tennis or jogging. Silk socks are still acceptable (no clocks, please), but the thin stretchable knit ones are more practical and easier to keep up. Don't wear heavy wool socks. Repeat: don't wear white socks.

Shoes

Shoes are either brown or black, with cordovan (what the Marines wear) thrown in as a compromise. There are two schools of thought concerning the wearing of brown shoes: that they should be worn only with brown or tan suits or that they can be worn with anything. This uncontroversial book does not take sides. If you feel comfortable in brown shoes, and if your wife will let you, wear them with anything.

Shoes should be leather and plain pattern, either the strap or the lace type. An alternative style is the short "flight" or "chukka" boot, which is permissible particularly if the wearer once actually flew planes. Plain loafers are now accepted. Avoid heavy shoes, those with box toes and high heels.

Shoes should be kept clean but not highly polished; shiny shoes are the mark of the traveling salesman. (President Nixon's valet shined even the soles of his employer's shoes. There may be a moral here.) Belts should be leather and match the shoes. Socks match the suit, not the shoes.

Miscellaneous

Hats are almost obsolete for daily wear. On very cold days when they have to be worn, almost anything will do; a knit ski cap, for example, will prove that its wearer is really a fun-loving boy. The ultimate hat is the Russian astrakhan.

The top coat is important. It should be tan, never blue, of the waterproof type that looks like a used pup tent. This is an English tradition, and the coat should have an English-sounding name. Burberry has a nice sound and has the historical cachet that Scott wore one when he went to the South Pole. A warning: when you pick up your London Fog at the checkroom, be sure you have your own, because they all look alike.

Accessories

The best rule for jewelry is, "When in doubt, don't." This applies even to the five-, ten-, and twenty-year pins the company gives out. In addition to the wedding band (which we can hardly cavil) we reluctantly allow the hideous university class rings; they have become the mark of the American businessman. Unless you feel naked without one, it is better to leave it at home. French cuffs and cuff links (conservative) are marginally acceptable. For certain types of jobs, such as controller or treasurer, they may be an advantage. Neat gold cuff links seem to go with money managing. If you must display your Phi Beta Kappa key, don't do it on company time.

Businessmen above a certain age are almost expected to wear glasses. It is common to sit in a conference where all the participants wear them. Glasses should be framed—rimless glasses look stuffy—and of moderate size. This rule applies only to men; women can, and do, get away with anything. Unfortunately this tolerance for prosthesis does not extend to hearing aids.* If you need a hearing aid, we suggest that you wear one anyway; only by familiarity will the present prejudice be overcome.

THE DRESS CODE—SPECIAL

The basic dress code varies geographically and professionally. In the Sun (or heat rash) Belt, places like Atlanta and Houston, people still change to summer uniform, although there is an increasing trend to stay with the same medium-weight suits all year round. The preferred summer suit is a lightweight cord (the distinguished white linen is a thing of the past). Lightweight ties, madras

---

* The reason may be the shocking crudity of hearing aids, which are little more than amplifiers. Whereas we expect a man with glasses to see well, we expect a man with a hearing aid to hear poorly.

or linen, are worn with summer suits. Lightweight summer shoes should be conservative.

Some parts of the country—those with tourist business, like Arizona, Florida, and Hawaii—defy the standard dress code. Sports clothes are aggressively worn at all corporate levels. If you're transferred to one of these favored regions, the easiest thing is to report in standard uniform. This will not be remarkable; after all, they all wear it when they go to headquarters. Local dress is best acquired locally, following the lead of the natives. There is a surprising diversity in regional codes—bolo ties in Arizona, for example—and it is cheaper to conform after the fact.

Certain professional groups modify the standard code. Those with an academic leaning, such as economics and research types, prefer slacks and blazers to business suits. The aim is an academic look—more precisely, to look like what people think college professors look like. (Actually, college professors usually wear chino pants and a sports shirt that looks as if it had come from a missionary barrel.)

The Corporate Secretary, in his position as corporate master of ceremonies, has the option of setting an example of the latest style (which nobody will follow), even white suede shoes.

For some reason corporate lawyers dress differently. It may be a matter of warning coloration, like the eye spots on the wings of the tiger moth or the clerical collar. Lawyers wear glasses with heavier, darker frames than other people. They always carry expensive leather dispatch cases—as far as I know even to the bathroom. The most characteristic item, however, is their shoes. Lawyers wear heavy black wing-tip shoes with a sole thickness of about a half inch. The reasons for this cultural deviation are not known; it may be taught in law school along with business ethics.

People in "creative" situations like advertising and interior design try to show creativity in their dress and are apt to show up in necklaces and purple pants. Don't copy.

Speech and Manners

After clothes, the most obvious outward visible signs of a businessman are his manners and his speech: the Emily Post and Nancy

Mitford things. We confine this discussion to two aspects of manners: interpersonal relations during the business day and table manners which show up at the business lunch. Happy-hour manners are covered in the section on drinking.

Interpersonal manners are usually informal in American business—"call me Hank"—but there are two recognized forms of address: Mr. and Sir. (The title "Dr." is sometimes used, more often in a research laboratory than in an office.) When talking *about* anyone higher in the organization, refer to him as Mr._____, for example, "Mr. Liedtke," or perhaps use the whole name, "Bill Liedtke" (this is mild name dropping). To use the first name alone can be confusing (and *is* name dropping)—there are a lot of Bills in this world. When talking to a higher-up, use Mr. unless he specifically asks you to use his first name. "Sir" is used as a convenience title in such statements as "Yes sir," "No sir," and "No excuse, sir." The double form "Yes sir, Mr. Liedtke" is a bit much.

Male-female addressing is less well defined except between businessmen and their secretaries. The Miss/Mrs./Ms. thing is untidy. Most businesswomen will make it easy for everybody by announcing early, "Please call me Janet." The form of address between man and secretary is best left to the woman. Some secretaries insist on calling their bosses "Mr." while some would rather be on a first-name basis. If your secretary calls you Mr. Holmes, you call her Miss Watson.

Table manners in the American business community are free-form. They seem to be uncorrelated with education or rank. I have seen a Ph.D. attack his red snapper Pontchartrain with fork *and* knife as if the thing were trying to fight back or at least to get away. One friend, now a vice president, starts his breakfast by chopping up his fried eggs like a housewife chopping celery, using the tines of his fork as a miter box. Another friend always leaves a restaurant, however classy, with a toothpick sticking jauntily out of his mouth like FDR's cigarette holder. The result of all this variant behavior seems to be tolerance. Since so few businessmen know the "rules," anything goes; if you prefer to eat your peas with a knife, you may be on to a good thing.

Good manners are more than a code of behavior; at their best they demonstrate consideration and respect for other people. By this criterion, American businessmen rank high: most are courteous, kind, and tolerant of other people and are not snobbish. The observation of strict rules of conduct in such matters as the use of eating tools can be used, as it is in Europe, to support class distinctions. I may be uneasy at times because of my friends' unstructured table manners, but on the whole I prefer the American way.

Business is tolerant of speech and accent differences. There is no received or proper pronunciation as there is in England to divide people into "U" and "non-U" categories.° Almost all accents are accepted: New England, Midwestern, Southern, Southwestern. A foreign accent can be an asset, particularly in a woman, where it is "cute." One accent which is a handicap is the "jive" talk of the black community. A Mexican-American accent may also be a liability. Neither of these is much heard in the business world; indeed, many companies conduct classes for minority people to improve their diction.

Precision of speech is spotty. As we have seen, it is possible to graduate from an American university without being able to construct a proper sentence. The same thing goes for the spoken word. Some businessmen take pride in speaking well and even attend classes on the subject, but they are a minority. At that, the average businessman expresses himself almost as well as some local TV commentators and better than most student-athlete interviewees—"you know." There are still a few who recognize the properly used subjunctive and make a distinction between "like" and "as" and "shall" and "will," but they are an endangered minority.

As we have seen, written business communication tends to founder in a sea of businessese. Spoken communication can have the same problem if the speaker thinks in businessese rather than in English (or American). Another problem of verbal communication is the excessive use of technical jargon. Computer people, economists, mathematicians, and scientists are prone to this failing. The listener may start by being impressed by implied knowledge, but he may end by being frustrated and angry.

° Nancy Mitford, *Noblesse Oblige,* New York: Harper & Row, 1956.

INTERESTS AND IDEOLOGY

With its continuing fight against government regulation and interference, business management would be expected to strongly support the conservative ideology, which is supposed to be against big government. This is often true (certainly business supports more conservative candidates than liberals), but it is not inevitable. The liberals do get some support from business leaders, particularly in the East. IBM is a huge company which is traditionally in the Democratic camp and which hasn't suffered. At middle-management levels, businessmen are more consistently conservative. Perhaps liberalism (or socialism) is more easily embraced when one is financially secure.

Among his peers, the young businessman is reasonably safe in taking a conservative position. A party label is not necessary; in fact, foreigners claim there is no ideological difference between the two major American parties. Historically, the conservative position is represented by the Republican party in most of the nation and by the Democrats in the Deep South. Now we have liberal Republicans and conservative Democrats to confuse the issue. Rather than announcing a party label, it is safer to be for free enterprise, less government, and lower taxes and to vote for the "man, not the party."

Few businessmen are students of political science, or more might question the usual conservative allegiance. Business has *not* automatically prospered under Republican administrations and suffered under Democratic ones. General national prosperity is much more conducive to business health than any favorable laws, even tax laws. As we have seen, the biggest government obstacle to business growth is not always the legislative or executive branches but, more often, the entrenched bureaucracy and the regulatory bodies which continue from administration to administration. Not all businesses support the Republican party.

Among most businessmen, political discussions tend to be naive; they're restricted to trading anecdotes about government stupidity. Important items such as supporting favorable candidates or lobbying for helpful legislation are left to top management, to the professionals, and to the chamber of commerce.

If businessmen's conversations on politics are usually short and superficial due to limited knowledge and depth of interest (if this seems unfair, ask your favorite businessman to name any four members of the president's cabinet), what do they talk about in a social, nonconference situation? Apart from domestic subjects—children, school, house hunting, barbecue recipes—main topics are the stock market and sports. The young businessman must have at least a nodding acquaintance with these subjects.

Stock market discussions tend to be cyclical—common when the market is going up and rare when it is going down. Most management people have private market speculations apart from their company stock and options, and they like to talk about their successes. More dangerous, they like to give free advice or "tips." Scientific people are particularly insistent, because they have just figured out (on company time) a statistical way of beating the market. These schemes usually work well in a rising market and poorly in a falling market. Options are the latest fad. The executive floors are haunted by systems involving combinations of stock and option ownership which are fool-proof winners. Most of these schemes seem to sacrifice the possibility of big gains to insure against big losses. Market discussions are fun, particularly when everybody seems to be winning. Unfortunately, really successful investors tend to be listeners rather than talkers, and it is hard to glean their secrets.

While political discussions are shallow and market conversations cyclical, talk about sports is constant and spirited. Hunting and fishing are good topics and in the Good Old Boy tradition, but they don't have the conversational staying power of football, baseball, and (locally) basketball and hockey. The same man who can't remember the name of his state senator may well know the names and batting averages of all the members of his favorite baseball team. Football, both college and professional, is king in the winter, and big-league baseball reigns in the summer except in parts of the Sun Belt and the Midwest, where football always dominates.*

* In the Southwest, where football fever is highest, it is permissible to stoutly dismiss baseball as a dull game. It is safer to check local opinion before taking such a position.

Vicarious sports participation has at least three major manifestations: statistical analysis, Monday morning quarterbacking (fire the coach), and betting. Betting usually involves modest sums and often a sentimental attachment to a college team, which can present favorable investment opportunities. Before important sports feast days, such as those when the World Series or the Super Bowl games are played, some sort of lottery involving final scores will make the rounds. These sporting bingo cards are initiated by the lower orders. Traditionally, popular managers are asked to participate. This offers a cheap way to show that one is really a good guy. Besides, one just might win.

Even if the young businessman would rather curl up with a good book or listen to music, he had better learn something about baseball and football or he is going to be cut off from a lot of friendly give and take. A foreigner working in America who was brought up on, say, soccer or cricket may find it painful to sit through the tribal dog feast which is an American college football game but he should do it if he is to understand his colleagues.

The Grapevine

Some businessmen readers may be chuckling at this point in the narrative. "Politics, the market, sports, these are not what *we* talk about over our traditional three martinis." There is one other great topic: corporate gossip, usually involving personalities. We haven't mentioned it earlier because the topic is not recommended. It can be painful not to join the good clean fun, and you may get stuck with a round of drinks while the others are talking, but we discommend the topic as too dangerous. It is dangerous because of the "grapevine."

The grapevine (etymology uncertain) is an informal organization for the gathering and dissemination of fact and rumor within an organization. This transmission system is maintained by lower-ranking employees, but its sources (and sinks) exist at all levels. All large organizations—military, government, jails, and corporations—have this informal intelligence apparatus. In the army its output used to be called "latrinograms." Much that goes through the grapevine is false, *but* the traffic is so heavy that the fraction that is true does monitor almost everything that goes on in a company. Run-of-the-mill accomplishments of the grapevine would be to report a general raise or a plant closing before management reports it. Specifically, any snide remark made among close business friends will probably be reported to the target the following day.

As the grapevine is run by and for the lower orders as a sort of protest and defense mechanism, it is quite possible for a businessman to pursue his career and be only vaguely aware of its existence. This is a mistake. For self-protection and information a connection should be established either through a friendly employee or, better, through a colleague who is already tied in. Incidentally, a secretary is not a good interface. Secretaries tend to be "givers" rather than "getters," and delicacy may prevent them from telling you choice items you would most like to hear. The grapevine is there; use it.

PARTICIPATORY SPORTS

With the current interest in physical fitness, it is no bad thing to be involved in sports as a participant and not just to talk about them. This trend is recent. It used to be enough to talk vaguely about the good old days on the high school football team (which preferably resulted in a trick knee proscribing further athletic activity). Today, businessmen want to be, and want their colleagues to be, lean and hard. That they fall short of this ideal is obvious and irrelevant. If you really don't like to participate or are a poor athlete, an acceptable "out" is to claim that you jog every morning before breakfast. For those who want to join the rat race, some sports are more acceptable than others.

The best sports activities are visible, are done during the lunch hour, and involve equipment that has to be carried in and out of the office. Squash is the best sport; it is usually played at a private athletic club and involves a racket which is curious-looking and which excites comment when left negligently on top of a filing cabinet. The disadvantage of squash (apart from finding a place to play) is that it is a difficult game and, unless learned at an Eastern prep school or college, is almost impossible to pick up. An alternative is to carry a squash racket around and *not* play. The danger, of course, is that some eager enthusiast may challenge you to a game. Handball is more widely played, but it is also a demanding game and has the further disadvantage of not using obvious exotic equipment.

The ideal business sport is one which has the advantages of squash but which is easier for a beginner to learn. There is such a game. Racquetball has taken over. It is played with a racket which can be carried around (actually an ugly thing that looks like a cross between a carpet beater and a fraternity paddle), and it is easy enough that a man with some athletic ability and aggressiveness can soon learn to play a passable game. It is played on squash or handball courts and, by a sort of Gresham's law, is driving the older games out.

It may be that the most important advantage of indoor sport to a businessman is not physical but the opportunity to relate to other businessmen in a congenial atmosphere. A lot of men never really grow up; unconsciously they want to retreat to their youth, specifically to the high school locker room. (This is particularly true of Good Old Boys.) A downtown athletic club can recreate this atmosphere: the smells of steam and liniment and sweat, the sound of dark green tin locker doors slamming, the chance to sit naked on a hard wooden bench and revert to a sophomoric conversation level. In such a situation a businessman can feel very close to his fellows. It can help his career.

The traditional business sport is golf; the new "in" sport is tennis. The problem with these games for the young businessman is that they are not played during the business day and that playing partnerships have been established years ago and are fixed. Tennis requires ability to play a congenial game. Unless one happens to like the sport, golf can be taken up later. Since all walking and most exercise have been eliminated from golf, it can be played by octogenarians.

Companies often sponsor team sports such as softball, basketball, and, most often, bowling. Because these are mostly organized for nonbusiness people, there is not really much advantage to a businessman in participating. About the only reason to play is simply to have fun.

BOOZE—THE DRINKING GAME

In spite of the increasing popularity of racquetball and the passion for fitness, the most popular indoor sport of the businessman is drinking. Not all businessmen drink alcoholic beverages, but most do. Those who don't are respected for their convictions or pitied for their infirmities. What is *not* tolerated is for teetotalers to criticize their drinking friends.

It is hard to overestimate the importance of drinking in the business community—the Harvard Business School has a bar where students can relax and learn the drinking game. There is an inclination to drink in a business setting which is almost pathological. People who don't, and who don't even want to drink at home, do so on a business trip. Even teetotalitarian Baptists may join the party if they are far enough away from home. People in business or in public life are *expected* to drink. Most people feel more comfortable even about the president of the United States if they know he takes an occasional snort. This was true even during prohibition.

There are advantages for a businessman's joining the cocktail-hour crowd. It is by definition a social occasion. It is also democratic and is about the only time when high-ranking and low-ranking people can talk to each other comfortably. To put together a drinking party is the easiest thing in the world; no special skills or equipment are required as they are, for example, to put together a bridge or tennis foursome. Any number can play, and there are no special physical requirements. For some old stagers, drinking and the talking that goes with it is about the only game they can still handle, and some of them handle it very well. The rules of the drinking game are simple and can be covered under three headings: drinking, talking, and paying.

Typical business settings for drinking are the business lunch, travel, and a stay away from home. There are other special occasions, such as the president's Christmas party or the office party.

Anyone who is invited to the first type of party can be expected to know the rules of the game; anyone trapped into the second type is on his or her own. When flying first class (where drinks are free) or when riding in a company plane with an open bar, the operating rule is simple: drink as much as you can safely handle. When traveling tourist class (where drinks are not free), it may be prudent to save the expense account for later events.

Drinking

The subject here is not how to drink but what to drink. Certain spirits and mixtures are "in" and others are "out." Suppose you are on a business trip and your party has arrived at its destination, has checked in at the executive motel, and is now gathered around a table in the lounge. The waitress, who seems to be dressed only in camiknickers, approaches with her pad and stands at your right shoulder. You are under the gun! You are expected to make the first order, and what you say may raise or lower you in the eyes of your fellows; it may set the drinking pattern for the evening. Let your order be quick, simple, and an "in" drink. The table shown here is a handy reference guide.

	Liquor	*Mixer*	*Cocktail*
"IN"	Bourbon Scotch Gin Vodka Beer	Water, soda, rocks As above Tonic, rocks As above	Martini Bloody Mary (lunch)
O.K.	Irish Brandy Rum Tequila Sherry	Water, soda, rocks As above Cola, ginger ale Rocks	Manhattan Old-Fashioned Margarita
"OUT"	Cordials (except after dinner) Aperitifs	Sweet soda, 7-Up, bouillon, etc.	Anything fancy involv- ing fruit or color, e.g., Golden Cadillac

There may be other schools of thought, but this is a safe working list. Bourbon and scotch are standbys. For some reason, scotch has an academic implication: research directors and economists will probably order it. In Texas, bourbon and Coke is tolerated, in England, Scotch and ginger ale, either of which is probably a mistake. Gin or vodka and tonic are pretty much summer drinks. Vodka has the advantage (?) of being tasteless and odorless and is often preferred for lunch in a Bloody Mary (vodka and tomato juice). Martinis, gin or vodka, are the drinking man's drink, if only because he can see how much liquor he gets. (This isn't fool-proof. In New York you may get served a small shot of gin on an ice cube when you order a martini.) Gin on the rocks is the final extrapolation of the dry martini. Beer is always acceptable.

The specification of a brand name such as "Johnnie Walker Black" or "Virginia Gentleman" is allowed and indicates experience in the drinking game. It will cost more, and there is a chance you will get bar liquor anyway and that you won't know the difference.

Order O.K. rather than "in" liquors or cocktails if you prefer them or if you want to use your choice as a conversation piece. "They serve a very good margarita here." Stay away from the "out" group. The man who orders a sloe gin fizz is marked as a poor drinker, certainly not a Good Old Boy. If you get too far out, the waitress may come back and tell you that the bartender doesn't know how to mix the thing (swill implied). Businesswomen should be particularly careful to observe these rules. When a woman orders a Jack Rose or a Harvey Wallbanger it confirms the *a priori* hunch most men have that most women don't know how to drink.

There are exceptions to the rules. Englishmen can order sherry without censure; most Americans know the stuff and realize that it is potent if you drink enough of it. Other foreigners can order just about anything and get away with it. The chairman of the board can drink anything he likes. My chairman drank something called "bullshots," which are vodka and canned bouillon. All company planes carried the ugly little cans of the mixer. I have even had otherwise civilized employees confide to me that it "really is a good drink." Sometimes the environment calls for a different approach—a wine bar might, for example, or one of those fancy restaurants that serve what they claim is Polynesian food and specialize in fruit and rum drinks (which can be good).

Talking

To drink without talking is boorish. One of the delights of gathering around a table or bellying up to a bar is that it provides a relaxed atmosphere for talk when the inhibitions are desensitized. In any social gathering there are "givers" and "takers." The giver is generous, he laughs honestly at other people's stories, he tells his own, he is willing to take the chance of making a fool of himself—in short, he has a good time. The taker doesn't have much to say (he may be the Cautious Man we described earlier), he laughs when he thinks he should, and he is deathly afraid of doing something wrong. The worst kind of taker is the one who is obviously making mental notes of the proceedings. Be a giver if you can. Most people love to forgive another person's indiscretions and even like him better for them.

Topics of conversation are the usual ones: sports, politics, business, and stories, either risqué or historical. Stay away from gossip if you can. Don't make the mistake of saving something up to tell Old Joe next time you have a drink together. Saved items are apt to sound much different after a gestation period and are usually best left unsaid.

Paying

When the time comes to pay up, rank raises its ugly head. When one member of the group obviously outranks the others—a department head, say, drinking with some of his staff—he will normally pick up the tab. If you are drinking with two vice presidents, let them fight it out. These payment rules make good sense. The ranking man can probably put the whole fringe binge on his expense account under the heading of "entertainment," while the others are only partially covered. The name of the game on a business trip or at a business lunch is to stick the company with the cost.

When there is no obvious leader, the usual thing is to split the bill equally. Even if you don't drink—if your total consumption has been two ginger ales—pay your share. This may not seem fair, but it is done; it spreads the load on everybody's expense account. On a long trip where different people pay at different times, keep mental running notes and pay your share. The money you might save is not worth the chance of being labeled a freeloader. Occasionally you may go on a trip with someone who really likes to pay—the last of the big spenders. Let him have his fun.

Wine and After-Dinner Drinks

Some businessmen know and enjoy good wines; most do not. On business trips, conditions for proper wine drinking rarely exist. Typically, the group heads for a restaurant after a session in the lounge or at the bar. To drink good wine after several martinis is a waste of money, but wine waiters still manage to move a lot of the stuff to such groups. "We ought to have wine with our dinner— after all, we *are* on expense accounts." If you are lucky, there is a wine snob in the group who will take charge. He may get carried away and order such an expensive wine that he feels obliged to pay for it. Too often the total knowledge of the gang is that red wines go with something and white wines with something else. As a compromise they wind up with a Portuguese rosé in a bottle that looks like an old-fashioned stone bed warmer. They would have done better with beer.

After dinner comes the after-dinner drink. All the drinking rules are forgotten. Imagination replaces conformity. The man who earlier raised an eyebrow at the ordering of ginger ale with bourbon now orders an outrageous substance called peppermint schnapps; The man next to him orders a coffee liqueur. Why this drastic lowering of standards? We don't know. Maybe it is just late and to hell with it.

SEX

Back in another age when I was an undergraduate, there were certain books in the school library with marked sections for special reading. It was not necessary to know the page numbers—just turn to the ones with worn edges. (It didn't take much to rouse us. I recall a passage in a Faulkner novel where a young lady in a compromising situation was being walloped with a hairbrush on her bare behind. Bristles down yet? Wow!) I don't think that this section of this book will be overly worn. Sex in business, at least at the physical level, is not very good copy.

Some of the Jungle Fighters may have to prove their virility by making (sometimes successful) passes at the resident females. Some more staid types may feel middle age creeping up on them and decide they had better do something before it gets too late. Good Old Boys make a few hectoring passes, up to and including fanny patting, to maintain their role. As far as the usual office sexual activity is concerned, that is about it. Most businessmen are married, have other things on their minds, and are too smart to get out of line on company time. There is probably more action at lower levels such as the stock room or the typing pool than on the executive floors. When a middle-management man does get out of line, when he gets overly involved with one of the female employees, he is more apt to be pitied than censored. The other businessmen know that the financial consequences of such entanglements can be severe, and they keep their priorities in order.

Occasionally there flashes through the business scene a girl with real sex appeal—one who doesn't mind using this advantage to further her own ends. The men in the office enjoy the novelty as a diversion and as a conversation piece; the other women bite their tongues. I had one of these delightful creatures as a secretary once. Her big act was serving coffee. The exercise was done without bending the knees, the cups being placed, preferably, on a low surface. There was something about this act that made grown men wheeze. As secretaries go, she had to rank high in the top ten of the world's worst, but we kept her on the payroll until she herself decided it was time to move on to better things.

Away from home, on business trips, the businessman has more scope. He can make casual arrangements which won't have sticky carryover. If a man has a regular beat, he can set up cosy repeat performances to fight loneliness on the road. Unfortunately, most business trips involve more than one person, and the travelers tend to chaperone each other. Not too many years ago, it was usual for a junketing group to head for a local "skin" show after dinner, and this could lead to bigger things. Now even this program has lost some of its appeal. The bored strippers can hardly get down to much less than what the cocktail waitress (who was prettier) was wearing, so why bother? It is easier and cheaper to go back to the motel room and curl up with a good copy of *Playboy* or *Penthouse*.

Secretaries

The passive side of the boy-girl relationships is more interesting. Until recently, the only visible females in the business world were secretaries. Special relationships and traditions, almost a feudal system, have grown up between businessmen and their secretaries, not only because they were the only females around, but also because of the special one-on-one situation between man and secretary. As more women rise in the business world, there should develop a healthier give and take between the sexes based on friendship and ability.

Women are as conscious of rank as men. A personal secretary assumes the honorary rank of her boss. The secretary to a vice president is paid more than, and looks down on, the secretary to a department head, much the same way that a colonel's wife feels free to snub a captain's wife. In some cases the secretary maintains this superior attitude toward the department head himself. This vicarious assumption of rank and power can exist only where there is a special relationship between the woman and her boss. Such a relationship does not always exist. Some businessmen prefer to have only objective, "businesslike" contacts with their help. Some secretaries, good ones, are not above reminding their bosses just what their job description entails. (This friendly objective approach is promoted by secretaries' organizations.) The old-fashioned special connection, which is still common, between employer and employee, satisfies each one's complementary desires: she to be in a position to "mother" her boss or to employ innocent blackmail against him, he to be "mothered" or to be loved.

Many businessmen want, may even need, to be loved by their secretaries—not in any vulgar, carnal sense, but rather in the sense of having the secure knowledge that she knows that he is wise, wonderful, generous, and fair. Many women will accept this role and even identify with it, in the teeth of contradictory evidence. To do so gives them a hold over their boss, which continues as long as the healthy state of his ego depends on her continuing approval and deference. He upholds his side of the implied bargain by always being polite, proper, and considerate, by getting her raises, and by speaking well of her to others. "Octavia is the best secretary in the company, I don't know what I would do without her." She loyally brags about him. A mutually satisfying mutual admiration society.

The "mothering–mothered" connection is more common than the prophet–discipline arrangement. It arises usually out of simple laziness on the part of the boss, and the desire to protect, as one would a stray puppy, on the part of the secretary. When I recall the things I had my secretary do for me—correct my spelling, remember appointments, anniversaries, even people's names—I am ashamed. These are things that a reasonably competent eighteen-year-old should be able to do for himself. This mother–son, or keeper–backward child, relationship is symbiotic if slightly perverted. It makes life easier for the man and protects him against stupid mistakes. It gives the woman satisfaction and security: as long as she is willing to do part of his thinking for him, he doesn't want to lose her.

Do secretaries usually admire their bosses? I think they often like them but rarely admire them. They work too closely together. Familiarity does not necessarily breed contempt, but it sure can shatter illusions. If there is a stuffed shirt under the gray flannel vest, she sees it; if he writes inane memoranda in businessese, she has to type them. She monitors his vacillations and deceits, she has to smell his foul pipe. It is almost as difficult for a secretary to admire her boss as it is for a wife to admire her husband.

INDEX